In the Beginning

MOREHOUSE COLLEGE

In the Beginning

The Martin Luther King, Jr. International Chapel at Morehouse College

---

A *Festschrift* in Honor of Lawrence Edward Carter, Sr.

Echol Nix, Jr., Editor

MERCER UNIVERSITY PRESS | *Macon, Georgia*

MUP/ H904

Published by Mercer University Press
1400 Coleman Avenue
Macon, Georgia 31207

9 8 7 6 5 4 3 2 1

Books published by Mercer University Press are printed on acid-free paper that meets the requirements of the American National Standard for Information Sciences—Permanence of Paper for Printed Library Materials.

ISBN 978-0-88146-530-3
Cataloging-in-Publication Data is available from the Library of Congress

Contents

Foreword vii
Acknowledgements ix
List of Contributors xiii
1. Models of the Scholar-Activist Type: Lawrence E. Carter, Sr. in the Shadows of Benjamin Elijah Mays and Martin Luther King, Jr., *by Lewis V. Baldwin* 1

2. "Be the Change You Wish to See": An Essay on Education and Personalism, *by Thomas O. Buford* 19

3. Dr. Lawrence Edward Carter, Sr. and My Journey to Christian Allegory, *by Delman L. Coates* 33

4. A Letter to the Dean: Autobiographical Reflections and Lessons Learned, *by Jason R. Curry* 47

5. Lawrence Carter, Sr. and the Boston Personalist Tradition, *by Norm Faramelli* 55

6. The Morehouse Gospel: Howard Thurman, Martin Luther King, Jr., and Prophetic Black Christianity, *by Peter Goodwin Heltzel* 65

7. Living Your Dreams, *by Barbara Lewis King* 81

8. Forgiveness as Self-Defense, *by Rabbi Douglas E. Krantz* 91

9. "Correcting Jesus": A Sermon, *by Bill J. Leonard* 97

10. "Unexpected Judgment": A Sermon,
by Otis A. Maxfield 103

11. Morehouse College and the King Chapel Ministry:
A Personal Retrospective, *by Echol Nix, Jr.* 115

12. The Twilight of Personalism at Boston University:
The Testimony of a Participant-Observer,
by Harold H. Oliver 121

13. The Vocation of a Modern-Day Prophet:
Dr. Martin Luther King, Jr., *by Peter J. Paris* 133

14. African-American Liberal Arts Education and
the Cultivation of Virtue, *by Samuel K. Roberts* 141

15. Cultivating a Culture of Peace,
by Prince El Hassan bin Talal 159

16. It's Not Easy Being Dean: From Kelsey to
Carter and the Case for the Importance
of Religion in the Historically Black College
and University Context, *by Harold Dean Trulear* 167

17. The Civil Rights Movement and the Role
of Nonviolence in Promoting Healthy
Communities, *by Edward P. Wimberly* 175

18. Ripping the Veil, Weaving Meanings:
The *Text*ures of Therapeutics of African
Diaspora Formation, *by Vincent L. Wimbush* 185

19. A Biography of God's Dream, *by Virgil Wood* 203

Foreword

Hugh M. Gloster, Jr., M.D.

My father, Dr. Hugh M. Gloster, Sr., founded the Martin Luther King, Jr. Chapel at Morehouse College. During Founder's Day weekend in February 1978, Hugh M. Gloster Hall, an administration building, and the Martin Luther King, Jr. Memorial Chapel were both dedicated with a series of events, which included a symposium, dedication ceremony, and banquet. The symposium was moderated by Dr. Robert Brisbane of the Morehouse College Political Science Department and featured Dr. Ralph Abernathy, Dr. Joseph Lowery, Rev. Jesse Jackson, and Mrs. Coretta Scott King. United Nations Ambassador and former mayor of Atlanta, Andrew Young, was the keynote speaker at the dedication ceremony in the chapel, and the Rev. Dr. Thomas Kilgore, Jr., chair of the Morehouse College Board of Trustees and pastor of the Second Baptist Church in Los Angeles, California, was the banquet speaker held in the Walter Chivers Dining Hall.

As president of Morehouse, my father often visited chapels, cathedrals, and churches around the world. He understood the importance of religion on college campuses, especially as young people develop intellectually and spiritually. After an extensive, nationwide search, Dr. Lawrence Edward Carter, Sr. was invited to be the first Dean of the Chapel on July 1 1979. My father spoke at the investiture service in October that year and he said that Larry Carter was the "best young college chaplain in the country." He also described Dr. Carter as "richly endowed, being a dynamic speaker, an able scholar, and a dedicated Christian." My father's predecessor, Dr. Benjamin E. Mays was also present during the service and delivered the invocation

Originally named the "Martin Luther King, Jr. Memorial Chapel," Dean Carter later asked the Board of Trustees to change "Memorial" to "International." The change in name captures the broad and far-reaching dimensions of Dr. King's message of peace, nonviolence, and civil and human rights and reflects Dean Carter's own approach to ministry. The chapel services are mostly in the Protestant tradition but the vision of the chapel is much more diverse and ecumenical, embracing people of other faith traditions.

This book is a lasting tribute to the hard work and creative efforts of Dean Lawrence Carter, to the legacy of Dr. Martin Luther King, Jr., and to the educational mission of Morehouse College.

Acknowledgments

Howard Thurman observed that "we are never left to ourselves alone." Indeed, we are surrounded by others whose understanding, support, and encouragement sustain us during long days and nights. This book is a product of such surrounding by others. Dr. John R. Silber, president emeritus of Boston University, assisted in a tremendous way by requesting the help of the Boston University Office of Sponsored Programs in identifying corporations and foundations for assistance. Joan Kirkendall, an expert on sponsored research at Boston University, was also very helpful. Judy Romano and Brianne Pochard in the Grants Office at Furman University and Dr. John Beckford, Vice President for Academic Affairs and Dean, deserve special mention for their leadership and administrative assistance.

Appreciation is extended to the staff at the James B. Duke Library at Furman for acquiring books, full text articles, digital microfilm, online encyclopedias, newspapers, magazines, periodicals in print, and unlimited access to computers in an adjoining room for editing, research, and printing. Many conversations were held with Morehouse College administrators, Board of Trustee members, faculty, staff, and alumni. Some of these include: Drs. Robert Michael Franklin, Wiley Perdue, John S. Wilson, Abraham L. Davis, Alton Hornsby, Marcellus Barksdale, Otis Moss, Jr., Amos Brown, and Calvin Butts. Also, the following people offered practical advice, critical thoughts, and valuable suggestions: Mrs. Barbara A.O. Wardlaw, Henry Goodgame, Roy Craft, Mrs. Brooks, John P. Brown, Jr., Seymour, Rev. Dr. Cameron Alexander and Rev. Dr. Charles G. Adams. Special appreciation is extended to my Morehouse friend and classmate, Rori Francis Blakeney, for his encouragement and for providing a needed alumni directory.

During the early phase of the writing process, Rev. Dr. Willie Roy Rogers, Sr. and his wife, Mrs. Janice Sikes Rogers, were instrumental in offering historical insights and served as important conversation partners from the beginning to the end. I am deeply indebted to Dr. Hugh

Morris Gloster, Jr. for providing the foreword of this book, and especially grateful to the contributing authors of the essays and sermons for choosing to honor Dean Carter and Morehouse College with their time and participation.

Heartfelt gratitude is due to Mrs. Rosetia Johnson Nix and McKenzie Grace Nix for their understanding and patience during the many hours "at the office" and for the necessary time "in the library." I fondly cherish the memory of my wonderful mother, Mrs. Annie Mae Nix, and the ongoing support of my father, Rev. Dr. Echol Lee Nix, Sr.; brother, Earnest; and sisters, Pamela and Keturah, as well as extended family members. James "Tee" Griscom, a Religion major at Furman University, provided tremendous technical assistance with the book's specifications and I appreciate the understanding and support of colleagues in Furman's Religion Department.

Words are not sufficient enough to express my profound and sincere thanks to Dr. Marc Jolley of Mercer University Press for initially embracing the idea and agreeing to publish the manuscript during a conversation with him in Montrèal, Canada. Thanks also to Marsha Luttrell, Publishing Assistant at Mercer University Press, and Mary Beth Kosowski, marketing associate at Mercer University Press, for providing thorough instructions and guidance regarding Mercer University's requirements.

In the Beginning: The Martin Luther King, Jr. International Chapel at Morehouse College would not have been published without the generosity of Dr. Vartan Gregorian, president of the Carnegie Corporation of New York, and Jeanne D'Onofrio, Chief of Staff and Operations. This publication was made possible in part by a grant from the Carnegie Corporation of New York. The statements made and the views expressed are solely the responsibility of the authors. Appreciation is also extended to the entire staff of the King Chapel, especially the Reverend Terry Walker and Mrs. Candice Hall-Wilcox. This book honors the continuing work of the campus ministry at Morehouse and Dean Carter's family, including Dr. Marva Griffin Carter, Carter, Jr., Mrs. Bernice Johnson of blessed memory, and others.

Howard Thurman was right in another way. During the process of writing and editing, I felt an abiding spiritual presence and blessed assurance that this book would be published. Like the Apostle Paul, I was convinced that God, who began his work through me, would bring it to completion (Philippians 1:6).

Echol Nix, Jr., Ph.D.
Greenville, South Carolina

MERCER
UNIVERSITY PRESS

Endowed by

TOM WATSON BROWN

and

THE WATSON-BROWN FOUNDATION, INC.

List of Contributors

Lewis V. Baldwin, Ph.D., Professor Emeritus, Religious Studies, Vanderbilt University, Nashville, Tennessee

Thomas O. Buford, Ph.D., Professor Emeritus, Philosophy, Furman University, Greenville, South Carolina

Delman L. Coates, Ph.D., Pastor, Mount Ennon Baptist Church, Clinton, Maryland

Jason R. Curry, Ph.D., Dean of Chapel, Fisk University, Nashville, Tennessee

Norm Faramelli, Ph.D., Professor Emeritus, Social Ethics, Boston University, Boston, Massachusetts

Peter Heltzel, Ph.D., Associate Professor of Theology, New York Theological Seminary, New York City

Barbara L. King, D.D., Founder and Pastor, Hillside International Truth Center, Atlanta, Georgia

Rabbi Douglas E. Krantz, Congregation B'nai Yisrael, Armonk, New York

Bill J. Leonard, Ph.D., Professor of Church History, Wake Forest University, Winston-Salem, North Carolina

Otis A. Maxfield, Ph.D., Former Senior Minister, First Community Church, Columbus, Ohio

Echol Nix, Jr., Ph.D., Assistant Professor of Religion, Furman University, Greenville, South Carolina

Harold H. Oliver, Ph.D., Professor Emeritus, Philosophy, Boston University, Boston, Massachusetts

Peter J. Paris, Ph.D., Professor Emeritus, Christian Ethics, Princeton Theological Seminary, Princeton, New Jersey

Samuel K. Roberts, Ph.D., Professor of Theology and Ethics, Union Presbyterian Seminary, Richmond, Virginia

Prince El Hassan bin Talal, Hashemite Kingdom of Jordan

Harold Dean Trulear, Ph.D., Associate Professor of Applied Theology, Howard University Divinity School, Washington, D.C.

Edward Wimberly, Ph.D., Professor of Pastoral Counseling, Interdenominational Theological Center, Atlanta, Georgia

Vincent Wimbush, Ph.D., Professor of Religion, Claremont Graduate University, Claremont, California

Virgil Wood, Ed.D., Pastor (Retired), Pond Street Baptist Church, Providence, Rhode Island

1
Models of the Scholar-Activist Type: Lawrence E. Carter, Sr. in the Shadows of Benjamin Elijah Mays and Martin Luther King, Jr.

Lewis V. Baldwin

"Whatever you do in this hostile world, be the best." This credo has long expressed the primary mission of Atlanta's Morehouse College,[1] and it has inspired Black leaders and activists from John Hope, Benjamin E. Mays, Mordecai W. Johnson, Samuel W. Williams, and Howard W. Thurman down to Martin Luther King, Jr., Lawrence E. Carter, Sr., and countless others who have followed them.[2] John Hope, the fourth Morehouse president, taught that the lack of education hampered the march toward freedom, a lesson learned and taken to heart by generations of "Morehouse men" and "Morehouse-related personalities."[3] The contention here is that Mays, King, and Carter are representative of the scholar-activist type that has always constituted the principal leadership model in the Morehouse tradition, and that their lives are instructive for all who seek to effectively combine academic excellence and intellectual vigor with an enduring sense of social responsibility and commitment.

---

[1] Linda Williams, "Molding Men: At Morehouse College, Middle Class Blacks Are Taught to Lead," *The Wall Street Journal* (5 May 1987): 4–5; and Edward A. Jones, *A Candle in the Dark: A History of Morehouse College* (Valley Forge, PA: Judson Press, 1967) 325.

[2] Lawrence E. Carter, Sr. uses the term "servant scholars" in reference to Mays, Johnson, Williams, and Thurman in *Walking Integrity: Benjamin Elijah Mays, Mentor to Martin Luther King, Jr.* (Macon, GA: Mercer University Press, 1998) xii (preface).

[3] Williams, "Molding Men," 4–5; Lawrence E. Carter, Sr., ed., *Walking Integrity: Benjamin E. Mays, Mentor to Generations* (Atlanta: Scholars Press and Morehouse College, 1996) xxviii (preface); and Lewis V. Baldwin, *There Is a Balm in Gilead: The Cultural Roots of Martin Luther King, Jr.* (Minneapolis: Fortress Press, 1991) 25.

The purpose of this essay is twofold. First, it highlights Lawrence E. Carter, Sr.'s treatment of Mays and King as intellectuals, clergymen, and social activists in some of his writings, speeches, and interviews with media sources. Second, Carter's role in keeping alive and advancing Mays's and King's legacies of ideas and struggle is discussed at some length. Here the discussion is grounded largely in Carter's sense of his own background and experiences as an African American in the South, and also in his work with various projects and institutions named for Mays and King. The three figures, considered jointly, are portrayed as educators devoted to translating the highest ethical ideals into practical action and practical reality.[4]

Carter views the American South as the initial context for exploring what became essentially a lifelong relationship between Mays and King. This is understandable since both Mays and King grew up in the South, exposed to the structures of White supremacy and Jim Crow. In the opening chapter of *Walking Integrity: Benjamin Elijah Mays, Mentor to Martin Luther King, Jr.* (1998), Carter discusses Mays's early education in a segregated school system in South Carolina, and traces his academic odyssey through Virginia Union University in Richmond, Bates College in Maine, and the University of Chicago.[5] Although Carter has not published books that seriously explore King's early training in the segregated public schools of Atlanta, he has often addressed King's

[4] Unlike Carter, Mays and King have received considerable attention as scholar-activists. This essay and others in this volume are designed to correct this pattern of omission. See Carter, Sr., ed., *Walking Integrity: Benjamin Elijah Mays, Mentor to Martin Luther King, Jr.*, 1–31; Dereck J. Rovaris, Sr., *Mays and Morehouse: How Benjamin E. Mays Developed Morehouse College, 1940–1967* (Silver Springs, MD: Beckham House Publishers, Inc., 1990) 24–142; Mark L. Chapman, *Christianity on Trial: African-American Religious Thought Before and After Black Power* (Eugene, OR: Wipf & Stock, 2006) 15–41; Baldwin, *There Is a Balm in Gilead*, 25, 168–74; and Rufus Burrow, Jr., *God and Human Dignity: The Personalism, Theology, and Ethics of Martin Luther King, Jr.* (Notre Dame, IN: University of Notre Dame Press, 2006) 17–265.

[5] Carter, Sr., ed., *Walking Integrity: Benjamin Elijah Mays, Mentor to Martin Luther King, Jr.*, 1–5; and Carter, Sr., ed., *Walking Integrity: Benjamin Elijah Mays, Mentor to Generations*, xxvi–xxviii (preface), 1–14.

academic pilgrimage and intellectual sources at Morehouse College, Crozer Theological Seminary in Pennsylvania, and Boston University, mostly in public speeches on the civil rights leader.

Born in Georgia, although raised in Ohio, Carter is quite sensitive to that vast complex of forces in the South—familial, experiential, and cultural—that shaped and informed Mays's and King's intellectual quests, educational values, and professional goals. He refers in some of his writings to the challenges that confronted Mays's parents, S. Hezekiah and Louvenia Carter Mays, both of whom were ex-slaves in South Carolina, and he makes special mention of Mays's upbringing in southern Black Baptist Protestantism, an experience reinforced by Louvenia's "serious prayer life" and "deeply religious" orientation.[6] Carter is equally mindful of King's upbringing in Atlanta's Ebenezer Baptist Church, and his understanding of the Mays' struggles also figures into his sense of the long periods of crisis that confronted King's parents, Martin, Sr. and Alberta Williams King, both of whom were from Georgia. Apparently, Carter has a deep appreciation for how the values and traditions of family, the Black Church, and the larger African-American cultural milieu of the South came together in the consciousness of both Mays and King with those of various academic institutions, thus preparing them for the intellectual and social justice challenges they confronted as intellectuals, race leaders, and international symbols of community.[7]

For Carter, education was also a vital part of the spiritual and cultural bond that united Mays and King. The image of Mays as an educator and scholar *par excellence*, and as "the mentor" to King, surfaces through Carter's reflections on this phenomenal figure. Mays's tenure as dean of Howard University's Divinity School and as a distinguished professor and president at Morehouse College is highlighted, and so are his many publications and his "responsible ethical pedagogy of poetic

---

[6] Carter, Sr., ed., *Walking Integrity: Benjamin Elijah Mays, Mentor to Martin Luther King, Jr.*, 1–2.

[7] Ibid., 1–10; and Lawrence E. Carter, Sr., George David Miller, and Neelakanta Radhakrishnan, eds., *Global Ethical Options in the Tradition of Gandhi, King, and Ikeda* (New York: Weatherhill, Inc., 2001) 21–133.

rebellion."[8] Carter singles out the hundreds of articles Mays wrote for the *Pittsburgh Courier* between 1946 and 1980, his *The Negro's God as Reflected in His Literature* (1938) and *The Negro's Church* (1933), a book he co-authored with Joseph W. Nicholson,[9] works which spoke to Mays's erudition, scholarly productivity, and importance as an example for Martin Luther King, Jr. Variously referring to Mays as "a one-man renaissance," "a candle in the dark," and "the great moral educator," Carter credits the Morehouse president with establishing "an early recruitment program" that "lured" King to that institution, and King became his "most famous student."[10] Carter's claims are supported by the testimony of King, who called Mays his "intellectual and spiritual mentor," and who always placed Mays among the great minds who "made me stop and think."[11]

---

[8] Here, Carter is suggesting that Mays's approach to education and teaching reflected his intense opposition "to institutionalized and traditional injustice of any kind." He quotes Orville Vernon Burton, who "was the first to refer to Mays's life as 'a rebellion of poetic elegance.'" See Carter, Sr., ed., *Walking Integrity: Benjamin Elijah Mays, Mentor to Generations*, 4–5, 13, 514; and Carter, Sr., ed., *Walking Integrity: Benjamin Elijah Mays, Mentor to Martin Luther King, Jr.*, 10.

[9] Virtually all of Mays's important published works appear in Carter's bibliographies. See Carter, Sr., ed., *Walking Integrity: Benjamin Elijah Mays, Mentor to Generations*, 15–16.

[10] Ibid., 9, 12; and Carter, Sr., ed., *Walking Integrity: Benjamin Elijah Mays, Mentor to Martin Luther King, Jr.*, x–xi (preface). Carter's image of Mays draws on Andrew Jones's *A Candle in the Dark. A History of Morehouse College* (Valley Forge, PA: Judson Press, 1967).

[11] King also called Mays his "spiritual and intellectual father," which means that he considered Mays a part of his extended family. See Carter, Sr., ed., *Walking Integrity: Benjamin Elijah Mays, Mentor to Martin Luther King, Jr.*, ix (preface); Martin Luther King, Jr., "Statement Regarding the Retirement of Dr. Benjamin E. Mays," unpublished version (1967), The Library and Archives of the Martin Luther King, Jr. Center for Nonviolent Social Change, Inc., Atlanta, Georgia, 1; Baldwin, *There Is a Balm in Gilead*, 26; Coretta Scott King, *My Life with Martin Luther King, Jr.* (New York: Henry Holt and Company, 1993) 83,

Carter has a longstanding interest in the rise of Mays and King as men of ideas and letters, and he clearly views their social praxis as largely an extension of their academic training and intellectual concerns. In the classroom and during what Carter calls his "legendary chapel talks every Tuesday morning" at Morehouse, Mays made King aware of "all the trends of modern thinking," and he was especially instrumental in introducing King to a liberal, Social Gospel theology.[12] Many of the idioms in King's public discourse came from Mays, thus providing more evidence in support of Carter's claims regarding King's intellectual indebtedness to the Morehouse tradition. While matriculating at Morehouse, King heard Mays say repeatedly that an unexamined life is not worth living, that if one has nothing worth dying for, one is not fit to live, and also that it is not how long one lives, but how well one lives—wise sayings that would find expression in King's sermons, speeches, and writings. Mays's insistence that "[i]t isn't a calamity to die with dreams unfulfilled, but it is a calamity not to dream," also left an indelible mark on King's thinking.[13]

169; and Calyborne Carson, ed., *The Autobiography of Martin Luther King, Jr.* (New York: Warner Books, Inc., 1998) 16.

[12] George D. Kelsey, who taught King philosophy and ethics at Morehouse, was equally significant in this regard. See Carter, Sr., ed., *Walking Integrity: Benjamin Elijah Mays, Mentor to Martin Luther King, Jr.*, x (preface); Carson, ed., *The Autobiography of Martin Luther King, Jr.*, 16; Carter, Sr., ed., *Walking Integrity: Benjamin Elijah Mays, Mentor to Generations*, 8; and Lewis V. Baldwin, *Toward the Beloved Community: Martin Luther King, Jr. and South Africa* (Cleveland: The Pilgrim Press, 1995) 8–9. The common view in much of the scholarship is that Mays, much like King's maternal grandfather and father, A. D. Williams and King, Sr., "were proponents of a Black social gospel." See Walter Earl Fluker, *Ethical Leadership: The Quest for Character, Civility, and Community* (Minneapolis: Fortress Press, 2009) 21; and Burrow, Jr., *God and Human Dignity*, 19, 42, 53–54.

[13] Some of these sayings can be found in Benjamin E. Mays's "What Man Lives By," in William M. Philpot, ed., *Best Black Sermons* (Valley Forge, PA: Judson Press, 1974) 36–39. Also see Baldwin, *There Is a Balm in Gilead*, 300; and Martin Luther King, Jr., "A Talk to a Seventh-Grade Class at George A. Towns Elementary School," unpublished version, Atlanta, Georgia (11 March 1964), King Center Library and Archives, 1.

Carter emphasizes certain of Mays's principles that King would embrace wholeheartedly as he sought to develop the intellectual language and categories he needed to articulate his theology and philosophy of life. Carter asserts that Mays "believed in the sacredness of all human personality," and that his "mission was to enhance human dignity and not degrade it." Carter goes on to note that Mays's mother is credited with "strengthening his conviction that the universe is essentially moral—never sustaining exploitation, war, and injustice."[14] Although King inherited these same principles from his parents, the Black Church, and his exposure to the Social Gospel and Personal Idealism at Crozer and Boston, he also owed much to Mays and Morehouse.[15] Morehouse College during Mays's years as president (1940–1967) was almost an exclusively Black setting in which human personality was uplifted and reinforced on so many levels, and students like King learned to think of the universe as essentially moral and friendly despite that wall of assumptions that the racist White society sought to impose on them.[16]

The Christian ministry afforded yet another spiritual and cultural link between Mays and King, as Carter has frequently suggested in his written statements, speeches, and interviews. Both men were ordained Baptist ministers, and Mays, who was thirty-five years King's senior,

---

[14] Carter, Sr., ed., *Walking Integrity: Benjamin Elijah Mays, Mentor to Generations*, 5.

[15] Carter, Sr., ed., *Walking Integrity: Benjamin Elijah Mays, Mentor to Martin Luther King, Jr.*, xii–xiii (preface); Burrow, Jr., *God and Human Dignity*, 69–73; Baldwin, *There Is a Balm in Gilead*, 22–23, 171–72; Clayborne Carson et al., eds., *The Papers of Martin Luther King, Jr., Volume I: Called to Serve, January 1929–June 1951* (Berkeley: University of California Press, 1992) 360–62; and Carson, *The Autobiography of Martin Luther King, Jr.*, 3–12.

[16] King made it clear as a seminary student, "It is quite easy for me to think of the universe as basically friendly mainly because of my uplifting hereditary and environmental circumstances. It is quite easy for me to lean more toward optimism than pessimism about human nature mainly because of my childhood experiences." Given the fact that King was essentially a child when he entered college, he was not likely to exclude Morehouse from those "hereditary and environmental circumstances" and those "childhood experiences." See Carson et al., eds., *The Papers of Martin Luther King, Jr.*, Vol. I, 360.

modeled for the youngster the kind of ministry that was intellectually sound, spiritually satisfying, and socially relevant. This, coupled with the influence of King, Sr., his father, helps explain why King accepted the call to ministry during his senior year at Morehouse.[17] Speaking of Mays and George Kelsey, his philosophy and ethics professor at Morehouse, King recalled that "I could see in their lives the ideal of what I wanted a minister to be,"[18] a point that supports Carter's comments on the central role of these men and Daddy King himself in the shaping of what he labels the "powerful prophetic preaching tradition at Morehouse."[19] Mays helped convince King that the ministry provided the best opportunities for him not only to "serve God and humanity"[20] as a whole, but to assume a leadership role in the liberation and empowerment of his own people, especially in a culture in which "The Negro," as James Weldon Johnson put it, was "the most priest-governed group in the country."[21] In other words, Mays, as Carter rightly suggests, was among those elders

[17] Carter, Sr., ed., *Walking Integrity: Benjamin Elijah Mays, Mentor to Generations*, 8, 510; and Carter, Sr., ed., *Walking Integrity: Benjamin Elijah Mays, Mentor to Martin Luther King, Jr.*, ix–x (preface), 2.

[18] Carson, ed., *The Autobiography of Martin Luther King, Jr.*, 16; King, "A Talk to a Seventh-Grade Class," 1; and Scott King, *My Life with Martin Luther King, Jr.*, 83.

[19] Interestingly enough, Carter includes Martin Luther King, Sr.—or "Daddy King," King, Jr.'s father—among the shapers of this tradition. See Carter, Sr., ed., *Walking Integrity: Benjamin Elijah Mays, Mentor to Martin Luther King, Jr.*, 12.

[20] Martin Luther King, Jr., "My Call to Preach," unpublished statement delivered before the American Baptist Convention (7 August 1959), The Martin Luther King, Jr. Papers, Special Collections, Mugar Memorial Library, Boston, Massachusetts, 1; Carter, ed., *The Autobiography of Martin Luther King, Jr.*, 16; Carson et al., eds., *The Papers of Martin Luther King, Jr.*, Vol. I, 363; and Baldwin, *There Is a Balm in Gilead*, 280.

[21] James Weldon Johnson, *God's Trombones: Seven Negro Sermons in Verse* (New York: The Viking Press, 1969; originally published in 1927) 3.

who persuaded King, by word and example, that his gifts and commitment could best be expressed through the ministry.[22]

Carter insists that Mays and King shared the fruits of not only the Morehouse preaching tradition, but also the larger Black preaching tradition. Although highly educated, Mays drank from the wellsprings of that tradition, as he even learned from untrained Negro preachers, thereby taking in the full range of resources that that tradition had to offer. Carter writes:

> Dr. Mays told [me] that in the early 1930s, before the age of the tape recorder, the nature of his sociological study of *The Negro's Church* forced him to transcribe by hand the sermons of hundreds of Black preachers who had neither the benefit of education nor had come under the tutorial influence of White teachers. Dr. Mays reported how he unconsciously imbibed his measured speaking rhythm from listening to and transcribing the sermons of these non-lettered Black preachers.[23]

As Carter has shown, the influence of Mays, King, Sr., and generations of Black preachers came together in King, Jr's preaching. King's "clear, rich voice," which carried the sound of a marvelous instrument, proved unmistakably that his "style of preaching grew out of the tradition of the southern Baptist ministers, with cadences and timing which he had heard from his father and other ministers as long as he could remember."[24] Despite their sense of the need for an educated Black clergy, Mays and King respected the raw, natural talents that unlettered Black preachers brought to the pulpit, and they insisted on taking the best that these preachers had to offer, in terms of wisdom and technique, and on making this a part of their own homiletic delivery. Therefore, Carter is right in suggesting that the Black preaching tradition accounted in great

---

[22] King, "My Call to Preach," 1; and Baldwin, *There Is a Balm in Gilead*, 280.

[23] Carter, Sr., ed., *Walking Integrity: Benjamin Elijah Mays, Mentor to Generations*, 14.

[24] Ibid.; Carter, Sr., ed., *Walking Integrity: Benjamin Elijah Mays, Mentor to Martin Luther King, Jr.*, 12; and Scott King, *My Life with Martin Luther King, Jr.*, 5.

measure for Mays's and King's effectiveness as orators, and also for the many successes they achieved as social change agents.

But Mays and King brought far more to their positions as ministers and leaders of their people. Carter calls Mays "an unbiased race man," "a race leader," or "a self-styled servant-scholar" who had a concern for justice, equality of opportunity, and better race relations, and whose "liberating praxis" helped dismantle the walls of racial segregation. Carter says essentially the same about King, as he assesses the place of both leaders "in the twentieth century African-American struggle for civil and human rights."[25] According to Carter, Mays, who creatively paired "rebellion and responsibility," gave over 800 public addresses in the period from the 1940s through the 1970s, many of which targeted the issues of segregation and the need for authentic, participatory democracy. Carter further notes that it was Mays who "produced three generations of 'hell-raisers,'" from Howard Thurman to Martin Luther King, Jr.[26]

Mays's and King's assault on segregation in the Christian Church set the standard for what Carter sees as prophetic social witness, particularly in light of that institution's tendency to parade as the body of Christ. Carter holds that Mays's "entire public life existed in rebellion against" not only the Jim Crow "educational system" and discriminatory practices in government, but also segregation in the life of the church. Carter recounts Mays's reaction when told that the *Brown vs. Board of Education* decision, which outlawed segregation in schools, had resulted not from leadership on the part of the church, but from the highest court in the land:

> When informed of the decision, Dr. Mays publicly wept and said, "I had hoped this decision would come from my beloved Church and not from the courts." His greatest disappointment with the Christian Church was that it had become politically impotent, a tail light and not

---

[25] Carter, Sr., ed., *Walking Integrity: Benjamin Elijah Mays, Mentor to Martin Luther King, Jr.*, ix, xii (preface); and Carter, Sr., ed., *Walking Integrity: Benjamin Elijah Mays, Mentor to Generations*, 7.

[26] Carter, Sr., ed., *Walking Integrity: Benjamin Elijah Mays, Mentor to Martin Luther King, Jr.*, ix, xii (preface); and Carter, Sr., ed., *Walking Integrity: Benjamin Elijah Mays, Mentor to Generations*, 2–4, 6–7, 9, 11–12.

> a head light, and not always constructive in its understanding that the responsible society is the place where the Kingdom of God and social issues meet.[27]

Echoes of this same critique of the church filtered through the public discourse and proclamations of King, whose name, in Carter's estimation, was "synonymous" with "the civil rights movement."[28] As the conscience and spirit of the movement, King, inspired by his father, Mays, and others, declared, "Segregation in the Christian Church is the most tragic form of segregation, because it is a blatant denial that we are all one in Jesus Christ." King brooded over the fact that "eleven o'clock on Sunday morning is the most segregated time in America," and that "[t]he Sunday Schools are the most segregated schools in the nation."[29] Evidently, King's and Mays's persistent protests against segregation, bigotry, and intolerance in the church were significantly based on each other's examples and actions. There were mutual influences here that do not escape Carter, for the ways in which the public lives of Mays and King intersected and influenced and reinforced each other surface at times in his reflections on both men.

Carter is at his best when explaining how Mays and King found common ground around the philosophy and discipline of nonviolence. He acknowledges the "vital role" that Mays, Howard Thurman, Mordecai W. Johnson, and Samuel W. Williams, all "Morehouse men," assumed "in establishing the historic and philosophical link between Gandhi and King—a link that altered forever the social and political

---

[27] Carter, Sr., ed., *Walking Integrity: Benjamin Elijah Mays, Mentor to Generations*, 2, 13–14. Carter's analysis of Mays's struggle with racism and segregation in the Christian Church is borne out in Chapman, *Christianity on Trial*, 15–29.

[28] Carter, Sr., ed., *Walking Integrity: Benjamin Elijah Mays, Mentor to Generations*, xxvi (preface).

[29] Martin Luther King, Jr., "An Address to the National Press Club," unpublished version, Washington, D.C. (9 July 1962), The King Papers, Boston University, 6; Lerone Bennett, Jr., "Rev. Martin Luther King, Jr., Alabama Desegregationist, Challenges Talmadge," *Ebony* (April 1957): 81; and Baldwin, *There Is a Balm in Gilead*, 51.

fabric of the United States."[30] "Through their efforts," Carter continues, King "was introduced to Gandhian 'nonviolence,'" but Carter does not minimize King's role in establishing the principle and practice of nonviolence in American social and political life. He ultimately reminds us that "[t]he collective efforts of" all five of these "ordained Christian ministers of the Baptist Church, self-styled 'servant-scholars,' introduced and shaped the philosophy of nonviolence that became a pillar of the American civil and human rights movement."[31]

No scholar has gone as far as Carter in identifying nonviolence as a part of that Morehouse tradition that shaped both Mays and King. The "seeds of revolution," in the nonviolent spirit, Carter concludes, were "planted" by Mays "in the Sale Hall Chapel at Morehouse." Nonviolence was an important part of Mays's "inclusive philosophy" of life, and the power of his message was never lost in those Tuesday-morning chapel services. Referring to Mays "as an unarmed prophet who disarmed Jim Crow and created Black men in a laboratory of freedom," Carter maintains that King was standing squarely in this Morehouse tradition when he employed nonviolent methods in his struggle to eliminate social evil.[32] In making such claims, Carter is not oblivious to King's indebtedness to the broader traditions of Christian pacifism and to the *satyagraha* principles of Mohandas K. Gandhi.

---

[30] Carter, Sr., ed., *Walking Integrity: Benjamin Elijah Mays, Mentor to Generations*, xxvi (preface); and Carter, Sr., ed., *Walking Integrity: Benjamin Elijah Mays, Mentor to Martin Luther King, Jr.*, xii (preface).

[31] Carter, Sr., ed., *Walking Integrity: Benjamin Elijah Mays, Mentor to Generations*, xxvi (preface); and Carter, Sr., ed., *Walking Integrity: Benjamin Elijah Mays, Mentor to Martin Luther King, Jr.*, xii (preface). In a recent work on King, Gary Wills agrees with Carter's claims regarding King's indebtedness to Mays for his nonviolent praxis, noting that "King also benefited greatly from the theological mentoring and activist model provided by Benjamin Elijah Mays." See Richard W. Wills, Sr., *Martin Luther King, Jr. and the Image of God* (New York: Oxford University Press, 2009) 43.

[32] Carter, Sr., ed., *Walking Integrity: Benjamin Elijah Mays, Mentor to Generations*, xxvi–xxviii (preface), 4, 511, 514; and Carter, Sr., ed., *Walking Integrity: Benjamin Elijah Mays, Mentor to Martin Luther King, Jr.*, xii (preface).

Before, during, and after King's student days at Morehouse, Mays was the embodiment of the kind of sacrificial life and ministry needed to make nonviolent action redemptive and transforming. He always stressed the biblical connection between personal faith and sacrificial service, and, as Carter notes, quoting Lerone Bennett, Jr., Mays demonstrated the supreme spirit of both sacrifice and achievement by doing "with pennies, nickels, and dimes, what Harvard, Yale, and Chicago did with millions."[33] Evidently, King, as Carter declares, found a workable model in this kind of sacrificial service and triumph in the face of great odds, and he translated these values into a peaceful crusade that emphasized bearing the cross, sacrificial servant-hood, and redemptive suffering for the salvation of all humanity. The prophetic advocacy of Mays and King, around this need for a culture of peace and sacrificial servant-hood, stood as a much-needed corrective for Christians who constructed edifices of every kind to shield themselves from any form of crucifixion. Hence, Carter's characterization of both men as "servant scholars" takes on an added significance.[34]

In the mind of Carter, Mays and King actually became world figures who were devoted to the globalization of an ethical ideal—namely, the beloved community. Carter explains that Mays, as a very young man, actually left the South "to seek a new world."[35] According to Carter, Mays not only represented the National Baptist Convention, USA, Inc. at the founding of the World Council of Churches of Christ in Amsterdam, Holland in 1948, but also aided in finalizing a statement on "the idea of the responsible society," or that "world society" in which man is "a free being," "responsible to God and his neighbor." Furthermore, Mays was active in the debate "concerning the responsibility of the World Council to prevent South African churches from coming into the WCC segregated," and he was "universally associated with academic excellence"

[33] Carter, Sr., ed., *Walking Integrity: Benjamin Elijah Mays, Mentor to Generations*, 6, 12.

[34] Carter, Sr., ed., *Walking Integrity: Benjamin Elijah Mays, Mentor to Martin Luther King, Jr.*, xii (preface).

[35] Ibid., 2; and Carter, Sr., ed., *Walking Integrity: Benjamin Elijah Mays, Mentor to Generations*, 14.

as well.[36] As "an instrument of social change in America and around the world,"[37] Mays once again found common ground with Martin Luther King, Jr., for both held that "all life is interrelated." As Carter and other scholars have indicated, this idea of "the interrelated structure of all reality," which embraced the concept of a globalized and interdependent world, actually captured the essence of their international vision and grounded their activities in opposition to the global realities of racism, poverty and economic injustice, and war and human destruction.[38]

Carter's most extensive and profound statements on King as an international figure and symbol appear in *Global Ethical Options in the Tradition of Gandhi, King, and Ikeda* (2001), a book he co-authored with George David Miller and Neelakanta Radhakrishnan. In twenty short chapters, this book discusses the meaningfulness and relevance of Mohandas K. Gandhi, Martin Luther King, Jr., and Daisaku Ikeda for creating "a new global ethics" that addresses issues such as self-realization, altruism, cooperation, community, and ecological integrity. Carter also has spoken on this subject at churches, academic institutions, and on various television networks, including Singapore television. [39] He is especially interested in the possibilities for the actualization of King's beloved community ideal on a global scale, and he keeps Mays in focus as well when exploring this issue. Much of what Carter says, in *Global Ethical Options* and in his many speeches and interviews, supports King's account of his own role "as a citizen of the world," and as one devoted to the type of "revolution of values" that will eventually lead to "a new kind

---

[36] Carter, Sr., ed., *Walking Integrity: Benjamin Elijah Mays, Mentor to Generations*, 9–11, 13. Mark Chapman casts Mays in the position of "world leadership," and insists that Mays "emphasized the global implications of the American race problem." See Chapman, *Christianity on Trial*, 16–27.

[37] Chapman, *Christianity on Trial*, 22.

[38] Ibid., 25–27; and Martin Luther King, Jr., *The Trumpet of Conscience* (San Francisco: Harper & Row, Publishers, 1987; originally published in 1968) 69–70.

[39] Carter, Sr. et al., eds., *Global Ethical Options*, 11–133, back cover.

of man."[40] Apparently, Carter views King and Mays as precursors of the kind of thinking currently associated with globalization, or with global conversations that center around the emerging issues of laissez-faire economics, free market democracy, information technology, and ethical options for the oppressed, marginalized, and endangered segments of humanity.

Carter's treatment of the deaths and legacies of King and Mays is equally significant, for he considers both their relationship to each other and their impact on this nation and the world. He recalls that the bond between the two leaders was such that it "had been agreed for some time that if Martin Luther King, Jr. predeceased Mays, the latter would do King's eulogy and vice versa."[41] Significantly, Mays and Howard Thurman, another "Morehouse man," helped King to deal philosophically with the possibility of his death through their counseling and reflections on transcendence.[42] As fate would have it, King was assassinated on 4 April 1968, and Mays eulogized the civil rights leader five days later, after the funeral procession marched four miles from Atlanta's Ebenezer Baptist Church to Morehouse College.[43] Before an estimated crowd of 150,000, Mays spoke to King's significance as a modern prophet and as the conscience of the nation. "How strange," he declared, that "God called the grandson of a slave on his father's side," and commanded him to "speak to America about war and peace; about social justice and racial

---

[40] King, Jr., *The Trumpet of Conscience*, 31; James M. Washington, ed., *A Testament of Hope: The Essential Writings and Speeches of Martin Luther King, Jr.* (New York: HarperCollins Publishers, 1986) 241; Lewis V. Baldwin, *To Make the Wounded Whole: The Cultural Legacy of Martin Luther King, Jr.* (Minneapolis: Fortress Press, 1992) 286; and "Doubts and Certainties Link," unpublished transcript of an interview with Martin Luther King, Jr., London, England (Winter 1968), King Center Library and Archives, 5.

[41] Carter, Sr., ed., *Walking Integrity: Benjamin Elijah Mays, Mentor to Martin Luther King, Jr.*, 28. This account is also given in Scott King, *My Life with Martin Luther King, Jr.*, 306.

[42] Baldwin, *There Is a Balm in Gilead*, 146; and a Private Interview with Dr. Philip Lenud, Nashville, Tennessee (7 April 1987).

[43] Carter, Sr., ed., *Walking Integrity: Benjamin Elijah Mays, Mentor to Martin Luther King, Jr.*, 28.

discrimination; about its obligation to the poor; and about nonviolence as a way of perfecting social change in a world of brutality and war."[44] For Carter, the eulogy was symbolic of that which had bonded Mays and King in life and in struggle.[45]

As Carter and others have noted, that cultural and spiritual bond actually extended up to the death of Mays on 28 March 1984. Carter reports that Mays's body reposed in state at the Martin Luther King, Jr. International Chapel on the campus of Morehouse College, and the funeral was held at that same location.[46] Evidently, the relationship between Mays and King, as Carter describes it, was as symbolic as it was substantive. The two leaders found unity in death, and they, in Carter's estimation, had become the authors of legacies that would intersect and not only enrich the Black Church and Morehouse traditions, but also challenge humanity around the values of justice, peace, human dignity, community, and participatory democracy.

On so many levels, Carter has sought to advance the legacies of Mays and King, while also standing in the shadows of both historic figures. Carter concludes that Mays's legacy is most evident in the impeccable character and dedication he brought to his activities in the private and public spheres, an observation equally fitting for King, who, according to Carter, became the great champion of nonviolent strategy and human freedom.[47] Since Mays's death, Carter, consciously and perhaps unconsciously at times, has confronted the question of his own role in keeping the memory of Mays and King alive in word and deed, especially considering the great degree to which he has been involved in the life of Morehouse College over the last three decades. The unfinished agenda of Mays's and King's holy crusades affords much of the inspiration for Carter's work as an academic and preacher at Morehouse,

---

[44] Scott King, *My Life with Martin Luther King, Jr.*, 307.

[45] Carter, Sr., ed., *Walking Integrity: Benjamin Elijah Mays, Mentor to Martin Luther King, Jr.*, 28.

[46] Ibid., 29–30.

[47] Carter, Sr., ed., *Walking Integrity: Benjamin Elijah Mays, Mentor to Generations*, xxvi (preface), 12–13.

and for his public advocacy in the interest of justice and peaceful coexistence between people in the national and international contexts.

When Carter became a professor of Religion and the first Dean of the Martin Luther King, Jr. International Chapel at Morehouse in 1979, Mays was in his eighties and still very much alive. Carter obviously related to Mays as a son would to his father, and he learned from and received impelling spiritual and moral power from the elderly gentleman. Mays's mere presence on the Morehouse campus ran like an electric charge through the atmosphere. Carter recalls those times when Mays occasionally appeared at the King Chapel for special events, appearances that were always greeted with thunderous applause. On one such occasion in the early 1980s, Mays entered "the great nave" of the King Chapel "unescorted" and "late for baccalaureate and commencement, aided only by a walking cane." "When Mays came into full view of the audience," Carter recounts, "a spontaneous standing ovation of 2,500 people interrupted the proceedings, continuing until Mays took his seat." Mays "smilingly acknowledged the applause by waving his cane." For Carter, this was yet another indication of the "universal admiration which Mays commanded."[48]

Mays the universal man is the image highlighted whenever Carter speaks and writes about the legacy of the former Morehouse president. This is why Carter has so often evoked the memory of Mays in sermons in scores of churches, during radio and television interviews in the United States, Asia, and Africa, and in speeches delivered in some thirty-five countries and in more than a hundred colleges, universities, seminaries, and divinity schools. Carter's role in editing a *Festschrift* "in recognition of the centenary of the birth of Dr. Mays" in 1995 will stand as perhaps his most important contribution to the preservation of Mays's legacy. As Carter has stated, this *Festschrift* was completed in the "spirit of unity to a cause, historical respect for leaders of the past, and a profound reverence and awe for the personal dynamic of King, Mays," and other great

---

[48] Carter, Sr., ed., *Walking Integrity: Benjamin Elijah Mays, Mentor to Martin Luther King, Jr.*, 29.

"Morehouse men."[49] While serving as a visiting professor at Bates College in Lewiston, Maine from 1996 to 2002, Carter conducted annual seminars at the Benjamin Elijah Mays Institute, frequently drawing on the contents of this *Festschrift*. Also, Carter started and raised funds for the Morehouse College International Hall of Honor, which features an oil portrait of Mays, along with more than a hundred other great leaders who figured prominently in nonviolent struggles for civil and human rights.

Carter's contributions to the preservation and advancement of the King legacy actually began before he arrived at Morehouse. While at Boston University, the institution from which he received the Ph.D. in Pastoral Care and Counseling, Carter served as Executive Director of the Martin Luther King, Jr. Afro-American Center. But his greatest contributions have come in connection with his teaching and activities as a professor and as Dean of the Martin Luther King, Jr. International Chapel at Morehouse. Carter covers the life and thought of King in courses at Morehouse, and Mays inevitably comes into focus during lectures and group discussions. Thousands of young "Morehouse men" have benefited from these efforts. In 1979, Carter started the Martin Luther King, Jr. Chapel Assistants Preseminarians Program with five hundred students at Morehouse. At his urging, the National Council of Churches set up an Ecumenical AmeriCorps Scholarship Awards Program at the King Chapel in 1998.[50] Carter also secured a gift of 100,000 dollars from the National Baptist Convention, USA, Inc., and used this to erect a statue of King on the Plaza of the King Chapel at Morehouse. This is the only major statue honoring King in the state of Georgia.[51] In recent years, Carter has led in the induction of hundreds into the International Collegium of King Preachers and Scholars, and in 2006 was involved in the decision to purchase some seven thousand King documents as yet another step in safeguarding the King legacy at Morehouse.

---

[49] Carter, Sr., ed., *Walking Integrity: Benjamin Elijah Mays, Mentor to Generations*, xxviii (preface).

[50] Lawrence E. Carter, Sr., "An Autobiographical Sketch," unpublished document, the author's files (Summer 2007): 1–2.

[51] Ibid.

Many of Carter's efforts in promoting the King legacy have occurred on an international level. In sermons, speeches, and radio and television appearances in England, Canada, Japan, New Zealand, Australia, South Africa, and other parts of Africa and Asia, King's name and historic significance have been evoked by Carter. The book *Global Ethical Options*, alluded to earlier, grew largely out of Carter's desire to remind people worldwide of King's importance as an international figure, whose ideas are still meaningful for addressing contemporary global problems.[52] Surprisingly, the book has not gotten the kind of attention it deserves, especially in an age when humans are desperately in need of more reliable paths to openness, enlargement, and peaceful coexistence.

Carter stands today as evidence that the Morehouse tradition and its history of producing great leaders did not die with Mays and King. That tradition is secure and is still evolving, and many of those "Morehouse men" who have studied with Carter, and those who now sit at his feet, will, undoubtedly, build on it and advance it to greater heights of excellence. This remains a hopeful sign in a nation and a world in which new scholar-activists are needed to take the lead in addressing global terrorism, post-Cold War ethnic cleansing, genocide, the nuclear threat, and other enormous challenges of this new century and millennium.

---

[52] Carter, Sr. et al., eds., *Global Ethical Options*, 11–133.

2

"Be the Change You Wish to See": An Essay on Personalism and Education

Thomas O. Buford

Introduction

For Dr. Lawrence E. Carter, Sr., education is more than the training of the mind to be an intellectual artist. Those who do so are satisfied with theory, with system, with logical perfection. But, neither is education lodged in the world of other human beings. That kind of education arises from human experience and the wisdom embedded in it. It is no more than common sense. Certainly, education is concerned with both theory and human experience. However, those who aim at either or both are shortsighted. Education also involves faith in God, the love of God and of other persons. And education involves change both in yourself and in the world in which you live; it requires that you be the change you wish to see. To achieve that vision requires discipline practicing the way of justice, respect for persons (nonviolence), and love. They, in turn, require moral imagination, knowledge, and discipline. Informed faith without works is dead, to paraphrase the Book of James's famous insight.[1] Edu cation is the disciplined action of the whole person. That vision animated the educational philosophy of Boston University Personalism. Dr. Carter's intellectual and theological background rests, in part, in the Boston Personalist tradition, in that vision. In this paper I shall lay that out, hoping to capture something of the richness of the educational vision that surrounded and influenced him at Boston University.

Personalism deeply influenced education in America during the first two-thirds of the twentieth century. Its influence was felt through the liberal Protestant consensus, which was the intellectual framework for higher education, and which they helped forge.[2] During the twentieth

---

[1] See James 2:26.

[2] For a full discussion of the significance for higher education of the liberal Protestant consensus, see George Marsden, "The Soul of the American

century forces eroded that consensus, and by the late 1960s its influence was weak. Many of us can remember the attack in the late 1960s on the Establishment waged by counterculture forces, specifically Woodstock. The result is that something is now missing that was in place fifty years ago. Let's call it the Center, the content of which was a theological understanding of the persons and their world, certain books, and the commitment to educating the intellect to know. Along with that Center went a view of person and an understanding of what moral education could mean if it were attempted. What I want to do is consider a part of what has been relegated to the background, specifically that view of persons and their moral education. My reason for this is more than historical; we may have cast aside a Personalist (that form of Personalism known as Boston Personalism) view of education, particularly moral education, but Dr. Carter does not. He believes that it should be given greater consideration; indeed, he is the incarnation of it. What is this Boston Personalism that so deeply informs his life?

Committed to the metaphysical thesis that Person is first, working within the Liberal Protestant Consensus, and believing that our minds are capable of grasping reality (to some degree), Boston Personalists have followed two roads in developing their thought: *ratio* and *poeisis*. The former is represented by Bowne and Brightman with their emphasis on reason (empirical coherence, for Brightman), and the latter by Bertocci with his emphasis on creativity. Though Bowne and Brightman were deeply concerned with education, it was Bertocci who wrote on the subject, and his focus was on moral education. My interest, however, is not in developing Bertocci's position. Rather I shall state the essentials of a Personalist view of *moral* education within the *poeisis* tradition. To do that I shall address this question: "Must one *know* to be good?" I shall discuss that question by examining the life of the developing moral person and the place of knowledge in that life. As this discussion unfolds, we shall see the educational ideal of Boston Personalism.

University," in George M. Marsden and Bradley J. Longfield, eds., *The Secularization of the Academy* (New York: Oxford UP, 1992) 9–45; and George M. Marsden, *The Soul of the American University, From Protestant Establishment to Established Nonbelief* (New York: Oxford UP, 1994).

Structure of Persons

We turn first to the life of the developing moral person. What can we say about that life? Humans are creative-finders. Being instinctually deprived and thus open to the world in a way that animals are not, they create structures for themselves.[3] They may be stable, as in traditional societies, or unstable and open to change, as in modern societies. Yet in their effort to overcome their instinctual deficit in their relation to the world and to provide safety for themselves, they craft a world, including institutions. The exercise of this capacity requires imagination and embodiment. This means that selves must "come up with," imagine both what is not already available to them in the world and ways of realizing those possibilities. The realization of the possible requires embodiment, the suggestiveness of the "medium" in which we live physically and socially. Selves and institutions are nothing more than abstractions if they remain only in the imaginative mind of the artist and on the drawing board of the draftsman. They must be instantiated by "artists" in contexts that will support them. But what is the place of creative-finding in the formation of our moral personhood?[4]

First, as a creative-finder a person is an agent. We not only initiate actions but we have the potentiality to act in a wide variety of ways. We shall call these "activity potentials." An activity potential is that which a person is able to do in a situation that calls for it. Persons have the

---

[3] See Arnold Gehlen, *Man in the Age of Technology,* trans. Patricia Lipscomb (New York: Columbia UP, 1980); and Max Scheler, *Man's Place in Nature,* trans. with intro. Hans Meyerhoff (New York: Beacon, 1961). See also Thomas O. Buford, *Trust, Our Second Nature: Crisis, Reconciliation, and the Personal* (Lanham, MD: Lexington Books, 2009).

[4] For what follows, we shall be heavily dependent upon the work of Peter A. Bertocci, especially his essay "The Essence of a Person," *The Monist* 61/1 (January 1978): 28–41. Bertocci, Bowne, and Brightman believed that the starting point in our search for the nature of the person is experience and reasoning within experience. It makes no sense to go beyond what experience supports, they argued; yet we must seek the most coherent account of experience as we find it. They wanted to achieve the most inclusively systematic hypothesis regarding the nature of persons, their identity, and their unity.

following activity potentials: "sensing, remembering, imagining, thinking, feeling, emoting, wanting, willing, oughting, and aesthetic and religious appreciation."[5] To possess the activity potential of sensing means, for example, that one has the potentiality to see the color of the Aegean sea, even though one has never actually seen it. If one were in a position to see it, one would be able to do so. It is also possible for a person not to possess an activity potential. A blind person does not have the activity potential of sight. We call these activity potentials a complex unity because rarely is one potential developed without involving the others. Persons do not simply see; they also think about what they see, appreciate what they see, and remember what they see. And we must remember that, as agents with activity potentials, those potentials actualize in a suggestive and limiting context. For one to sense, there must be something that is sensed. We cannot sense a red male cardinal as just any color we arbitrarily choose. The bird sets limits to the actualization of my activity potential, seeing.

Second, as creative-finders we are self-conscious of this complex of activity potentials as belonging to ourselves. And as belonging, these activity potentials are owned. They are mine. However, the fact that they belong to me does not mean they are consistent with each other or that they work well together. Rather, they "belong" in the sense that they are all owned by one person, me. But what is the person to whom these activity potentials belong? For them to belong to me, there must be a unifier to whom they belong. To ignore belonging as implying a unity leaves us with simply unrelated experiences as the activity potentials actualize their potentiality. That could leave us with the following oddity: I could hit my finger with a hammer today and I could remember tomorrow that I hit my finger with a hammer yesterday and the two experiences have nothing to do with each other. But, of course they do; I connect them. Both belong to me and I am aware of that. The self cannot be only a succession of experiences, as Hume contended. There can be no succession of experiences without the experience of succession. Unless there is someone to whom they belong and who acts as unifier, change and the interrelation of the activity potentials are incoherent. A

[5] Ibid., 29.

person is a unity-in-continuity. Does this mean that a person is an entity that has the capacity to possess these characteristics? No, a person is not an entity; a person is nothing other than the experiences he or she has. No unchanging, mathematically identical soul unifies our activity potentials. While the complex unity of activity potentials is nothing apart from the self, the self is not reducible to this complex unity. The self is "a self-identifying unity in change, a self-identifying being and becoming."[6] We find that we are a self-conscious unity amid complexity. What does this mean?

Third, as creative-finders our identity is rooted in our experience of the continuity of "nows." We are self-consciously aware that we are both self-identifying and being-becoming. We are self-conscious of ourselves as complex unities who have identities and that remain through change. "The unity that is undeniable is the complex now of self-experience, a present that is no mathematical point but a saddle-back span, a telic moment *erlebst* that gives way to another moment."[7] How are these "nows" to be interpreted? They are our experience of ourselves as temporal beings. The most rudimentary experience we have of ourselves is our now, our duration. As enduring, we are continuous with the past and the future. For this reason, we call this view a temporalistic view of the person. But how are the nows connected to form our ongoing continuous selves? It seems at first sight that reason is the best candidate to connect them. But reason is not the experiential basis for our conviction of a continuous self, an identity. What evidence do we have that there is an identity among our nows, that we are the same persons at the beginning of Franz Liszt's *Les Preludes* as we are at the end of it?

On the one hand, the experiential basis of our belief that we are identical through change is the experience of "again." The "now" that I am conscious of recurs again. "Againness" is rooted in memory, especially recall, as in recalling a person's name. This is the power both to form an image, an individual in the midst of the flux of sensation, and to recognize now the reoccurrence of that individual. On the other hand, as we connect our nows as happening again, we may be in error. But to be

[6] Ibid., 30.

[7] Ibid., 30–31.

in error requires the identity of persons. Only persons are able to refer an experience to an object or to claim knowledge of an object. If my student advisee, Reed, says that he is better suited to being a salesman rather than an accountant, Reed believes something and refers it to himself. He may be wrong about himself. Let's assume that he is, and that he would make a better accountant than a salesman. The error was dependent on something being in Reed's consciousness: "only a being who can be aware of x, continue to be and become as he refers the x experienced beyond itself, and thus be the 'locus' of whether or not his reference is correct—only such a unity-in-continuity, only such a being-becoming, can render the very occurrence of error intelligible."[8] Only a person who remains self-conscious through nows, who has identity, can be in error.

Fourth, and finally, as creative-finders we direct our lives towards ends. We want to become doctors, salesmen, laborers, or whatever, and we work toward those goals. We may be wrong or "misdirected" about those goals. But we must believe that persons who purposively and imaginatively guide their successive experiences relative to ends are continuous and self-identical through those telic successive experiences. Thus, as a creative-finder I am an interrelator of nows, a self-identifying, imagining interrelator whose nature it is to act and be acted upon. A person as being-becoming is deeply rooted in the constitutive imagination focused on the "medium" within which it lives. What are we to make of a person as an interrelator that forms her *personality*?

Let's consider the nature of personality, how it arises, and then its relation to persons. A personality can be defined as "that organization, by a self-identifying person, of those psychophysical wants and abilities that uniquely characterizes his expressive and adaptive adjustments to his environment."[9] How does the personality arise? Personalities are not mere products of their environments or mere unfoldings of capacities. Personality develops due to persons' responses to and understanding of themselves and their public environment. As human beings, persons have needs, tendencies, potentialities, and interests. Individuals select from

---

[8] Ibid., 32.

[9] Peter A. Bertocci, "The Person, His Personality, and Environment," *Review of Metaphysics* 32 (1979): 606.

their own capacities and telic tendencies. We select among these tendencies and the environmental options available to us. Telic tendencies include drives, propensities, needs, and motives, both innate and learned. Such tendencies are psychophysiological in character and include the "bodily me" as well as some aspects of self-identity and ego enhancement discussed earlier. Telic tensions, conflicts, and anxieties do not occur between individuals and their environments (social and physical). Rather, "they have their locus within the person whose dynamic, telic nature encourages the different meanings and values he gives to what surfaces in his constant interaction with *some* environment."[10]

Personalities are the products of knowing-wanting agents who interact with their private and public environments in the attempt to satisfy their own selections and abilities. What is the relation of person and personality? There is an interrelator (Descartes's crucial insight is correct), but this interrelator is not a timeless, unchanging, substantially identical being. Persons are being-becomings. They objectify themselves, become, in relation to their environment. In so doing their activity potentials through interaction with the total environment are formed into a relatively coherent becoming. This is the personality. No personality, no person. Likewise, no person, no personality.

We can now understand "poeisis," the metaphor drawn from art and its relation to the formation of personality. Both the imagination and medium play central roles in the formation of both the person and personality. If the self is to be understood as a complex time-binding interrelation of activity potentials, the act of relating is an act that brings something into existence that was not there before. The person is agent; but the person is deeply the constitutive imagination on the basis of which the "medium" (the total environment) is explored and the elements of the self are both interrelated and related to that medium. No image, no relations; and no relations, no personal identity.[11] Further, the

---

[10] Ibid., 608.

[11] Vico is right. The central imaginative universal is Jove. From it, all else human develops. The self finds itself in and through sacred story. See Stephen Crites, "The Narrative Quality of Experience," *Journal of the American Academy of Religion* 39 (September 1971): 291–311.

self that forms its personality as it interacts with its environment must consider possible ends towards which to move, and that requires the creative imagination. It could be that the self forms its personality dyadically, as in traditional societies. But even then it recognizes itself as numerically other than the persons in their community. Or it could be that the self forms its personality monadically, as in modern, industrial society. In that case it attempts to form its personality independently of other persons even though it may be influenced by them. The modern personality is the peculiar development of the self as it relates to the specific environment—social, political, economic, moral—that is found in the West since the 1600s. Thus, the temporalistic personalist helps us to understand how the self develops a personality and, in so doing, helps us to develop the metaphor of "medium" that is necessary to the imaginative development of the self, to creatively finding a self.

In sum, we now have before us an interpretation of the person as creator-finder. We have seen that the imagination and "medium" are central to the self's formation of itself as a personality. To bring into existence what was not there before, a person must imagine possibilities. The self is constrained by a "medium," which, as we have seen, both suggests and constricts by setting boundaries. Now we must discuss that which directs and unifies the activity potentials of the self, its telic and regnant ideals.

Values and the Good

At the heart of the Personalist view of persons is that they are complex time-binding unities with regnant ideals. As moral agents, persons are "capable of thinking and conducting [themselves] in accordance with the ideals of truth and value."[12] But how do these ideals arise? To understand that, we must discuss the Good and its place in the life of persons as creative-finders. Persons are willing, feeling, emotive, wanting selves, as well as oughting ones. This means that oughting is an activity potential. Oughting does not arise from knowledge; neither does it arise from the person herself, as if it were made by that person or by society. As

---

[12] Peter A. Bertocci, "A Personalistic Philosophy of Education," *Teachers College Record* 80/3 (February 1979): 489.

Bertocci says, "...any person mature enough to conceive alternatives, who decides that x-value is better than y-value, *never* experiences 'I ought to choose y' (even though it may turn out that he does choose y)."[13] But what ought persons to choose?

What is the good for persons? This good has two components, the first of which is that persons are ends. This means that,

> were persons not capable of thinking and willing in relation to the alternatives consonant with their affective-emotive tendencies, they would have no reason for treating themselves as ends; they could reasonably be treated as things. Only that person can be an *end in* himself who can be an end *for* himself. This is the baseline of a personalistic theory of the good and therefore of education.[14]

However, this is not enough. It remains empty until a person

> decides what values and ideals are the best for persons,...until we articulate an ideal of personality that ought to be realized as far as possible (meliorism) in the context of the raw materials [read "medium"] of personal experience. ...The personalist's next question must be: How shall we reason about the actual good open to persons, by which all educational choices, formal and material, ought to be guided?[15]

We must keep in mind that values are the wantings, strivings of persons. But some wants are prized over others. We must evaluate them in the situations in which we find ourselves. As we do so, we find them forming patterns. "Any value pattern we discover will be a description about persons in their world, or of the world with persons left in it. The ideal of the life good to live will be a consequence of man's relating himself in thought and action to his own activity-potentials and to his environment, as conceived and as it really is."[16] Once we see this, we find that some values are cardinal and support the development of others. These cardinal ones are existence, health, and truth-values. These values are not concoctions of impulse that can be dismantled in preference to

---

[13] Ibid., 490.

[14] Ibid., 491.

[15] Ibid., 492.

[16] Ibid., 494.

others. "To live at all is to live 'in connections' we can't escape; our problem—the fundamental one in education—is to discover the framework, so to speak, of connections among our value—and disvalue—experiences."[17]

To live lives good to live also requires that we discipline ourselves by our ideals. That is our character. "Character…is a simple word for a person's complex, learned, moral dispositions to face value conflicts that inevitably or purposely arise in and around his efforts to discover and increase values in his own life and that of others."[18] Succinctly, persons ought to discover the best of which they are capable and strive to achieve it in the face of whatever difficulties present themselves in their environments.

The achievement of these values, however, also involves affiliative and vocational values. Persons find that their values are not only deeply "rooted in, but rendered more worthwhile by, their associations with others."[19] And "the job one has, the work one does 'for a living,' may well take its place alongside of family-experience as the gymnasium in which most persons shape their personalities."[20] However, vocation is broader than work to earn a living. It is one's calling, which is to actualize the purpose that allows for the full actualization of his individuality.

And what is the interrelation of these values? There is no hierarchy here. Our lives move and change as we creatively grow within and in response to our environments. Different values come to the front to guide us at different times in our lives. It is best to think of a symphony of values. "Hence the question always is: Which orchestration of values will not foreclose values unnecessarily?"[21] As Bertocci says, "The goal in life, the meaning of happiness, cannot be 'serene' fulfillment but a melioristic 'creative insecurity.' …His task, ultimately of self-education, is the task of finding where he is, and how far he can go, in relation to

[17] Ibid., 497.
[18] Ibid., 499.
[19] Ibid.
[20] Ibid., 501.
[21] Ibid., 503.

the total human venture in value realization."[22] "The moral life consists not in a flight from insecurity, but in risky but blessed creativity, guided by a larger, imperfect vision of what man and the universe can be."[23] Though the Personalist can develop a view of the life good to live on the basis of a person's *Lebenschauung*, it points to grounding in a view of Being as Person.

Knowledge, the Good, and Persons

The universe is deeply moral and we can know its structure through the revelation of God in the Judeo-Christian tradition. But we are not left to faith alone. Appealing to German Romantic thought, particularly Kant and Hegel, we can argue that the universe is moral and knowable by reason and experience. Nature is God's creation and, by our own devices, notably science, we can learn what God placed there. Humans, made in the image of God, are best guided by reason as they interpret experience as well as being instructed by it. But left to reason and experience alone, persons drift and find no stable meaning in life. (Scientific standards and procedures are not enough to build a life on.) Only on the basis of their purposive, aiming, valuing activity can persons find meaning. But values are not private or limited to society. Written in the heart of reality are moral patterns that are universal and available to all persons. By grasping these moral values, a person can integrate them into her life, thereby finding the meaning that seems so elusive. Though a person, thinking philosophically, can grasp them, any person through the Judeo-Christian faith, particularly the Protestant tradition, can grasp them and find in them meaning for their lives.

This reformulation of the tradition of the calling aids persons to find answers to the deepest questions of their lives, specifically: Who am I? What am I to be? What am I to do? And in answering them, one supposedly overcomes the truncated and splintered personality and finds rich identity. What gives our lives unity are values, purposes that

---

[22] Ibid., 504. See Peter A. Bertocci, *Religion as Creative Insecurity* (New York: Associate Press, 1958; Westwood, CT: Greenwood, 1973).

[23] Peter A. Bertocci, *Education and the Vision of Excellence*, University Lecture 1959–1960 (Boston: Boston UP, 1960) 26.

transcend us and to which we commit ourselves. Writing in 1908, Josiah Royce, the great Harvard philosopher, wrote,

> …the answer to the question, "Who are you?" really begins in earnest when a man mentions his calling, and so actually sets out upon the definition of his purposes and of the way in which these purposes get expressed in his life. …To sum up, then, I should say that a person, an individual self, may be defined as a human life lived according to a plan.[24]

Further, we search for "some cause, far larger than ourselves, to which we are fully ready to be loyal."[25] When we find that cause, we come to our full moral consciousness, we find unity for our lives, and we also find our calling. It should not be assumed that the cause to which one is loyal will actually fully and finally unite and integrate one's life. Edgar S. Brightman wrote in 1925 that "…our incomplete and fragmentary minds give rise to an ideal of a full and complete personality, that this ideal is the only one that fulfills the demands of coherent thinking, and hence that the perfect personality is real."[26] And what is the relation of that cause, that which is supremely valuable to that perfect personality, to God? God is the home of universal values. They are the fundamental principles in terms of which God created, sustains, and redeems the world. And only they can provide the unity a purposive, aiming person seeks. Though our limited, finite, individual minds seek unity, only God is fully integrated, unified personality.

Conclusion

A Personalist answer to our question can be seen within the central personalist concern regarding the education of the whole person. The whole person rests on character and truth, the two rails on which the moral personality travels. Let's summarize by focusing on the original question, "Must one *know* to be good?"

---

[24] Josiah Royce, *The Philosophy of Loyalty* (New York: Macmillan, 1908, 1918) 168.

[25] Ibid., 170.

[26] Edgar Sheffield Brightman, *An Introduction to Philosophy* (New York: Holt, 1925) 210.

Person is a time-binding, complex unity of activity potentials, governed by ideals, "a fighter for ends" (William James).
For persons to be good, to be rich, full personalities, they must *know* those ideals that give their lives coherence.
If one were to claim to be virtuous and did not know that the values chosen were the best for the fully developed personality, that person cannot escape the charge that they could be acting badly while they thought there were acting virtuously.
Hence, o*ne must know the good to be good.*

Indeed, for Dr. Carter, one must know and seek "to become the change" that knowledge requires. His disciplined life is animated by Micah's prophetic vision, "He hath shewed thee, O man, what is good; and what doth the Lord require of thee, but to do justly, and to love mercy, and to walk humbly with thy God?" (Micah 6:8, KJV).

3

Dr. Lawrence Edward Carter, Sr. and My Journey to Christian Allegory

Delman L. Coates

The Rev. Dr. Lawrence Edward Carter, Sr., affectionately known as "Dean" by his students, is singlehandedly responsible for guiding me as an undergraduate student to pursue doctoral studies in Religion. I met him my first week at Morehouse College during Freshman Orientation in fall 1991. During an orientation session for the Martin Luther King, Jr. International chapel assistants program, Dean Carter gave those assembled a copy of Cain Hope Felder's *Stony the Road We Trod,* which had just been released. I shall never forget reading Dr. Felder's introduction sitting there in the King Chapel office, and decided that day that I would pursue a Ph.D. in New Testament and Early Christianity. Dean Carter impressed upon us the importance of "an informed ministry," and encouraged those of us who were so inclined to prepare ourselves to pursue a terminal degree in Religion. Taking that charge seriously, I began taking courses in Greek, Hebrew, French, and German my first year at Morehouse in order to prepare myself for later doctoral studies. I am indebted to Dean Carter for his guidance and mentoring during those formative years of my intellectual development.

The journey to expand my theological horizons, however, was not as smooth as I had anticipated. Early on as a freshman Religion major, I experienced a rather considerable tension between the Christian understandings I had inherited from my Christian upbringing, and the academic, "higher critical" approach to the study of Christianity I was learning and had come to embrace. I recall wrestling intellectually with whether my Christian beliefs, as I understood them, could be reconciled with the academic study of Christianity and the Bible I was being taught. All around me I observed other students going through a similar struggle. On the one hand, there were those who opted to reject critical theological and historical studies, choosing to remain in the safe theological confines of the faith communities that nurtured them, and on the other hand, there were those who opted to reject the belief systems that nurtured them in favor of the more informed and enlightened "scientific" approach to the study of religion. This choice between the life of the spirit and the life of the mind was never unacceptable to me; however, as an 18-year-old product of a Black Baptist, evangelical Christian background, I had neither a language nor the theological tools to help me negotiate these two worlds that I valued so much. As a preacher and aspiring scholar, I found myself yearning for a way to be authentically Christian and unashamedly academic at the same time.

The process of resolving this tension began for me in an "Introduction to Religion" course with Dean Carter during my freshman year at Morehouse. In response to a question I raised about the apparent contradictions in the Bible, and the apparent similarities between biblical narratives and myths found in other ancient, Near Eastern religions, Dean Carter and guest lecturer Charles Finch helped me understand that the "truth" of the ancient religious mythologies (including the Christian myth) is found in "deeper, spiritual meanings" rather than a presumed "historical fact." I shall never forget that lecture because it served as the catalyst for helping me reconcile my devotion as a Christian, and my commitment to the academic study of religion in general, and Christianity in particular. That lecture in fall 1991 led me to do some informal research on patristic exegesis and interpretation, and resulted in my subsequent interest in early Christian allegorical interpretation. In many ways, my academic interest in "allegorical interpretation," "spiritual exegesis," or "non-literal interpretation" was rooted in my own spiritual and theological quest to reconcile my faith with my academic studies, and I would later come to understand that the interpretive method I used had as much to do with interpreting the self and my location in the world, as it did with interpreting a text.

My subsequent thinking about ancient (and modern) interpretive practices came as a result of reflecting on the way in which I had used scriptural interpretation as a means of authorizing my own socio-religious position in the world. If, as Vincent Wimbush states, "the logical and provocative place from which to begin the critical-interpretive task…

is not with a focus upon text, but upon construction of world,"[1] then it seemed appropriate to regard hermeneutics as much about the interpretation of the self as the interpretation of written texts. Was it possible, I began to wonder, that some ancient interpreters similarly read texts as a means of giving voice to their own subjectivity and appropriated particular interpretive methodologies in order to engage and critique prevailing discourses? If that was the case, then I wanted to explore the intersections between hermeneutics, ideology, social location, and power in my study of the ancient world. I would later discover, however, that the traditional scholarly approach to the study of early Christian allegorical interpretation did not lend itself to the exploration of these questions.

The history of scholarship on early Christian allegory has focused the categories of analysis upon the theological appropriateness of the method for biblical interpretation, obscuring our ability to consider these broader questions about the strategy's social and cultural function. The debate over allegorical interpretation has a history that extends back into the early centuries of Christian history.[2] The terms, issues, and categories of the contemporary debate regarding allegorical interpretation, however, can be located in a more recent historical context that has its genesis in the theological and political environment of early Protestant theology

[1] Vincent Wimbush, "Reading Texts as Reading Ourselves: A Chapter in the History of African-American Biblical Interpretation," in *Reading from this Place: Volume 1 Social Location and Biblical Interpretation in the United States*, ed. Fernando F. Segovia and Mary Ann Tolbert (Minneapolis: Fortress Press, 1995) 95–108. See also Vincent Wimbush, "Reading Darkness, Reading Scriptures," in *African Americans and the Bible: Sacred Texts and Social Textures*, ed. Vincent Wimbush (New York: Continuum, 2000) 1–43, for his argument that the academic field of biblical studies be reframed so as to place intentional and critical focus "on the *phenomenology of social cultural formation and the creation and uses of sacred texts*" (14).

[2] Karen Jo Torjesen, *Hermeneutical Procedure and Theological Method in Origen's Exegesis* (Berlin and New York: Walter de Gruyter, 1986) 1. See also Elizabeth A. Clark, *The Origenist Controversy: The Cultural Construction of an Early Christian Debate* (Princeton, NJ: Princeton University Press, 1992); and Adolf Von Harnack, *Der Kirchengeschichtliche Ertrag der exegetischen Arbeiten des Origenes* (TU 42, 3 1918) 8.

and scholarship. An understanding of this history will help us to understand the current state of the problem.

Traditional approaches to the study of Christian allegory begin with the assumption that the practice is an "insane activity," a "refuge of unskillfulness," and a "persistent problem" characterized by "ambiguity," "indeterminacy," "unpredictability," and a lack of fidelity to the historical dimension of knowledge.[3] The comparativist strategies used to evaluate the legitimacy of allegory's theological content are rooted in a long history of Protestant polemics against Catholicism and Judaism.

In many ways Martin Luther is responsible for laying the foundation upon which the contemporary objection to the practice is based.[4] Beginning with the assumption that allegory is primarily a method for interpreting the Bible to discover spiritual truths, Luther rejects the use of allegory to derive the theological meaning of the Bible.[5] Since so much of Luther's biblical theology was informed by the sociopolitical realities of his day, such as European nation-states struggling to secure political sovereignty from the Catholic Church in the late fifteenth and early sixteenth century,[6] his thinking was largely influenced by these developments. The loss of monarchical-ecclesiastical power on the eve of the

---

[3] John Whitman, *Interpretation and Allegory: Antiquity to the Modern Period* (Leiden: Brill, 2000), 3, 4, 6. Philip Rollinson, *Classical Theories of Allegory and Christian Culture* (Pittsburgh, PA: Duquesne University Press, 1981) 21; R. P. C. Hanson, *Allegory and Event: A Study of the Sources and Significance of Origen's Interpretation of Scripture* (Richmond, VA: John Knox Press, 1959) 367–69. For Whitman, allegory is a practice "on a collision course with itself" that ends in failure.

[4] Torjesen, *Hermeneutical Procedure and Theological Method*, 1.

[5] Ibid. Also David Dawson, *Allegorical Readers and Cultural Revision in Ancient Alexandria* (New Haven: Yale University Press, 1992) 1, 15. See Martin Luther, "Concerning the Letter and the Spirit," for a critique of the spiritual interpretation of the scriptures that was popular in the Catholic Church.

[6] See Steven Ozment, *The Age of Reform 1250–1550: An Intellectual and Religious History of Late Medieval and Reformation Europe* (New Haven and London: Yale University Press, 1980) 182–222, 245–89, for a survey of the social, political, and economic conditions that provided fertile soil for Protestant thinking.

Reformation foreshadowed Luther's efforts to provide a theological basis for undermining the hegemony of the Catholic Church that was already taking place throughout Europe. Luther's biblical theology, and his view of allegorical interpretation in particular, must be connected then to the rejection of late medieval (Catholic) piety and papal claims to temporary power that were current at the time.[7]

Luther's method of biblical exegesis was designed to counter the figurative reading of the Bible that was current in the Church. He argued that the meaning of the Bible was conveyed in the "simplici puraeque et naturali significationi verborum, quam grammaticus et usus loguendi habet quem Deus creavit in hominibus."[8] Luther here is asserting that the divine meaning of scripture is attained in the simple, natural sense of the text.[9] The importance of Luther for subsequent criticism of allegorical interpretation lies in his view that the power of the scriptures to provide theological training and education is not to be found in the figurative or allegorical sense of the scriptures, but rather, in the grammatical sense of the text.[10] Luther transforms the theological basis for

---

[7] Ozment, *The Age of Reform 1250–1550*, 205. See also Heinrich Finke, "Die Nation in den spatmittelalterlichen allgemeinen Konzilien," *Historisches Jahrbuch* 57 (1937): 323–38; Joseph Lortz, *Die Reformation in Deutschland*, vols. 1–2 (Freiburg im Breisgau: Herder, 1962), 1962); and Etienne Delareulle, *L'église au temps du Grand Schisme et de la crise conciliare* (Paris: Bloud et Gay, 1962). I make this assertion in recognition of the fact that at various points in his intellectual development, Luther thought of his theology as coterminous with the Catholic Church. For example, he concludes his "Disputation Against Scholastic Theology" by saying, "In these statements we wanted to say and believe we have said nothing that is not in agreement with the Catholic church and the teachers of the church" (in *Martin Luther's Basic Theological Writings* (Minneapolis: Augsburg Fortress, 2012) 20).

[8] Torjesen, *Hermeneutical Procedure and Theological Method*, 1; citation from Martin Luther, *De Servo Arbitrio*, WA 18, 700.

[9] Torjesen, *Hermeneutical Procedure and Theological Method*, 1, 2. Luther further writes, "Sic placitum est Deo, ut non sine verbo, sed per verbum tribuat spiritum, ut nos habeat suos cooperators, dum foris sonamus" (*De Servo Arbitrio*, WA 18, 600).

[10] Torjesen, *Hermeneutical Procedure and Theological Method*, 2.

accessing the message of scripture by consolidating the multiple senses of scripture of late medieval biblical theology into a single, grammatical sense of the text that is accessed through the natural meaning of words.[11] Luther's claim for the sufficiency of the natural sense of the text as the standard for Protestant exegesis was a reaction to papal political hegemony in Europe and to the perception that medieval exegetical practices served to buttress that authority.

Given the centrality of the Catholic Church in late medieval society,[12] Luther's critique of medieval exegetical practices (i.e., allegory) had sociopolitical implications that set the stage for subsequent generations of Protestant thinkers to continue his "revolution against Rome and traditional religion."[13] Positive associations between Protestant theology, Renaissance humanism (with its focus upon knowledge of the "original" languages, attention to text criticism, satirical and polemical attacks upon the Church and the clergy, and an increasing spirit of European nationalism), and Enlightenment thought over the next few centuries sharpened the critique against allegory.[14] Critics contended that the practice did not conform to the emerging intellectual and scientific expectations of the day. Future debates over the appropriate method for interpreting the Bible would center upon how the one, primary sense of

---

[11] Hans W. Frei, *The Eclipse of Biblical Narrative: A Study in Eighteenth and Nineteenth Century Hermeneutics* (New Haven: Yale University Press, 1974) 23, 24.

[12] Ozment, *The Age of Reform 1250–1550,* 22.

[13] Ibid., 231.

[14] For a discussion of the interaction between Renaissance humanism and Protestant thinking, see ibid., 290–317; James K. McConica, *English Humanists and Reformation Politics Under Henry VIII and Edward VI* (Oxford: Clarendon Press, 1965); Johan Huizinga, *Erasmus and the Age of Reformation* (New York: Harper, 1957); Bernd Moeller, "Die deutschen Humanisten und die Anfange der Reformation," *ZKG* 70 (1959): 46–61; Paul O. Kristeller, *Renaissance Thought: The Classic, Scholastic, and Humanist Strains* (New York: Harper & Row, 1961); and Alain Dufour, "Humanisme et Reformation: Etat de la question," in *XIIe Congrés Internationale des Sciences Historiques, Vienne, 29 Aout–5 Septembre 1965: Rapports* (Horn/Wien: Verlag F. Berger, 1965) 3:57–74.

the scriptures is to be defined and accessed.[15] This would be the focal point for subsequent criticism of allegory as an interpretive methodology.

Efforts to understand the world in a newly scientific way during the seventeenth and eighteenth centuries influenced subsequent Protestant reflection on biblical interpretation and effectively reshaped the criteria upon which exegesis would be based. In this environment, exegesis had to be accommodated to the scientific understanding of the world that was gaining intellectual supremacy. The convergence of theological apologetics and scientific epistemology caused future scholarship on allegory to be preoccupied with the relationship between method, interpretation, and history. In other words, the basis of the critique against allegory during this period was its lack of fidelity to the literal, grammatical, and historical or "scientific" dimension of scripture.[16] According to Torjesen, the basic criticism of allegorical interpretation by the seventeenth century is not that it is fanciful, but rather that allegory depreciates history.[17] Hans Frei has shown that biblical interpreters during this period had to wrestle and come to terms with the evolving secular/scientific concept of history, leading many interpreters to conflate theological meaning and historical fact.[18]

By the late nineteenth century, critics of allegory used other grounds for rejecting the practice. As the scientific method was becoming foundational in other fields of inquiry, allegorical interpretation was expected to conform to the canons of scientific methodology—objectivity, consistency, and repeatability.[19] The new question regarding allegory was whether the practice met the new intellectual expectations concerning methodological legitimacy. Unable to deny that Christian allegorists possessed a systematic concept of method that was applied when interpreting the Bible, nineteenth-century critics contended that allegory

---

[15] Torjesen, *Hermeneutical Procedure and Theological Method*, 1.

[16] Ibid., 2.

[17] Ibid.

[18] Frei, *The Eclipse of Biblical Narrative*, 17–50. See also Torjesen, *Hermeneutical Procedure and Theological Method*, 2.

[19] Torjesen, *Hermeneutic Procedure and Theological Method*, 2.

could not meet the "scientific" standard for interpreting the scriptures.[20] By the mid-1920s, scholars began to concede that allegory was a scientific methodology. The difference, however, was that it was "scientific" according to Hellenistic standards.[21] Says de Faye, "L'allégorie était le moyen reputé, savant, scientifique, philosophique de discerner dans les écrits antiques et vénérés à titre d'oracles une philosophie et une théologie."[22] The basis for the critique of allegory, then, centers not upon its qualifications as a method, but rather upon the theological result that is achieved when this "Hellenistic" or "foreign" (*étranger*) method is applied to the scriptures. According to de Faye, "Lorsqu'on lit, soit les commentaries de notre auteur soit ses homilies, il est naturel qu'on se demande comment il a pu alterer le sense des Écritures au point d'y substituer un sens philosophique entièrement étranger aux auteurs sacrés."[23] De Faye's essential critique of allegory is now that it utilizes non-Christian sources that result in the substitution of Hellenistic philosophical doctrines for doctrines that should be theological in nature.[24]

This new critique of allegorical interpretation belongs to the era of criticism initiated by Adolf von Harnack in the late nineteenth century. In *Handbuch der Dogmengeschichte* (1883), Harnack argued that early Christian theological and exegetical traditions suffered from the influence of Hellenistic thought.[25] This kind of argument presupposes a radical difference between Christianity and its environment. Scholars interested in the issue of Christian allegory now sought to isolate early Christian exegesis from its historical context by distinguishing the supposed continuity between Judaism and Christianity from Hellenistic culture. To achieve this goal, scholars endeavored to determine the "sources" behind ancient Christian exegetical practices. By distinguishing

---

[20] Ibid., 2.

[21] Ibid., 3.

[22] E. de Faye, *Esquisse de la pensée d'Origéne* (Paris: Leroux, 1925) 40, quoted in Torjesen, *Hermeneutical Procedure and Theological Method*, 3.

[23] E. de Faye, *Origéne, sa vie, son oeuvre, sa pensée*, vol. 1 (Paris: Leroux, 1923) 94, quoted in Torjesen, *Hermeneutical Procedure and Theological Method*, 3.

[24] Torjesen, *Hermeneutical Procedure and Theological Method*, 3.

[25] Ibid.

Jewish sources or patterns of interpretation from Hellenistic sources, these scholars attempted to determine what aspects of ancient Christian interpretation are uniquely "Christian," and what aspects derived from "pagan" sources. The apologetic and theological interests involved in this endeavor use comparative methodology to subordinate those forms of interpretation considered "later," "pagan," or "non-Christian." When it comes to the study of early Christian allegory, the interests of the comparative enterprise have been driven by particular ideological and theological agendas that have masqueraded as disinterested scientific inquiry.

The history of the discourse on early Christian allegory reveals the methodological dilemma posed by traditional approaches to the study of Christian allegory. In the history of scholarship on early Christian allegory, the evaluative criteria for assessing the appropriateness of the strategy have tended to focus on the theological dimensions of the practice. Using comparative methodology as the primary analytical resource for attempting to understand the "sources" behind allegorical interpretation, these scholars have limited our understanding of the broader cultural-critical functions of the practice. While claiming to be a disinterested "scientific" inquiry, scholars seeking to identify the "sources" and "theological structure" of early Christian allegory have merely been advancing a theological agenda that obscures the topic at hand.

The scholarly disparagement of allegorical interpretation is most often rooted in a Protestant critique of Catholic theology and hermeneutics. For Protestant historians and theologians, allegorical interpretation represents a kind of hermeneutical "decay" from more pristine forms of Christian interpretation. When situated against the broader cultural and philosophical "background" of the Greco-Roman world, the comparative interests that inform the assessment of early Christian allegory have as their presupposition the view that allegory represents a departure from earlier, more essentially Christian forms of interpretation. In Quasten's *Patrology*, for example, a historiographical narrative is told that traces the beginnings of Christianity in a "Palestinian" milieu and eventually spreads to more "Hellenized" parts of the Roman Empire.[26] As Christianity penetrated the Greco-Roman world, it is supposed that there was a greater need to make the tenets of Christianity intelligible to a new "Hellenized" audience. The growth of Christian communities in these Hellenized circles increased the need for catechetical instruction that corresponded to the new intellectual climate, necessitating the training of teachers for that purpose. "Thus were created the theological schools, the cradles of sacred science."[27]

This is the supposed cultural backdrop against which the Christian allegorists, often referred to as the Christian "Platonists," enter the stage of history. It is a narrative in which the city of Alexandria figures prominently as the "birthplace of Hellenism" and as the cultural incubator for figures such as Origen of Alexandria. The city of Alexandria is caricatured as a "...pot boiling with diverse teachings, all eclectic in nature: the Gnosticism held by Basilides, the Neoplatonism of Ammonius Saccas and Plotinus, the Hellenistic Judaism that followed in the tradition of Philo, and the esoteric and Platonist Christianity of Clement and Origen."[28] Here, Oriental, Egyptian, and Greek cultures commingled and syncretized, giving birth to a rich new intellectual mind. Hellenistic-Judaism in Alexandria, expressed chiefly in the extant writings of the philosopher/exegete Philo, had the greatest influence on the biblical exegesis of later Alexandrian Christians such as Clement and Origen. This "context," then, is supposed to assist the student in understanding the "content" of allegorical interpretation.

While Christian allegorists considered their theological views and hermeneutical method to be within the pale of accepted Christian teaching,[29] the supposed contextualization of their views within the cultural and philosophical environment of ancient Alexandria is intended

---

[26] Johannes Quasten, *Patrology: The Ante-Nicene Literature After Irenaeus*, vol. II (Westminster, MD: The Newman Press, 1952).

[27] Quasten, *Patrology*, 1.

[28] Justo L. Gonzalez, *History of Christian Thought*, vol. I (Nashville, TN: Abingdon Press, 1970) 191.

[29] Origen [225], *On First Principles*, Preface (Eugene, OR: Wipf and Stock, 2012), 2.

to show the derivative nature of his appropriation of the Christian tradition. According to the historiographical narrative, allegorical interpretation served a kind of "missionary" function—namely, to make the biblical traditions of Judaism and Christianity intelligible to the Hellenistic mind. While Christian allegorists were not the first to employ the strategy, this view regards allegory's chief function to be exporting or transmitting the Christian tradition to a more philosophically minded audience.[30] As Christianity entered Alexandria towards the end of the first century, it developed in close contact with the "Greek," "Jewish," and "Egyptian" religious and philosophical milieu that characterized the environment there. As a consequence, these Christian philosophers adopted the method of textual interpretation that was popular within "Hellenized" circles because, as Gonzalez says, "they were convinced that a literal interpretation was in many cases unworthy of God."[31]

By "contextualizing" modern scholarship on Christian allegory, it becomes clear that the analysis is informed by a long tradition of Protestant critique against the (Catholic) view of multiple levels of scriptural meaning.[32] I have attempted to show that, beginning in the sixteenth century, the Protestant interpretive tradition waged a consequential attack on allegorical exegesis, setting the stage for the "scientific, grammatico-historical exegesis" of later periods.[33] Silva writes,

> By the time that Farrar wrote his *History of Interpretation* (1886), it was clear that the allegorical method had completely lost respectability in the scholarly establishment. One could no longer expect such a method to shed any light on the meaning of a text. One now had to pay

[30] Gonzalez, *History of Christian Thought*, 3–10.

[31] Ibid., 3.

[32] See Moises Silva, *Has the Church Misread the Bible?: The History of Interpretation in the Light of Current Issues*, vol. 1 (Grand Rapids, MI: Zondervan Publishing House, 1987) for the revival of literary treatments of the Bible in modern ecclesial and academic settings leading to a shift away from a concern for the "figurative sense" of the scriptures.

[33] Silva, *Has the Church Misread the Bible?*, 52.

> exclusive attention to the text's historical meaning, that is, the meaning *intended* by the biblical author.[34]

Scholars used comparative methodology to present Christian allegorical interpretation as an aberration in the history of Christian scriptural exegesis. In critiquing the manner in which historians of early Christianity apply these comparative assumptions, Jonathan Z. Smith contends that the comparison of early Christianity with the traditions of the late antique world is more about distinguishing Protestant Christianity from those characteristics of Catholicism that Protestants consider objectionable.[35] In order to prevent any association between early Christianity and the "later" Hellenistic cultural traditions, scholars have developed a discourse of difference that gives "the Christian apologetic language of the 'unique' its urgency."[36] When it comes to the study of early Christian allegory, "allegory" becomes one of the code words for a later, "Catholic" form of interpretation that represents the corruption of an imagined original Christian mode of interpretation.

Knowledge of the apologetic environment that has defined the study of early Christian allegorical interpretation necessitates a reconfiguration of the scholarly inquiry. Rather than seeking to disprove the allegorical claims about the Bible or rejecting the practice because it did not conform to modern (Protestant) theological categories, I have sought to focus upon the social, rhetorical, and cultural functions of such allegorical

---

[34] Ibid., 52, 53 (emphasis mine).

[35] Jonathan Z. Smith, *Drudgery Divine* (Chicago: University of Chicago Press, 1990), 43.

[36] Ibid., 40. In *The Ideology of Religious Studies*, Timothy Fitzgerald argues that the "scientific" study of religion has been informed by a theological impulse that has obscured and informed the categories and methods of analysis. Fitzgerald traces this theological impulse he calls "liberal ecumenical theology" from the beginnings of the modern "scientific" study of religion through its current manifestation in religious studies departments. Even as the "scientific" study of religion sought to oppose established, dogmatic Christianity, Fitzgerald asserts that "religious studies has been fundamentally imbued with theological principles of the liberal ecumenical kind." See Timothy Fitzgerald, *The Ideology of Religious Studies* (New York/Oxford: Oxford University Press, 2000) 3–53.

claims. That is, what was at stake for certain early Christians when they asserted that the Bible was to be understood allegorically, and how did they use allegorical interpretation to authorize their own subjectivity over-and-again other competing discourse? My research had concluded that ancient allegorists used allegorical interpretation as a resistance strategy to subvert competing discourses and to give voice to an alternative subjectivity. The theological and exegetical categories used by Christian allegorists were tools for carving out social and ideological space in the midst of competing cultural discourses.[37]

These observations call into question the traditional framing of early Christianity that enables scholars to use the Greco-Roman cultural milieu as an implicit criterion for marking the decline of the "original" Christian tradition. It calls into question the comparison of early Christianity with so-called "Greco-Roman" religious and philosophical traditions that has become such a mainstay in the study of Early Christianity, sets the stage for operating outside of the theological and apologetic paradigm that has informed many of the questions raised and the methods used in the study of early Christianity. By reconceptualizing the functions of early Christian allegorical interpretation, I advocate a kind of methodological freedom to raise new questions about historical meaning in general, and interpretation in particular. When we think about issues of interpretation, the theological and exegetical paradigm we have received does not adequately and completely account for the "meaning" interpreters seek to disclose. What is needed is the courage to fathom a new comparative enterprise and the boldness to think about the

---

[37] According to David Dawson, "Ancient allegorical compositions and interpretations constituted fields on which struggles between competing proposals for thought and action took place. The very tensions between literal and nonliteral readings that characterized ancient allegory stemmed from efforts by readers to secure for themselves and their communities social and cultural identity, authority, and power.... Instead of reveling in the absence of meaning, these ancient allegorists tended to use apophatic claims *rhetorically*, as a way of justifying their own application of allegorical readings that were designed to show what the real meanings were" (*Allegorical Readers and Cultural Revision*, 2, 3).

task of the historian in a new way.[38] Rather than comparing the "sources" of early Christian allegorical interpretation, an alternative comparative approach might compare certain kinds of socio-ideological practices, interests, dynamics, and agendas of cultural interpreters past and present, so as to understand the cultural-critical dimensions of ancient interpretive practices.[39] My journey to these conclusions began with my encounter with Dr. Carter at Morehouse College. Indeed, it was a transformative encounter for which I am forever grateful.

---

[38] See Mae Henderson, "Borders, Boundaries, and Frame(work)s," in *Borders, Boundaries, and Frames: Essays in Cultural Criticism and Cultural Studies* (New York: Routledge, 1995); and George Lipsitz, "Listening to Learn and Learning to Listen: Popular Culture, Cultural Theory, and American Studies," American Quarterly 42 (1990): 615–36.

[39] See my dissertation titled "Resistance Reading: Reconsidering the Functions of Early Christian Allegory" (New York: Columbia University, 2006), for an alternative theory of the functions of early Christian allegorical interpretation.

4

A Letter to the Dean: Autobiographical Reflections and Lessons Learned

Jason R. Curry

> For this reason, ever since I heard about your faith in the Lord Jesus and your love for all the saints, I have not stopped giving thanks for you, remembering you in my prayers. I keep asking that the God of our Lord Jesus Christ, the glorious Father, may give you the Spirit of wisdom and revelation, so that you may know him better. (Ephesians 1:15–17)

I am Dean of the Fisk Memorial Chapel at Fisk University. Previously, I served as Dean of the Fisk Chapel from 2003 to 2008, and left in summer 2008 to become the Academic Dean at Payne Theological Seminary in Wilberforce, Ohio. In fall 2009, I gladly accepted President Hazel R. O'Leary's invitation to rejoin the "Fisk Family" and resume duties as Dean of the Chapel. My decision to return was heavily influenced by my own vocational interests coupled with prayer, meditation, and reflection. Even though I spent a year enjoying the beautiful city of Wilberforce, Ohio, I knew in my heart that it was time to leave the Buckeye State.

As I reflect on my one-year residency in Wilberforce, I vividly remember the heavy snow falling on the tall cedar trees in the winter, and I recall brown and curious deer walking freely around the campus, unaware of the intense theological conversations, such as Clement of Alexandria's notion of spiritual knowledge (*gnosis*), occurring in the seminary classrooms. To me, the landscape of Wilberforce is representative of the best of God's majestic brilliance expressed in nature; however, the God who speaks simultaneously through nature as *Logos* also speaks to human beings. I discerned the "Word of God" speaking to me and inviting me to return home to Fisk. I gladly and readily accepted the invitation, and I looked forward to continuing the work that was placed upon my heart in 2003.

The decision to return to my spiritual home at Fisk was not a difficult one to make. While considering the invitation, I remembered the many talented students and soloists in the Jubilee Singers who performed in the chapel on select Sunday mornings. I also remembered the enthusiasm and excitement of young preachers who embraced the call on their lives and were in school to learn as much as they could to be better proclaimers of the good news (or "*euangelion*" in Greek). I further recalled the many days and nights spent counseling individuals, couples, and families in the basement of the Fisk Memorial Chapel. Many of their personal challenges, anxieties, and fears were overcome through critical and honest conversations, and with emotional and spiritual support, understanding, and prayer. Moreover, I could not forget the powerful and inspiring sermons from the chapel pulpit by outstanding preachers such as the Rev. Dr. Robert Michael Franklin, Rev. Dr. Calvin Butts, Bishop Vashti McKenzie, and the Rev. Dr. Cheryl Townsend Gilkes, among others. Their sermons empowered administrators, faculty, alumni, staff, students, and community friends. Fisk University was and is a special place. It remains one of three "spiritual homes," along with the Agape AME Church in Brooklyn, New York, and Morehouse College.

I fully affirm Fisk University's motto: "Her sons and daughters are ever on the altar," and I am convinced that whatever administrative success I have as Dean of the Chapel can primarily be attributed to: (1) the providential hand of God constantly healing, guiding, and sustaining me during days of crises and jubilation; and (2) the instruction and encouragement from the Rev. Dr. Lawrence Edward Carter, Sr., Dean of the Martin Luther King Chapel at Morehouse College. Both have shaped my life in meaningful and wholesome ways and have strengthened my life and ministry at Fisk. To paraphrase an African-American spiritual, "if it weren't for the good Lord *and* Dean Carter on my side, I don't know where my ministry would be today."

I will first elaborate on the "Spirit of God" and then discuss Dean Carter's lasting influence. In my opinion, the refrain of a famous hymn by Doris Akers captures the sentiment and mood of what takes place weekly at the Fisk Memorial Chapel. In the initial sentence of her hymn, Akers writes: "There's a sweet, sweet spirit in this place, and I know that it's the spirit of the Lord." The "sweet, sweet spirit" is evident in public and silent prayers of students who believe that God makes a way out of no way for them to continue their college matriculation despite financial crises and other difficult circumstances. The "sweet, sweet spirit" is evident in the tithes and offerings presented on Sunday mornings—often meager, yet meaningful expressions of love, dedication, and generosity. I am aware that many of these financial gifts are from student-refund checks and work-study jobs.

Moreover, the "sweet, sweet spirit" is evident in the willingness of nationally renowned clergy who accept the invitation to the chapel even though the honorarium pales in comparison to what they might normally receive for preaching. The "sweet, sweet spirit" is apparent in the worship services attended by students who are from African Methodist Episcopal, Baptist, Missionary Baptist, Primitive Baptist, Catholic, and Presbyterian churches. Indeed, the "sweet, sweet spirit" is in God's abiding presence as we comfort each other when students unexpectedly depart this life, when beloved members of the staff leave the university to pursue other vocational opportunities, and when we attempt to press on and do great work, without much media attention. In all these instances, I have witnessed a "sweet, sweet spirit" in the chapel. God's providential hand provides for us and protects us from dangers seen and unseen, and to God be thanks and glory and honor!

As Dean of the Chapel, I mentor other college students and future seminarians, just as I was once mentored. As a college student at Morehouse, I met many professors and ministers who profoundly influenced my growth and development as a Christian thinker, but no one has had more influence on me than Dean Lawrence Edward Carter, Sr. I accepted a call to ministry after my freshman year at Morehouse and worked faithfully in the King Chapel all four years. Morehouse is also sacred space and is my third "spiritual home," as mentioned earlier. I preached my first sermon in the George Sale Hall during a mid-week worship service led by the Martin Luther King, Jr. International Chapel assistants. I became a chapel assistant and befriended other students on campus who are now colleagues. Some of them have an essay or sermon in this volume.

As a result of Dean Carter's instruction, I was introduced to "axiology," the philosophical study of value. Axiology is concerned primarily with two kinds of value, mainly ethics and aesthetics. Ethics investigates the concepts of "right" and "good" in individual and social conduct. Aesthetics studies the concepts of "beauty" and "harmony." The value of an education in general, and at Morehouse in particular, cannot be overstated. There is a continuing need and purpose for historically Black colleges, and Morehouse ranks in the top tier, providing a quality education while nurturing one's spirituality and social consciousness. A word often used at Morehouse is "mystique." This word is difficult to define but seems to be a quality that many Morehouse men possess that compels them to be agents for social change and to make a desperately needed contribution to the world. Although Dean Carter is not a Morehouse graduate, he clearly embodies and promotes the "Morehouse Mystique." Dean Carter's theoretical and holistic understanding of Christianity and spiritual formation has had a profound impact on my ministry as well as the ministries of many former chapel assistants.

In *The Republic*, Plato argues that the realm of the Forms, as opposed to the attributes of particular things, constitutes the essence of a being. In my opinion, neither Dean Carter's awards nor his scholarly publications have had the greatest influence on my development as a minister. Rather, it is the "essence" of who he is (or his "ontology") that shines and illuminates a path for others who are seeking to find their way. Dean Carter's background in the area of pastoral care and counseling influenced my own decision to enter the Ph.D. program in Religion and Personality at Vanderbilt University. As I reflect on my relationship with Dean Carter over the years, I well remember his ability to teach psychological concepts discussed in his "Psychology of Religion," but I also appreciate those psychodynamic theories incarnated in his own personality and through teacher-student exchanges during classroom encounters and office appointments. How much he knew became more important to me after I knew how much he cared for the academic discipline and for his students.

I vividly remember a conversation Dean Carter and I had at the George Sherman Union at Boston University after I completed the Master of Divinity degree at Harvard Divinity School and prior to my admission to the Ph.D. program at Vanderbilt. During our hour-long conversation, I informed him that I was a bit apprehensive about entering a Ph.D. program in Religion because of challenges I had faced in the Master of Divinity program. Although I was familiar with the historical-critical methodology in religious and biblical studies—including redaction criticism, postcolonial hermeneutics, and its emphasis on race, class, and gender—I was a bit reluctant to enter another academic program that would challenge my traditional understanding and interpretation of sacred texts.

During our lunch conversation, Dean Carter did not dwell on the theories or techniques in the field of psychotherapy, and he did not criticize my traditional beliefs or dismiss me as a Christian fundamentalist. Instead, he concluded that I was not a fundamentalist, although I embraced fundamental beliefs, such as the existence of God and the divine nature of Jesus Christ. Most of all, Dean Carter simply accepted me and demonstrated Carl Rogers's psychotherapeutic notion of "unconditional positive regard." He listened to my challenges by utilizing the Freudian practice of "evenly hovering attention" and determined that my anxiety about entering the Ph.D. program was rooted in an "unconscious internal conflict." In terms of further graduate study, I thought my intellectual growth would lead to the demise of my religious beliefs and spirituality. However, Dean Carter's understanding of pastoral care and counseling, and his role as a college chaplain, helped me achieve better insights regarding the nature of my problem and helped me resolve a conflict that was preventing my intellectual as well as spiritual growth. Over the next year, he assumed the role of "diagnostician" and "therapist" by helping me to understand myself better. In the end, I decided to pursue the Ph.D., with an emphasis on pastoral care and counseling, and eventually graduated with honors.

In the first chapter of Paul's letter to the church at Ephesus, the Apostle gives thanks to God for the members of the early church. He goes on to say that the Christians in Ephesus would remain in his prayers. Like the Apostle Paul, I, too, give thanks to God for the leadership and the "Christian witness" that exist in the Martin Luther King, Jr. International Chapel at Morehouse College. I also give thanks to God for allowing Morehouse College to serve as a "third" spiritual home for me, as the number "3" is significant. The King Chapel is where I first heard the homiletical brilliance and divinely inspired and powerfully delivered sermons of Civil Rights icons such as Otis Moss, Jr., Thomas Kilgore, Gardner Taylor, and Hosea Williams. They spoke "wisdom through the ages" and they spoke "truth to power." Morehouse is where I began to discard the clothing of an ignorant and irrational self-hatred that I wore as a young, African-American man growing up in a Northeast inner-city and depressed community. The brotherhood that developed during orientation week with several of the hundreds of students I met during my years there continues today. Professors and campus speakers constantly reminded us that God's plan for African-American men does not include senseless violence, criminal activity, illiteracy, substance abuse, unemployment, political apathy, social alienation, moral indifference, incarceration, or irresponsibility.

Morehouse is where members of the faculty and administration readily embrace the role as surrogate fathers and your brother's keeper, and it is where students are expected to follow Dr. Benjamin E. Mays's insistence on doing a job so well "that the living, the dead, and the unborn could not do it any better." Like other professors, Dean Carter encouraged us to aim high and to master the skills of reading, writing, research, and debate and argumentation. However, he also encouraged a balance between "head and heart" (borrowing a phrase from Howard Thurman's autobiography), meaning one should temper intellect with sensitivity, care, and love. Like Paul, I thank God for affording me the opportunity to be influenced by the life and ministry of Dean Carter. Also, like Paul, I learned that a minister can combine theological scholarship and ministry by having a desire for God and a love for learning. I learned that the facts and data of the social sciences can be useful because the sciences are not necessarily contradictory to religion. For me, the sciences can reveal the genius of God's creation and show that we are wonderfully made and how to discover what is true, good, and beautiful.

Furthermore, I learned that a good professor should conduct research so that human thought can be advanced through the accumulation and application of knowledge. However, a good professor should never be too busy to listen to the problems of his or her students. I learned that one should strive to attain the terminal degree in his or her chosen field, but one should also abandon rank and title in worship centers. Dean Carter teaches: "You are fast becoming who you're going to be." Therefore, I work diligently so that some part of my future will produce rewards based on what I am doing now. Like the one discussed in Jesus' "Parable of the Talents" (Saint Matthew 25:14–30), I pray that the gifts I have might somehow, through God's grace, be a blessing to someone else. Following Dean Carter's example, I hope that some aspect of my academic and ministerial career might be helpful to others and will serve as a "thank you" to him.

5

Lawrence Carter, Sr. and the Boston Personalist Tradition

Norm Faramelli

Lawrence Carter was at Boston University ("BU") in the 1970s, which was the last major phase of Boston Personalism. Although his work at BU was primarily in pastoral care and pastoral counseling, it is clear from his work that he is influenced by Boston Personalism. This influence is evident in *Walking Integrity: Benjamin Elijah Mays, Mentor to Martin Luther King, Jr.*, a centennial *festschrift* in honor of Mays, which he edited along with an illuminating introduction. *Global Ethical Options: In the Tradition of Gandhi, King, and Ikeda*, coauthored with George Miller and Neelakanta Radhakrishnan, also reflects the influence of Boston Personalism. In *Global Ethical Options*, the authors develop an ethical framework for global citizenship and planetary care that is based primarily on the moral laws as they emerged in Boston Personalism.

Carter's doctoral dissertation at Boston University was on "Motivation and Preaching: Context, Analysis of Sermons by Two Preachers in Light of Abraham H. Maslow's Theory of Need-Values." In his dissertation, he compared the differences between two prominent preachers, one White and one Black, Otis Aubrey Maxfield and William Augustus Jones, Jr. (Jones had worked with Martin Luther King, Jr. in 1961 on the split from the conservative Baptists to form the Progressive National Baptist Convention.) Carter wanted to assess, using statistical comparisons, the basic differences between White and Black preaching in light of Maslow's theory of needs. Carter was somewhat critical of the hierarchy of needs in Maslow; nevertheless, the desire for self-realization of all people has played an important role throughout Carter's ministry.

Although Carter has spent his career at Morehouse College, he has lectured worldwide along with many visiting professorships at major universities. It is clear that the work of Martin Luther King, Jr.—as expressed in nonviolence and social justice—is a common thread in Carter's own vocation. It is also clear that the links between Howard Thurman, who was Dean of Boston University's Marsh Chapel from

1953–1965, and Benjamin Mays, president of Morehouse College, are interwoven in Carter's experiences.

Key to Boston Personalism and Why Martin Luther King, Jr. Went to Boston University

In his work on *Personalism: A Critical Introduction,* Rufus Burrow, Jr. affirms that Boston Personalism is "the most reasonable philosophical basis of two critical beliefs in Afrikan American religio-cultural tradition: that God is personal and cares about us and that all persons have been etched into their being the image of God and thus are heirs to a legacy of absolute dignity and worth."[1]

When Martin Luther King, Jr. went to BU, his intention was to work with Edgar S. Brightman, which he did for a year. However, in 1953, Brightman died and King was mentored by L. Harold DeWolf, Walter Muelder, and many others at BU. King spoke positively of his Boston University experience in *Stride Toward Freedom.*[2] He was impressed with White men like Allen Knight Chambers and Dean Walter G. Muelder who were pacifists and were concerned about racial and economic justice. King saw that they had a "deep faith in the possibilities of human beings when they allowed themselves to become co-workers with God." King added: "It was at Boston University that I came to see that [Reinhold] Niebuhr had overemphasized the corruption of human nature. His pessimism concerning human nature was not balanced by optimism concerning divine nature. He was so involved in diagnosing man's sickness of sin that he overlooked the cure of grace."

In another work on Martin Luther King, Jr. and Boston Personalism, Burrow makes a strong point that King integrated his religious tradition and experiences in the Black Church with the philosophical

---

[1] Rufus Burrow, Jr., *Personalism: A Critical Introduction* (St. Louis, MO: Chalice Press, 1999), from the dedication.

[2] See Martin Luther King, Jr., "My Pilgrimage to Nonviolence," in *Stride Toward Freedom: The Montgomery Story* (New York: Harper and Row, 1958) 100.

foundations of Boston Personalism.[3] King did not need to go to Boston University to learn about a personal God or the inherent dignity of each person; he already experienced that in the Black Church. The grounding of those beliefs in a philosophical, theological, and ethical framework was the type of Personalism that King and Carter experienced at Boston University.

It is difficult to point out specifically how Mays was connected to King, other than to say that Mays recruited him to come to Morehouse College, and that Howard Thurman, Benjamin Mays, and King's father were probably the three most important mentors to Martin Luther King, Jr.[4]

Benjamin E. Mays and Martin Luther King, Jr.

In his work on Mays, Carter notes that Mays was influenced by the Social Gospel theology of the 1920s and 1930s. Mays's emphasis was on "the Negro's God" who was an active participant in the struggles against slavery, segregation, and other forms of discrimination. Carter views Mays as "a forerunner of Black Liberation Theology."[5] Mays was able to balance an inherent desire to rebel (as articulated in his *Born to Rebel*) with a strong sense of responsibility. That is why when he was a participant in the first Assembly of the World Council of Churches in 1948, he worked on the document with Walter Muelder and others who articulated "the idea of a responsible society."

According to Walter Muelder, the idea of a responsible society contained several components that were expressed in Mays's work before

---

[3] See Burrow, Jr.'s *God and Human Dignity*, chapter 2. The connections between the Black Church experience and Boston Personalism were well developed in a lecture by Lewis V. Baldwin in April 2007 at Boston University (Center for Practical Theology): "Martin Luther King, Jr. and Boston Personalism."

[4] Carter, Sr., ed., *Walking Integrity: Benjamin Elijah Mays, Mentor to Martin Luther King, Jr.*, chapter 8.

[5] Carter, Sr., ed., *Walking Integrity: Benjamin Elijah Mays, Mentor to Martin Luther King, Jr.*, 7.

and after 1948. These motifs were the role of religious norms in a just and free society, particularly the creative purposes of God and his concern for personal and social salvation. They were also seen in the conception of man—his dignity, rights, and self-realization in community with others. Other motifs were the interpenetration of the political, economic, and social spheres of society. These responsibilities were needed in interpersonal relations, community activity, and on the national and international levels.

The authors in Carter's centennial *Festschrift*, written in honor of Benjamin Mays, offer an array of views, including but not limited to: Mays's life story as noted in *Born to Rebel*; Mays as preacher and debater; his academic and educational philosophy, as well as his relation to students; his deanship and presidency at Howard University and Morehouse College, respectively; his spiritual rebellion and work for racial justice; his book on *The Negro's God*; and, above all, his mentoring of Martin Luther King, Jr.

In his preface to the *Festschrift* in honor of Mays, Carter writes:

> The name of Mays's most famous student, Martin Luther King, Jr., is synonymous with the philosophy of nonviolence, and the Civil Rights Movement in the United States, a philosophy and a movement influenced by the example and teachings of India's Mohandas K. Gandhi. Not so well known, however, are the names of four other men associated with King and his alma mater, Morehouse College in Atlanta, and their vital role in establishing the historic and philosophical link between Gandhi and King—a link that altered forever the social and political fabric of the United States. These Morehouse men were Howard Washington Thurman '21, Benjamin Elijah Mays '67 (hon.), Mordecai Wyatt Johnson '11, and Samuel Woodrow Williams '37. Through their efforts, Martin Luther King, Jr. '48 was introduced to the philosophy of "nonviolence." The collective efforts of these five ordained Christian ministers of the Baptist tradition, self-described "servant-scholars," introduced and shaped the philosophy of nonviolence that became a pillar of the American civil and human rights movement.[6]

---

[6] Ibid., xii (Preface).

The theme of nonviolence as expressed in Gandhi and King is one that has influenced Carter throughout his ministry. Many of his lectures and university appointments are focused on this theme. He also consistently seeks to work on an interfaith level with the various traditions in world religions.

Evolution of an Ethical Framework in Boston Personalism

During the time when Carter was at Boston University, the Boston Personalists had accepted the theology and philosophy of their predecessors, but the cutting-edge work was not in philosophy or theology. It was in social ethics. Walter Muelder, a student of Edgar S. Brightman, was impressed with Brightman's *Moral Laws* (1933), but he thought they were too limited to personal interactions and lacked a social context. With the encouragement of Brightman, Muelder moved Boston Personalism in a direction of communal and social ethics.

Brightman was very well known for his work on the limited power of God, as seen in his controversial work *The Problem of God*, where he spoke of God limited in power but abundant/infinite in grace and love. Brightman is well known for his work on *Philosophy of Religion* (1940), which is perhaps his most popular book. His least popular and probably least read book is *Moral Laws*, where he lays out a scientific and rational basis for ethics. It was Brightman's work that the Boston Personalists used to build an ethical framework.

The moral laws of Brightman are divided into three categories—Formal, Axiological, and Personalistic:

The Formal Laws
The Logical Law (a consistent will)
The Law of Autonomy (Self-imposed ideals are obligatory.)

The Axiological Laws
The Axiological Law (consistent values)
The Law of Consequences (Consider and address foreseeable consequences.)
The Law of the Best Possible (Do your best in each situation/improve conditions.)

The Law of Specification (Develop values that are directly relevant to the situation.)
The Law of the Most Inclusive End (Consider a coherent life in which the widest range of value is realized.)
The Law of Ideal Control (Control empirical values with ideal values.)

The Personalistic Laws
The Law of Individualism (Realize in one's experience the maximum value of which one is capable in harmony with moral law.)
The Law of Altruism (Respect persons as ends in themselves, as far as possible, and cooperate with others on the production and enjoyment of shared values.)
The Law of Ideal Personality (Judge and guide all acts by an ideal personality.)

These laws are rooted in Kantian philosophy, but unlike Kantians, Boston Personalists take consequences seriously. These laws are regulative and not prescriptive. DeWolf and Muelder used these laws to shape their social ethics. But in order to accommodate these laws to a wider social context, DeWolf and Muelder needed to expand Brightman's laws, so they added three communitarian laws, which, Muelder noted, "place the free and responsible person in the context of a free and responsible society." These three laws are: the Law of Cooperation (cooperate in the production and enjoyment of shared values—already in Brightman but moved from the Personalistic to the Communitarian category); the Law of Social Devotion (all persons ought to devote themselves to serving the best interests of the group and to subordinate personal gain to social gain); the Law of Ideal Community (all persons ought to form and choose all of their ideals and values in loyalty to the ideal [in harmony] with other Moral Laws of what the whole community ought to become and to participate responsibly in groups to help them similarly choose and form all their ideals and choices); and the Metaphysical Law (one seeks to know the source and significance of the harmony and universality of these laws—the coherence of the moral order).[7]

Later on, another Boston Personalist, Paul Deats, added two more: the Law of Conflict and Reconciliation and the Law of Fallibility and Corrigibility. These two added laws are defined as follows:

> Conflict and Reconciliation—All persons, in their own lives and in the life of groups to which they belong, ought to accept conflict in the course of seeking to formulate and achieve the ideals of personality and of community, and to work through conflict with others, "friends" and "enemies" alike, toward consensus, justice, and reconciliation.
>
> Fallibility and Corrigibility—All persons ought to expect to make, and suffer others to make, mistakes, and even intentional misdeeds, as well as to experience failure and defeat, without being overcome or losing hope. When mistakes are recognized, and repentance expressed and forgiveness asked, the way is open for resources, human and divine, to be available.[8]

These laws are analogous to many traditions of natural law, since they are rooted in human reason and are linked to the notion of a "common good" that is prominent in Roman Catholic social teachings. Some refer to these as principles or ethical guides instead of moral laws. Nevertheless, they were designed as a system to provide comprehensiveness and coherence.

Carter and the Development of Global Ethical Options

---

[7] See Burrow, Jr., *Personalism: A Critical Introduction,* 200–25, for the evolution of the Personalist ethical framework. See also "21st-Century Ministry Booklets Vol. 6," in *The Significance of Walter G. Muelder's Social Ethics: The Present Status of Personalism* (Newton Centre, MA: Boston Theological Institute, 2006), which contains articles by N. Faramelli, T. Massaro, S. J., Ruy O. Costa, and James A Nash.

[8] See Paul Deats, "Conflict and Reconciliation in Communitarian Social Ethics," in *The Boston Personalist Tradition in Philosophy, Social Ethics, and Theology,* ed. Paul Deats and Carol Robb (Macon, GA: Mercer University Press, 1986).

The framework for ethical analysis laid out in *Global Ethical Options* is based on the laws that evolved in the Boston Personalist tradition. In addition to his reliance upon the work of Brightman, DeWolf, Muelder, and Deats, Carter is also indebted to the work of Peter Bertocci, who integrated Boston Personalism with psychology, which has always been of great interest to Carter. The authors in *Global Ethical Options* refer to the ethical principles as "guides for critical thinking" and are "communitarian, not ego-centric" in focus. The structure of laws discussed by Carter, Miller, and Radhakrishnan are:

I. Formal Aspects (How ought we to choose?)
Consistency (self-respect)
Autonomy (conscience)

II. Axiological Aspects (What should we choose?)
Coherent Valuation (testing)
Consequences (foresight)
Best Possible (improvement)
Situational Relevance (specification)
Variety and Depth (truth-seeking)
Ideal Control (ideal norm)
Ecological Integrity (nature and value)

III. Personal Aspects (For whose sake do we choose?)
Self-Realization (individualism)
Altruism (reciprocity)
The Ideal Personality (ideal personhood)

IV. Communitarian Aspects (In what social context do we choose?)
Cooperation (mutual value creation)
Social Devotion (group's best interest)
Ideal Community (universal humans)

V. Praxis Aspects (How should we respond to conflict and defeat?)
Nonviolent Caring (dynamic interpersonalism)

Reconciliation (ideal progress)
Fallibility and Corrigibility (ideal realism)

VI. Ethical Ontological Aspects (What is the source of ethical obligation?)
Metaphysical Source (quest for the source of ethical obligation)
Ultimate Justice (character of the moral order)[9]

Utilizing the ethical framework from the Boston Personalists as a foundation, Carter and co-authors creatively integrate these ethical principles with examples from many other traditions, especially from the work of King, Gandhi, and Ikeda. It is important to note that Carter and his co-authors expanded the Boston Personalist framework with three additional categories. These important additions were: (1) Ecological Integrity (an axiological aspect), (2) Nonviolent Caring (a praxis aspect), and (3) Ultimate Justice (an ethical ontological aspect). Although Ecological Integrity was implicit in some of Brightman's work (cf. *Nature and Values* [1945]), it was made explicit in the work of another ethicist in the Boston University tradition, namely, James A. Nash (*Loving Nature: Ecological Integrity and Christian Responsibility*), whom the authors cite. The second addition is Nonviolent Caring (a praxis aspect). Although this approach was implicit in many of the Boston Personalists, it was not articulated as such in the formulation of the Moral Laws. Here, Carter includes Peter Bertocci, Walter Muelder, Howard Thurman, and Martin Luther King, Jr. as examples. The third addition is the category of Ultimate Justice, implied in the Boston Personalists and defined by the authors: "Every person ought to for all of his/her ideals and choices in relation to his/her conception of ultimate reality, which is the ground of ethical obligation." Or, as Martin Luther King, Jr. himself noted: "The moral arc of the universe bends toward justice."[10]

---

[9] See Carter, Sr. et al., eds., *Global Ethical Options*, where the entire ethical framework is spelled out, esp. p. 27. The book is dedicated to Walter George Muelder and Paulo Friere.

[10] Ibid., 130–35.

It was this framework of moral laws developed by Brightman and expanded upon by Muelder, DeWolf, and Deats that formed the basis of the approach followed by Carter, Miller, and Radhakrishnan. The expansions by the authors demonstrate that the ethical framework of Boston Personalism is still evolving. *Global Ethical Options* is an instruction manual intended to assist students in exploring ethical options that are consistent with the work of Gandhi, King, and Ikeda in order to foster global citizenship and planetary consciousness. This work is an excellent example of Carter's interfaith and cross-cultural focus, for which he is indebted to the four Baptist ministers from Morehouse College, as well as to Boston Personalism. It is also a fitting tribute to the brilliant career of Lawrence Carter, Sr., a career dedicated to justice, nonviolence, and the crossing of boundaries between the world's religions.

6

The Morehouse Gospel: Howard Thurman, Martin Luther King, Jr., and Prophetic Black Christianity

Peter Goodwin Heltzel

Martin Luther King, Jr. has been canonized as the heroic leader of the Civil Rights Movement, yet his visionary leadership was part of a much longer and deeper tradition—the Morehouse mystique—grounded in what I call the "Black Social Gospel." The Morehouse Gospel sought to be faithful to the Gospel of Jesus Christ in both its personal and social dimensions. It focused on seeking to embody God's love for the disinherited in the church, society, and the world. The Morehouse Gospel is mediated by a long tradition of Christian theologians, including Benjamin E. Mays, Mordecai W. Johnson, Howard W. Thurman, Martin Luther King, Jr., and Lawrence Edward Carter, Sr.

In this chapter, I argue that King's leadership succeeded because of his embodiment of the Morehouse Gospel. He was the product of a mighty Morehouse legacy that included his grandfather, A. D. Williams, and his father, Martin Luther King, Sr., both Morehouse graduates. Morehouse President Benjamin Mays mentored King during his undergraduate days, inspiring him to serve humanity.[1] While there were many churches in Atlanta that embodied the Black Social Gospel (e.g., Ebenezer Baptist, Big Bethel AME, Wheat Street Baptist, and Friendship Baptist), it was Morehouse that became the most strategic educational community, forming hundreds of leaders in this prophetic theological tradition. Throughout his life, King continued to be shaped by this Morehouse tradition, including the time he spent with Howard Thurman, whom he first met during his doctoral studies at Boston

---

[1] For a thoughtful explanation of Mays's influence on the life and thought of Martin Luther King, Jr., see Carter, ed., *Walking Integrity: Benjamin Elijah Mays, Mentor to Martin Luther King, Jr.* Also see Benjamin E. Mays's important work, *Born to Rebel* (New York: Scribner, 1971).

University; Thurman's seminal volume *Jesus and the Disinherited* (1949) became a template for King's prophetic Christology.[2] King epitomized this Morehouse Gospel, including its vision of prophetic-mystical ministry, racial justice, and nonviolent love.

Martin Luther King, Jr. and the Morehouse Gospel

Through his Christian family, Ebenezer Baptist Church, and his Morehouse education, King was socialized into the Black Social Gospel. Historians of the Social Gospel have unfortunately treated it as an almost exclusively White phenomenon, focusing on White Northern preachers like Washington Gladden and Walter Rauschenbusch.[3] However, the Northern Social Gospel was developed within the framework of Christian theology conceived as exclusively a White, male, Euro-American enterprise. Thus, while the "Social Gospel" sought to embody social justice, it was largely blind to the problem of White racism. Since the trans-Atlantic slave trade exposes the moral contradiction of Christianity in the United States, we need a new historiography of North-American Christian movements that begins with the encounter between African Americans and European Americans.

The "Black-White encounter" model of American religious history provides a framework that can actively deconstruct Christian theology's Whiteness and Western-ness, while highlighting the moral vision of the prophetic Black Christianity.[4] On the underside of a White Euro-

---

[2] Howard Thurman, *Jesus and the Disinherited* (Boston: Beacon Press, 1976).

[3] Samples of some of the traditional accounts of the Social Gospel movement include Charles Howard Hopkins, *The Rise of the Social Gospel in American Protestantism, 1865–1915* (New Haven: Yale University Press, 1940); William R. Hutchison, "The Americanness of the Social Gospel; An Inquiry in Comparative History," *Church History* 44/3 (September 1975): 367–81; and Ronald C. White, Jr. and C. Howard Hopkins, *The Social Gospel. Religion and Reform in Changing America* (Philadelphia: Temple University Press, 1976).

[4] On the "encounter of Black and White Christianity" model for the study of the history of world Christianity, see David W. Wills, "The Central Themes of American Religious History: Pluralism, Puritanism, and the Encounter of Black and White," *Religion and Intellectual Life* 1 (Fall 1987): 30–41.

American modernity emerged a robust tradition of social justice Christianity in which racial justice was a central commitment—the Black Social Gospel.[5] While the Black Social Gospel emerged in northern urban centers like Chicago at the turn of the twentieth century, a more robust expression erupted in the South. In Atlanta, Georgia, a southern version of the Black Social Gospel emerged that was one of the most formative influences on Martin Luther King, Jr.'s vision of beloved community.[6] The Black Social Gospel ran like a mighty river through many generations of King's family. He wrote,

> I am many things to many people: Civil Rights leader, agitator, trouble-maker and orator, but in the quiet resources of my heart, I am fundamentally a clergyman, a Baptist preacher. This is my being and my heritage for I am also the son of a Baptist preacher, the grandson of

---

[5] For King's connection to the Black Social Gospel, see Clayborne Carson, "Martin Luther King, Jr. and the African-American Social Gospel," in *African-American Christianity*, ed. Paul E. Johnson (Berkeley: University of California Press, 1994) 159–77. Reprinted *African-American Religion: Interpretive Essays in History and Culture*, ed. Tomothy E. Fulop and Albert J. Raboteau (New York: Routledge, 1997). Walter Earl Fluker also points to this Black Social Gospel tradition associated with Morehouse in *Ethical Leadership: The Quest for Character, Civility, and Community*, ch. 1. For the historical origins of the Black Social Gospel, see Ralph E. Luker, *The Social Gospel in Black and White: American Racial Reform, 1885–1912* (Chapel Hill and London: University of North Carolina Press, 1991); and Anthony Pinn, ed., *Making the Gospel Plain: The Writings of Bishop Reverdy C. Ransom* (Harrisburg, PA: Trinity Press International, 1999). On Morehouse College, see Jones, *A Candle in the Dark.*

[6] On the "southern" character of King's life and theology, my thought has been shaped by Lewis Baldwin. See Lewis V. Baldwin, "Understanding Martin Luther King, Jr. Within the Context of Southern Black Religious History," *Journal of Religious Studies* 13/2 (Fall 1987): 1–26; "Martin Luther King, the Black Church and the Black Messianic Vision," *The Journal of the Interdenominational Center* 12/1–2 (Fall 1984/Spring 1985); and *There Is a Balm in Gilead*, esp. 159–228.

> a Baptist preacher, and the great-grandson of a Baptist preacher. The Church is my life and I have given my life to the Church.[7]

King was the product of three generations of socially engaged Baptist preachers who sought to embody both the personal and social dimensions of the Gospel.

The son of Willis Williams, a revivalist slave preacher, Adam Daniel (A. D.) Williams (1861–1931), King's maternal grandfather, was a stalwart preacher of the Black Social Gospel. Williams served as the minister of Bethlehem Baptist Church in Covington, Georgia. Founded in 1847, Bethlehem Baptist Church was liberated in fall 1864, during General Sherman's March to the Sea.[8] Interestingly, A. D. Williams marked his first birthday on 2 January 1863, the day after the Emancipation Proclamation, even though the census of 1870 seems to indicate that he was born in 1881.[9] Thus, in King's family history we see a prophetic Christian attempt to work through the logic of the Emancipation Proclamation for racial justice in American society. Martin Luther King, Jr.'s religious heritage runs deep into the heart of the Southern Freedom movement.

On 14 March 1894, A. D. Williams accepted a call to serve Ebenezer Baptist Church in Atlanta, Georgia. Dealing with racial injustices in this growing Southern city, William's commitment to the social dimension of ministry was strengthened. Visionary civic activism was

---

[7] Martin Luther King, Jr., "The Un-Christian Christian," *Ebony* (August 1965): 77.

[8] General William Tecumseh Sherman of the Union Army was considered a liberator by most African-American communities during the Savannah campaign of 1864. Many African Americans from Georgia assisted General Sherman in the Savannah campaign, although they were not allowed to participate in armed combat. See Andrew Billingsley, "General Sherman and the Black Church," *Mighty Like a River: The Black Church and Social Reform* (Oxford: Oxford University, 1999), 22–34.

[9] On the debate concerning A. D. Williams's birth date, see "Introduction," *The Papers of Martin Luther King, Jr.*, Vol. 1: *Called to Serve: January 1929–June 1951*, ed. Clayborne Carson, Ralph E. Luker, and Penny A. Russell (Berkeley and Los Angeles: University of California Press, 1992) 4, 6.

seen as integral to Baptist ministry. William's activism was diverse and varied: he participated in the organization of the National Baptist convention in 1895; served as the chairman of the Committee on the Equalization of Teachers' Salaries; led voter registration campaigns; helped found a local chapter of National Association for the Advancement of Colored People (NAACP), which he would serve twice as president; and, in 1914, was appointed chairman of the finance committee of the Morehouse College Alumni Association. [10] For Williams, the minister was called to bear witness in all dimensions of community life. When an issue of injustice emerged in the community, Williams would be there with other ministers to bear witness to God's righteous reign of justice.

Martin Luther King, Jr.'s father, Daddy King, carried on this tradition of prophetic, activist ministry at Ebenezer. Both Morehouse men, A. D. Williams and Martin Luther King, Sr. "preached a social-gospel Christianity that combined a belief in personal salvation with the need to apply the teachings of Jesus to the daily problems of their Black congregations."[11] Marrying into the Ebenezer ministry, Martin Luther King, Sr. married Rev. Williams's only daughter in 1926 and became the minister of Ebenezer five years later when Williams passed away in 1931.

Martin Luther King, Sr. continued to proclaim the Morehouse Gospel from the pulpit of Ebenezer. While King, Sr. was refused admission to Morehouse twice, A. D. Williams successfully intervened on behalf of his future son-in-law. Williams, an officer in the Morehouse College Alumni Association, placed a call to the admissions office to

---

[10] Clayborne Carson writes, "Williams, along with other Black religious leaders, was a pioneering advocate of a distinctive African-American version of the Social Gospel, endorsing a strategy that combined elements of Washington's emphasis on Black business development and W. E. B. Du Bois's call for civil Rights activism." "Intro," *Papers*, 1:1–18. On the historical origins of the National Baptist Convention, including its formation in 1895 in which A. D. Williams played a pivotal role, see James Melvin Washington, *Frustrated Fellowship: The Black Baptist Quest for Social Power* (Macon, GA: Mercer University Press, 1986).

[11] "Intro," *Papers*, 1:26.

ensure King, Sr. a place at Morehouse. King, Sr. began his studies in fall 1926. While at Morehouse, King, Sr. became good friends with Howard Thurman, who distinguished himself as an eloquent writer and passionate leader.[12]

Daddy King's studies at Morehouse expanded his understanding of the social structures that composed the global urban landscape and inspired him to imagine new ways that the church could be a prophetic community. Morehouse pushed Daddy King to embody a more intentional and broad social witness in his pastoral ministry. Lucius M. Tobin, Professor of Religion at Morehouse, wrote that Daddy King was "one of the most progressive pastors in the city of Atlanta."[13]

Daddy King emerged as one of the ardent supports of the Black Social Gospel in Atlanta. King's annual address as moderator of the Atlanta Missionary Baptist Association on 17 October 1940 was a prophetic *tour de force*. Echoing Jesus' first sermon where he read from the Isaiah scroll, King, Sr. passionately proclaimed, "The church is to touch every phase of the community life.... We are to do something about the broken-hearted, poor, unemployed, the captive, the blind, and the bruised.... God hasten the time when every minister will become a registered voter and a part of every movement for the betterment of our people."[14] King, Sr.'s forward-thinking statement of hope that "God hasten the time when every minister will become...a part of every movement for the betterment of our people" anticipated a religiously based civil rights movement that is increasingly interpreted as a religious

---

[12] Ibid., 1:25. Cf. Martin Luther King, Sr. with Clayton Riley, *Daddy King: An Autobiography* (New York: William Morrow, 1980).

[13] Lucius M. Tobin (1898–1984), Letter to Charles E. Bratten, Dean, Crozer Theological Seminary, 25 February 1948, in *Papers*, 1:151.

[14] King, Sr., "Moderator's Annual Address, Atlanta Missionary Baptist Association," 17 October 1940, Christine King Farris Collection, as quoted in "Introduction," *The Papers of Martin Luther King, Jr.*, Vol. 2: *Rediscovering Precious Values*, July 1951–1955, ed. Clayborne Carson (Berkeley: University of California Press, 1992) 2.

revival for justice.[15] Prophetic ministers are called to lead the movement for justice.

Both graduates of Morehouse College, A. D. Williams and Daddy King mediated the Black Social Gospel to the young Martin Luther King, Jr., who began his studies at Morehouse at the age of 15. Young Martin had the vision, imagination, and courage to deepen this tradition of robust Black Christian witness. At Morehouse, President Benjamin E. Mays was able to be a mentor and example to the young King as he moved out of the towering shadow of Daddy King. The longtime president of Morehouse (1940–1967), Mays was influential on several generations of Morehouse men. Refined, erudite, and wise, Mays impressed upon King the importance of a strong personal faith, an active literary imagination, and passionate public service. King enjoyed conversations with President Mays after he addressed the student body at Tuesday-morning chapel services, and the two grew quite close to each other during King's years at Morehouse. Through these conversations and through his example, Mays mediated the Morehouse Gospel to King.

Throughout King's days at Morehouse, he was an energetic advocate for the poor in Atlanta. In "Kick Up Dust," a letter to the editor of the *Atlanta Constitution*, King wrote,

> We want and are entitled to the basic rights and opportunities of American citizens: The right to earn a living at work for which we are fitted by training and ability; equal opportunities in education, health, recreation, and similar public services; the right to vote; equality before

---

[15] On interpreting the Civil Rights Movement as a religious revival for justice, see David L. Chappell, *A Stone of Hope: Prophetic Religion and the Death of Jim Crow* (Chapel Hill, NC: University of North Carolina Press, 2004); Peter Goodwin Heltzel, *Jesus and Justice: Evangelicals, Race, and American Politics* (New Haven, CT: Yale University Press, 2009); and Charles Marsh, "The Civil Rights Movement as Theological Drama—Interpretation and Application," *Modern Theology* 18/2 (April 2002): 231–50.

> the law; some of the same courtesy and good manners that we ourselves bring to all human relations.[16]

Written during a period of White mob violence close to Atlanta, King wrote the editorial to take a courageous public stand on behalf of the rights and opportunities of African Americans.

Holy Scripture fired King's prophetic imagination during his Morehouse days. Professor George D. Kelsey guided King's biblical studies at Morehouse; King's only "A" at Morehouse was in Kelsey's Bible class during his junior year (1946–1947).[17] Kelsey wrote that King "stood out in class not simply academically, but in the sense that he absorbed Jesus' teachings with his whole being."[18] For King, Jesus' teaching of the Kingdom was more than an abstract ethical vision; it was a concrete way of life. While traditional evangelical theology emphasized Jesus' redemptive death on a cross "then and there," King emphasized the importance of Christians' taking up their own cross, in the struggle for justice "here and now."[19]

Graduating from Morehouse in 1948, King decided to pursue a deeper Christian life through divinity studies at Crozer Theology Seminary. When King arrived at Crozer Theological Seminary, he encountered the Social Gospel of Walter Rauschenbusch. King writes, "I came early to Walter Rauschenbusch's *Christianity and the Social Crisis*, which left an indelible imprint on my thinking by giving me a theological basis for the social concern which had already grown up in me as a result of my early experiences."[20] Rauschenbusch's theological vision provided words to describe much of the lived theology of King's youth at

---

[16] King, Jr., "Kick Up Dust," Letter to the Editor, *Atlanta Constitution*, 6 August 1946 (written during the summer after his sophomore year at Morehouse), *Papers*, 1:121.

[17] King, Jr., "Courses at Morehouse College," *Papers*, 1:40.

[18] Renee D. Turner, "Remembering the Young King," *Ebony* 43 (January 1988): 44 as quote in King, *Papers*, 1:155, n. 2.

[19] On King's theology of the cross, see Heltzel, "Martin Luther King, Jr.'s Theology of the Cross," *Jesus and Justice: Evangelicals, Race, and American Politics*, 45–70.

[20] King, Jr., *Stride Toward Freedom*, 91.

Morehouse and Ebenezer. King always articulated and embodied the Social Gospel in his own distinctive way as a Black Baptist from the South, focused on seeking to alleviate the concrete suffering of Black folks and to empower their subversive moral agency.[21]

During his graduate studies, King was inspired by the moral vision of the Hebrew prophets. King often invoked the prophets to give specific content to the discourse on justice and the righteousness of God. Commenting on Amos 5:21–24, King writes,

> This passage…reveals the deep ethical nature of God. God is a God that demands justice rather than sacrifice; righteousness rather than ritual. The most elaborate worship is but an insult to God when offered by those who have no mind to conform to his ethical demands.… God is a God that demands justice and sacrifice can never be a substitute for it.[22]

In this passage King lifts up the ethical imperative of the prophets, theologically grounding it in the nature and character of God.

The content of "justice" for King presupposes a *theological* account of the Living God. God's covenant with Israel reveals the righteousness of God, which is fully disclosed in Jesus of Nazareth. Justice understood as God's righteous reign of shalom presupposes God's specific way of dealing with the world as created as good, bound in a covenant of love. It is from such a theological account of justice, theologically grounded in the Hebrew prophets, with Jesus being chief among the prophets, that King sought to proclaim and embody the justice of God. As King writes, "Whenever Christianity has remained true to its prophetic mission, it has taken a deep interest in social justice. Whenever it has fallen short at this point, it has brought about disastrous consequences."[23] For King,

---

[21] The kingdom of God was one theme that was common between the White and Black social Gospel; however, King always emphasized that this was an inclusive community for all people: "God's final purpose is the building of a regenerated human society which will include all mankind in a common fellowship of well-ordered living." King, Jr., "What Christians Believe about History and the Future," *Papers,* 1:250.

[22] King, Jr., "God (Amos)," in *Papers,* 2:165.

[23] King, Jr., "Social Ethics (Psalms)," in *Papers,* 2:167.

Christianity was true to its prophetic roots when it engaged in the work of social justice, seeking to transform society through a collective embodiment of the prophetic imperative. Given America's legacy of slavery and segregation, racial justice should be central to the mission of the Church. The anti-racist struggle in society has both an outer and inner dimension. While King would work for social transformation, Howard Thurman emphasized the importance of inner transformation.

Howard Thurman: The Origins of Prophetic-Mystical Theology

One of the many ways that the Morehouse Gospel was mediated to King was through Howard Thurman.[24] Thurman, the African-American poet, preacher, mystic, and activist, applied the Gospel to the concerns of mistreated African Americans with his 1949 publication of *Jesus and the Disinherited*. Thurman's thought had a powerful impact on King's vision of the Beloved Community and his civil rights activism.

A worn copy of Thurman's classic *Jesus and the Disinherited* was carried in King's briefcase throughout his civil rights journey. In this work, Thurman interprets Jesus as a poor, marginalized Jew within the Roman Empire. Thurman writes, "How different might have been the

---

[24] For the influence of Thurman on King, see the following sources: Lerone Bennett, *What Manner of Man*, 2nd rev. ed. (Chicago: Johnson Publishing Company, 1976) 74–75; John J. Ansbro, *Martin Luther King, Jr.: The Making of a Mind* (Maryknoll: Orbis Books, 1982) 27–29, 272; Lewis V. Baldwin, "Understanding Martin Luther King, Jr. Within the Context of Southern Black Religious History," *Journal of Religious Studies* 13/2 (Fall 1987): 1–26; Baldwin, "Martin Luther King, the Black Church, and the Black Messianic Vision," 1–16; Walter E. Fluker, *They Looked for a City: A Comparative Analysis of the Ideal of Community in the Thought of Howard Thurman and Martin Luther King, Jr.* (Lanham: University Press of America, 1989); Walter Fluker, "Howard Washington Thurman and Martin Luther King, Jr.: Critical Resources in the Development of Ethical Leadership," in *Ethical Leadership, The Quest for Character, Civility and Community* (Minneapolis: Fortress Press, 2009) 11–32; and Larry Murphy, "Howard Thurman and Social Activism," in *God and Human Freedom: A Festschrift in Honor of Howard Thurman* (Richmond, IN: Friends United Press, 1983) 154–55.

story of the last two thousand years on this planet grown old from suffering if the link between Jesus and Israel had never been severed.... [For] the Christian Church has tended to overlook its Judaic origins,... the fact that Jesus of Nazareth was a Jew of Palestine."[25] Thurman connects Jesus' outsider status as a Jew with the outsider status of African Americans in White America, arguing that Jesus stands in solidarity with all those "whose backs are up against the wall."

In 1949, the year that Thurman's manifesto was released, King was in seminary at Crozer, writing outlines and papers on Jesus. In one of his outlines for class, "Who was Jesus of Nazareth?" King writes, "Jesus was a Jew. It is impossible to understand Jesus outside of the race in which he was born. The Christian Church has tended to overlook its Judaic origins, but the fact is that Jesus of Nazareth was a Jew of Palestine. So as we study Jesus we are wholly in a Jewish atmosphere."[26] This quote is an explicit recapitulation of Thurman's Christology, as Thurman wrote that "the Christian Church has tended to overlook its Judaic origins.... Jesus of Nazareth was a Jew of Palestine." Since Thurman was a family friend and King's statements so closely resemble Thurman's, it is highly likely that King, Jr. received a copy of the book the year it was published. Thurman's Christology provided a template for King's conception of Jesus and the earthly struggle for justice. Thurman's Christology of Jesus understood chiefly as a poor, disinherited Jew remained at the epicenter of King's vision of beloved community throughout his life.

In *Jesus and the Disinherited*, Thurman goes on to argue that Christians are called to make Jesus' dream of the Kingdom a reality today. This is precisely what King did through leading communities around America to work toward building the beloved community. Jesus' dream provided both the vision and the motivation for the church's prophetic mission in the world. Thus, a prophetic Christology was foundational to the theology that undergirded King's leadership of the Civil Rights Movement.

---

[25] Howard Thurman, "Jesus—An Interpretation," *Jesus and the Disinherited* (Boston: Beacon Press, 1976) 16.

[26] Martin Luther King, Jr., "Who Was Jesus of Nazareth?" 23 November 1949, Crozer Seminary, *Papers*, 1:245.

Thurman's relationship with King was personal, and he always sought to look out for King's well-being. During his doctoral studies at Boston University, Thurman invited King over to watch the World Series. When King was stabbed later in his career, Thurman went to meet with King in the hospital and encouraged him to take a month of convalescence to reconnect with God and restore his soul. Thurman loved King in concrete ways, praying for him and seeking to care for his soul.

Deep streams of mysticism permeated Thurman's theology. It is this subterranean mysticism that is Thurman's principle contribution to the Morehouse Gospel. This is why I think that the best way to understand the Morehouse Gospel is at once a "mystical-prophetic theology." While King's vision of beloved community emphasized the prophetic, toward the end of his life, we see a subtle movement toward the mystical.[27] King's recovery of the prophetic imperative and Thurman's recovery of mystical depth, both rooted in a mighty Morehouse tradition, lay down an important challenge for contemporary Christian theology and ethics. Thus, the Morehouse Gospel as a fully orbed "mystical-prophetic" theology is, as yet, a still unrealized possibility, not only for Black Christianity, but for the world Christian movement.

In addition to a mystical-prophetic vision and a commitment to racial justice, the Morehouse Gospel of Thurman and King is marked by nonviolent love. Thurman was the first advocate of the Black Social Gospel to go to India and meet with Gandhi, an experience he describes vividly in his autobiography, *Head and Heart.*[28] Thurman would be followed by Mordecai Johnson, Benjamin Mays, and Martin Luther

---

[27] Al Raboteau, "A Hidden Wholeness: Thomas Merton and Martin Luther King, Jr.," in *Fire in the Bones* (Boston: Beacon, 1995) 165. Raboteau writes, "At the time of his assignation, plans were underway for Martin Luther King, Jr. to make a retreat with Thomas Merton at Our Lady of Gethsemani Abbey. We shall never know what might have resulted from a dialogue between this Roman Catholic monk and this Black Baptist preacher whose lives still fascinate and inspire us twenty-five years after their deaths" (166).

[28] Howard Thurman, *With Head and Heart: The Autobiography of Howard Thurman* (New York: Harcourt, Brace and Company, 1979).

King, Jr. Gandhi helped the Black Social Gospel see nonviolent love as both a philosophy and a political strategy.

Mohandas Gandhi and Nonviolent Love

The nonviolent tradition of prophetic protest was mediated to the Black Christianity through the philosophy and activism of Mohandas Karamchand Gandhi (1869–1948). King had heard Mordecai Johnson, president of Howard University, deliver a moving lecture on Gandhi in 1950 during his last year at Crozer. Ever since then, he was drawn to Gandhi's vision of nonviolence and began to devour books about Gandhi. Through Gandhi's writing, King became persuaded that nonviolent love could be a collective force for social transformation.[29]

Many generations of advocates of the Black Social Gospel had pilgrimaged to India to meet with Gandhi and other nonviolent Indian activists. Howard Thurman was the first to go, meeting with Gandhi in 1935, followed by Benjamin Mays and Mordecai Johnson in 1936, so Gandhi's vision of nonviolent love was a central part of the Morehouse Gospel since the late 1930s.[30] King was also tutored in Gandhi's philosophy of nonviolence during the Montgomery and Nashville struggles by a number of activists who were associated with the Fellowship of Reconciliation, including Bayard Rustin, Glenn Smiley, and James Lawson. Thus, King was following trails well traveled when he, Coretta Scott King, and Lawrence D. Reddick traveled to visit India in 1959 to deepen their understanding of the freedom struggle in India.

---

[29] For discussion of Gandhi's nonviolent philosophy on the theology and strategies of Martin Luther King, Jr., see Ansbro, *Martin Luther King, Jr.: The Making of a Mind,* 1–7; Baldwin, "Martin Luther King, Jr., the Black Church, and the Black Messianic Vision," 97–98; Baldwin, *There Is a Balm in Gilead,* 171–73, 185–87; and J. Deotis Roberts, "Gandhi and King: On Conflict Resolution," *Shalom Papers: A Journal of Theology and Public Policy* 2/1 (Spring 2000): 29–42. See also J. Deotis Roberts, "The Fellowship of Kindred Minds: Gandhi, Bonhoeffer, and King," *Bonhoeffer and King: Speaking Truth to Power* (Louisville: Westminster John Knox, 2005) 61–74.

[30] William Stuart Nelson, a philosopher of religion at Howard University, also mediated the Gandhian tradition to the Black Social Gospel tradition.

While King's dream of beloved community was born in the fires of White racist violence in the Deep South, it could only be fulfilled through nonviolent protest. On the evening of 30 January 1956, when King's home was bombed in Montgomery, Alabama, he had to decide whether or not he would retaliate. King chose the path of nonviolence, embodying Christ's teaching to love one's enemies.[31]

From that point on, Gandhi's philosophy of nonviolence began to guide King's thought and activism:

> Then I came upon the life and teachings of Mahatma Gandhi. As I read his works, I became deeply fascinated by his campaigns of nonviolent resistance. The whole Gandhian concept of *satyagraha* (*satya* is truth which equals love, and *graha* is force; *satyagraha* thus means truth-force or love-force) was profoundly significant to me. As I delved deeper into the philosophy of Gandhi, my skepticism concerning the power of love gradually diminished, and I came to see for the first time that the Christian doctrine of love operating through the Gandhian method of nonviolence was one of the most potent weapons available to oppressed people in their struggle for freedom.[32]

With the principle of nonviolent protest, we see that King develops a political strategy to inspire people to collectively embody love through a coalition dedicated to realizing social justice, including the full participation of all people in democratic life. While violence led to destruction, nonviolent love was the way to redemption for all humanity. King wrote, "The way of acquiescence leads to moral and spiritual suicide. The way of violence leads to bitterness in the survivors and brutality in the destroyers. But the way of nonviolence leads to redemption and the creation of the beloved community."[33] The path of nonviolence marked King's democratic theologizing—it was only through the theory *and* practice of nonviolent love that beloved community could be realized.

---

[31] One of King's advisors who encouraged King to lead through a strategy of nonviolence was Bayard Rustin (1912–1987). See Bayard Rustin, *Time on Two Crosses: The Collected Writings of Bayard Rustin*, ed. Devon W. Carbado and Donald Weise (San Francisco: Cleis Press, 2003).

[32] King, Jr., "Pilgrimage to Nonviolence," in *Testament of Hope*, 38.

[33] King, Jr., "My Trip to the Land of Gandhi," in *Testament of Hope*, 25.

King's theology of love and justice provided a new global horizon through which the Morehouse Gospel could broaden its outreach. Throughout his years at Morehouse College, Lawrence Carter, Sr. has faithfully deepened and advanced the Morehouse Gospel. As a professor and Dean of the Martin Luther King, Jr. International Chapel at Morehouse, Carter has actively worked to build the beloved community, both in North America and around the world. Thurman's and King's vision of nonviolent love comes into focus in his class lectures, as well as in his sermons and lectures at churches and academic institutions throughout the country. Carter has also actively pursued the globalization of the beloved community vision as articulated and pursued by both Thurman and King.[34] To this end, he has invested his energy into ministries and projects that lead to positive social change, inspiring a new generation of leaders to join the struggle for the common good.

Conclusion

The Black Social Gospel changed the face of twentieth-century North American theology. One of its most robust expressions was at Morehouse College. Here a mighty tradition of prophetic Christian theology and ethics developed, creating the fertile soil that produced King the theologian, ethicist, and international leader. The Morehouse Gospel was characterized by a prophetic-mystical vision, a focus on racial justice, and a commitment to nonviolent love.

Like Gandhi's freedom struggles on behalf of the "untouchables," King recognized that the Black freedom struggle had implications for a global movement of human rights. For King, "It really boils down to this: that all life is interrelated. We are caught in an inescapable network of mutuality, tied into a single garment of destiny."[35] Our common humanity, knitted together by the living God, is the reason that humanity will prevail. As King continued to struggle for radical democracy, he was assassinated in Memphis on 4 April 1968, leaving us

---

[34] Carter, Sr. et al., eds., *Global Ethical Options,* 12.

[35] Martin Luther King, Jr. "Peace on Earth," in *The Trumpet of Conscience* (New York: Harper and Row, 1968) 69.

heirs to a new season of struggle to achieve a truly radical democratic vision—the beloved community.

After King, prophetic Christian theology must acknowledge its wounds if humanity is to heal and become whole once again.[36] By the grace of God, humanity's future lies in new global movements of the people of the world, wounded healers, who are united by the egalitarian ideals of love and justice. Inspired by Benjamin Mays, Howard Thurman, Martin Luther King, Sr., and Martin Luther King, Jr., Lawrence E. Carter, Sr. has faithfully continued to pass on and embody this Morehouse Gospel, inspiring a new generation of mystic-prophets, academic-activists, to work with prophetic imagination, jazz-like improvisation, and stout hearts in creating the common good throughout the world.

[36] See Peter Goodwin Heltzel and Corey D.B. Walker, "The Wound of Political Theology: A Prolegomenon to a Research Agenda," *Political Theology* 9/2 (2008): 252–55.

7
Living Your Dreams

Barbara Lewis King

This "lesson in living" is about finding your purpose. It is based on the idea that purpose can come through dreams. As a result of many years of ups and downs—and more ups than downs—I have learned things about myself. I can now answer the question, "What am I here for?" I believe every living person has a purpose. You may not be aware of your purpose and you may have been told things that affect your conception of it. Many of us come from homes where discouraging words were said, such as, "You will never be anybody," "You will never go anywhere," or "You will never do anything." On the other hand, there are those who heard, "Have faith in God because with Him, all things are possible," "It doesn't matter what the color of your skin is," and "Regardless of the comments, you have a purpose in life, whether you accept it or not." Either way, you are the one who gives direction to your life.

Many of us have a passion, an inner urgency, or a desire to accomplish something. Some are not aware of the potential they have to accomplish their goals. For those who do not believe, there are others who affirm with Jesse Jackson, "I am somebody." Whether you have reached your goal or not, a noble pursuit is to become aware of your potential and power. You are somebody—created by God—for a purpose.

In this "lesson in living," I want to discuss seven factors and twelve steps that can help you discover and fulfill your purpose. First, I will discuss the seven factors, namely: Feelings, Imagery, Recurrence, Dread, Change, Haunting, and Curiosity. An understanding of these factors may help you organize your dreams so you can make sense of them. Then, I will discuss twelve steps you can take to help fulfill your purpose as revealed in your dreams. These steps are: Desire, Decide, Love, Look Up, Work, Ask-Seek-Knock, Think, Speak, Listen, Accept, Dispose, and Rest. In combination with the seven factors, these twelve steps bring about powerful advances toward both understanding yourself and living your dreams.

What Are Dreams and Why Do They Matter?

A dream can start as a series of thoughts. On a physical level, dreams are thought to be images that come together in our mind, often while one sleeps. Images appear, ideas develop, and thoughts arise. On a spiritual and psychological level, dreams can result from a desired goal or purpose that motivates you to push on in spite of past or current obstacles, setbacks, or disappointments. In this respect, dreams can take the form of the joy one finds in his or her work. Dreams can inspire others almost as much as they inspire you.

Since dreams can reflect past experiences and give rise to future possibilities, it is unfortunate, yet common, that we often forget dreams or don't fully understand them. Some dream experts have estimated that we dream 150,000 dreams a year. Another way of thinking about the number of dreams we have is to consider a dream as an opportunity to enrich our lives. The good news is that it's not as hard as one might think to understand what the prophet Daniel in the Old Testament called "night visions." In fact, by paying attention to the following seven dream factors, you can discover signposts in your dreams that may enlighten you in ways you might not have imagined.

Factor 1: Feelings

The first factor you'll want to look for are strong feelings that result from dreams. Did a dream wake you up or shake you up? Did a dream touch you in an emotional way? Did it frighten you? Did it bring you peace? Ask yourself these questions in the aftermath of your dreams.

Factor 2: Imagery

The second factor is imagery. What were the images in the dream? Did you see anything that concerned you? When considering imagery, don't overlook or underestimate the role of culture. Sometimes your background or past history shapes the dream's imagery in certain ways.

Factor 3: Recurrence

How often must a dream return before you call it a "recurring" dream? If you've seen it more than once, it's safe to say it's recurring. Dream books may offer a meaning for recurring dreams. However, the problem with such books is that they give a general message about something that happens in a dream. For instance, if you dream about "falling out of a chair," the dream book gives you a broad or overarching meaning for falling out of a chair. The next step is to move from the "generic" to the "specific." What does "falling out of a chair" mean to you? One cannot always depend on a dream book to define such specificity.

Another important thing to remember about recurring dreams is that they relate to *you*. They may not necessarily apply to your sister or your brother but rather to *you* and something that you are specifically experiencing or about to experience. If you dream about water, you should question your relationship to water. If you dream about a tree, how do you relate to a tree? If you dream about falling, how does that apply to you? It may even be helpful to write your dream or dreams down. Writing the details down will help you remember and allow the opportunity to revisit the details and critically reflect on them.

Factor 4: Dread

Dread is a feeling of terror or anxiety. It's like a nightmare, but it can be a sign that you are ready for some kind of healing. Obviously, no one wants to repeat a nightmare, so it may be a reminder that there's something unpleasant in your life that you need to take care of, or something you've been doing that you really should quit or avoid.

Factor 5: Change

Another kind of dream occurs when you're contemplating change or when you're involved in something that you have no control over, such as the death of a loved one, or when you're undergoing a transition. Other changes may include leaving a job, contemplating a divorce, or a separation from a lover. Change can be a springboard for future dreams. And when you envision those dreams, whether layoffs, divorce, relocation, or other expected or unexpected transitions, perhaps there's something you can learn about the choices that you are making. In order to get anything out of the dream, you must remember that the dream is for and about you, no matter who else is in the dream.

Factor 6: Haunting

A dream that haunts you is one that will not go away. When a dream stays with you, it is embedded in the subconscious realm of your mind to nudge you to bring whatever it is to the forefront. This kind of dream might occur due to something triggered from memory and surfaces. It might be something you have strong feelings about, or maybe someone says something or reminds you of an experience that brings back memories. Regardless, these often pop up from a subconscious state in the form of a dream. A lot of dreams help us to realize who we are and who we don't want to be. That's where psychotherapy comes in. I am not a psychotherapist, psychoanalyst, psychiatrist, or psychologist; however, when dreams haunt you, they likely originate from a place where immediate action needs to take place.

There are people who are haunted with all kinds of situations that start in a subconscious way. For example, a teenager becomes pregnant out of wedlock. Her parents insist that she gets an abortion. What if she doesn't want an abortion? Let's say she conceives the baby, will she still feel the pain of her parents' rejection in a subconscious or subliminal way? She may even get married and realize this issue carries over into her marriage in a number of ways. Or she might get pregnant again and have mixed emotions about having another child. But then she might have a dream that nudges her to critically examine what's been haunting her. Instead of suppressing the dream, she should overcome what's haunting her. In the same way, when something from your past comes up from your dreams, it can be a source to help straighten out a present situation or prepare to deal with a future one.

In the Book of Daniel, when king Nebuchadnezzar had a dream about a mysterious stone (Daniel 2), he was filled with fear and wanted the wise men of the kingdom to explain to him the dream. None of them could interpret it so he ordered them to be put to death. Daniel rose to the occasion by boldly volunteering to interpret Nebuchadnezzar's dream. After the meaning was revealed to him, Nebuchadnezzar declared, "Blessed be the name of God forever and ever, For wisdom and might are His.... He reveals deep and secret things; He knows what is in the darkness, And light dwells with Him" (Daniel 2:20, 22 NKJV). Every time Daniel interpreted something, he would return thanks. We should, likewise, be in a constant state of thanksgiving and prayer. Go in the closet of your own mind and heart and pray. If you don't know how to pray, pray the Lord's Prayer in Saint Matthew 6:9–13. In doing so, you will come closer to finding the purpose God has for you.

There are not many people like Daniel who can interpret dreams. You can't seek counsel from everybody, and it's better to confide in someone you are comfortable with and someone you can trust. I recommend those who have been around awhile, like elders in your church or community. Go to your grandmother, for instance, or an aunt or uncle. Don't discount elders or wisdom through the ages. Another example of haunting is when you are visited by the spirit of someone who has passed away. A lady came up to me one Sunday and said, "My mother keeps coming to me in a dream and I don't understand because my mother is 'on the other side.'" It should not be surprising if parents or loved ones "reappear." My grandmother is always "coming to me." Sometimes I sing a song in the pulpit that my grandmother used to sing. She is still with me, still living in me, and still influencing me in many ways.

Factor 7: Curiosity

The seventh factor is curiosity. Curiosity is being genuinely concerned about something. It grows out of a serious desire to know something. Curiosity leads to reflection and meditation. The purpose of meditation is to help you calm down, center your thoughts, and listen to your intuitions. Intuitions may be the voice of God, helping you to discern the meaning of your dreams. Begin a dream journal, a log of what you dream about. Write in the present tense and date each entry. Try to hammer out two pages and, although the process may seem lengthy, it will be helpful in organizing your thoughts. On the first page, begin with a personal statement such as: "I am feeling...doing... hearing...seeing...tasting...." Then record the following information about the dream, if applicable. Such could include houses or buildings that appeared in the dream; people and places; colors; aromas; flowers, trees, or shrubs; shapes and numbers; gemstones; symbols and how they apply specifically to you; animals; traveling of any kind, or movement such as running or walking; emotions or feelings about yourself. Everything in this list won't be a part of every dream. The purpose, however, is to be as specific as you can and capture as many details as you can recall. Afterwards, turn the page and continue writing.

Now what? You've had the dream, you've entered it into your dream journal, and you've interpreted it. What will you do as a result of having this particular dream? Unless you do something meaningful with the information you obtained from the dream (and that doesn't mean it has to be something big), the dream you've just spent so much time interpr-eting will become just another episode in your subconscious. Therefore, it's now time to move on to the next step—acting on your dream to improve your life.

Finding Your Purpose in Life Through Dreams

When we thank God for "living in us," we acknowledge God as "I AM." I AM is an etymology for the God of Israel, YHWH, which is treated as a verbal form derived from "to be" and formulated in the first person, especially in Exodus 3:13–15, according to Bruce Metzger. Metzger also maintains that YHWH is a third-person form and may mean, "He causes to be," which refers to God in action.

We were all created for a reason. Genesis 1:1 says: "In the beginning, God created the heavens and the earth." We come from different backgrounds but, as different as our backgrounds might be, they are all intertwined in the vision God has for us. Each person is wondrously made and created in God's image (*imago Dei*). Jeremiah 29:11 says it best: "For I know the plans I have for you, plans to prosper you and not to harm you, plans to give you hope and a future."

Next, there are twelve steps to fulfilling your purpose. Before we begin, let's drop age as a barrier. It doesn't matter how old you are. When I was a little girl, my mother had a beauty shop and people ordered combs that I made. Therefore, if your child or teenager has an idea, don't discount the idea but encourage him or her to pursue it. As it relates to older people, I remember my "Grandma Moses," who started painting in her nineties. She sold all those paintings and bought a

Bentley luxury car and a million-dollar house. Dreams come true at all ages.

A big reason many people cannot fulfill their dreams is fear. In order to succeed, fear must be overcome. Fear can be overcome with faith. Hebrews 11:1 says: "Faith is the substance of things hoped for, the evidence of things not seen."

Step 1: Desire

Desire can result from God nudging you and saying, "Listen, I want to bring this through you." The scripture teaches that God will give you the desires of your heart. You are really in sync with God when you discern the voice of God saying, "This is what I want you to do, and only you can do it." What do you desire?

Step 2: Decide

Determination to decide follows desire. Deciding to act on your desires takes courage, faith, and determination. You must be determined to make it work. Say, "I am going to do this. I don't know how I am going to do this, but I am going to keep trying." Sometimes you need to check out your resources. Be resourceful. Look around and see what's available and then make a decision to use what God has given you. Don't worry about possible negative outcomes. Keep pushing and looking for a way. Don't remain in the sea of indecision. Make a decision and stop telling everybody about your dream because they won't all understand it. Just do it!

Step 3: Love

You must have passion about what you are doing. The power of love will dissipate anger, envy, and jealousy. Many people will get jealous but you should not be concerned about naysayers, including those in your family or close circle of friends. Although family and friends mean well, they don't always understand your passion, your calling, or your love for an idea or plan. Many dreamers encounter opposition. How do you respond to those who oppose your dreams—or, at least, don't understand them? Loving them "in spite of" is one way.

Step 4: Look Up

Your dream will come true if you keep your head up and persevere. I once opened a dress shop. I did not have a bank loan. However, when the idea of a tall girls' dress shop came to me in a dream, I pursued it. I ventured into the Galleria, an upscale mall. You must have the determination not to give up but to *look up*. What happens is unknowable, but attitude determines altitude.

Step 5: Work

Anything worthwhile takes hard work. The results may not be immediate but hard work does pay off. If you have to get a side job to accomplish your goals, don't let pride get in the way. There are many people who have come up from the bottom. If you have overcome obstacles, remember where you came from and keep working to make a difference for yourself and for others.

Step 6: Ask, Seek, Knock

Luke 9:11 says, "Ask and it will be given to you; seek and you will find; knock and the door will be opened." This New Testament affirmation parallels another one of old: "Trust in the Lord with all your heart and rely not on your own wisdom. In all your ways acknowledge him, and he shall direct your path" (Proverbs 3:4–5). Many of us have put a down payment on our dream and then let fear take over and stop us in our tracks. One of the best ways to begin focusing on the power of imagination is by asking for your dream. If you want clarity about your dream, just ask, like the Apostle Paul, "What would you have me do?" (Acts 9:6).

Step 7: Think

Thinking is the process used to reach a decision. You are what you think. What you think of yourself is more than what others think. "If you think you, you can!" Mark 11:23 says, "Whoever should say to this mountain be thy moved and fall into the sea and does not doubt in his heart but believes that what he says will be done, it will be done to him or her." Don't give up on your dreams. If you find yourself giving up, do whatever you can do spiritually to get back on track. It takes work to stay on track and work is a part of the process. The dream may seem difficult but there is hardly progress without struggle. Think seriously about the hardships involved and what course of action to take.

Step 8: Speak

Nothing will bring your dream forward until you speak it into existence. Speak it like you really mean it. The dream is yours, nobody else's. If somebody does not see what you see, remember that it is your dream. Go back to your original thought and say, "Wait a minute. This is what I am supposed to be doing." Don't let anyone turn you around. Once you speak your dream aloud, don't be surprised at what may happen. In Genesis 1, God said, "Let there be...," and everything that was not, became. There is power in a spoken word.

Step 9: Listen

If you have taken some steps and your dream has not come true, then maybe it's time to stop and listen. Listening is an important factor to make sure you are hearing the right thing. It is easy to listen to others as well as one's own interests and selfish desires. Listening to the voice of God, whether in a still, small voice or through other means, for confirmation is an important step.

Step 10: Accept

The word "accept" means you agree or assent to doing something. When you accept your dream, you agree to do whatever it takes to realize it. Accepting means becoming aware of what needs to be done and doing it. When you accept responsibility for your dream, you are prepared to see it through, regardless of potential barriers.

Step 11: Dispose

This means you are going to look and see what you can get rid of because there's something new coming. Many times goals are blocked by unforeseen and foreseen problems. Obstacles are going to come. You have to decide what you are going to sacrifice in order to realize your dream. Dispose of anything that is blocking your dream.

Step 12: Rest

When you have done all you can do, get some rest. The steps may not all fall into place as quickly as you would like. You may be at Step 10 and somebody else may be at Step 11. Take your time and engage in reflection, rest, and renewal of your mind, body, and spirit.

These seven factors and twelve steps can be useful in understanding and living your dreams. Apply these concepts to your life and remember that, with God, all things are possible. Just look at the founders of Morehouse College and the life and ministry of Dr. Lawrence Edward Carter, Sr.

8

Forgiveness as Self-Defense[1]

Rabbi Douglas E. Krantz

Judaism teaches us that the right of self-defense against a hostile pursuer is both obligatory and fundamental. Our Talmud, the great foundation of Rabbinic Judaism compiled in Babylonia—modern-day Iraq—around the year 600 of our Common Era, teaches: "If a person comes to kill you, rise early to kill him first."[2] The principle rooted in Rabbinic conviction is that the purpose of all of the rules in the Torah is that we shall "live by them."[3] Judaism is a religion that teaches us how we shall live in a world that is human, and often predatory.

---

[1] A version of this paper, although not delivered, was submitted as a part of the 6th Doha Conference on Inter-Religious Dialogue. Special thanks to John F. Heimerdinger for pointing out to me that most people underestimate the significance of forgiveness. Thanks also to Ivy Levien, Carolyn Salon, Robert Belson, Ellen Siev, and Jeffrey Klafter for listening to my ideas and offering suggestions. Special thanks to my colleague Rabbi Seth M. Limmer and to my assistant, Rosie Aronin, for their thoughtful critiques.

[2] Yoma 85a, Berakot 58a, Sanhedrin 72a יומא פ''ה.,ברכות נ''ח., סנהדרין ע''ב

If a man comes to kill you, rise early and kill him first. ותורה אמרה. בא להרגך השכם להרגו.

The principle comes from the rabbinic understanding of Exodus 22:1 where the right to kill a burglar who is prepared to commit murder is affirmed.

Also see: *Talmud*, Sanhedrin 74a סנהדרין ע''א

רבי יונתן בן שאול אומר. רודף שהיה רודף אחר חבירו להורגו, ויכול להצילו באחד מאבריו ולא הציל נהרג עליו.

Rabbi Yonatan ben Shaoul says: "If one is pursuing his fellow to slay him, and if the pursued could have saved himself by maiming the pursuer, but instead killed the pursuer, the pursued should be executed [for murder] on that account." Note that here the right of self-defense against a hostile pursuer is assumed, but the example offered is not readily adjudicable.

[156] See discussion on Leviticus 18:5 regarding the words וָחַי בָּהֶם in *Talmud* Sanhedrin, 74a.

Thinking about our human predatory nature and the right of self-defense, and the insistence that we are to live by our Jewish rules and laws, brings to mind the women who waited on customers at the Beverlywood Bakery in West Los Angeles, where my mother would take me as a young boy. The women who served us there had tattoos on their arms. They were survivors of the Nazi concentration camps of World War II. The women who sold the staff of life and sweet cakes to my family had legitimate grievances as a part of their life experience.

I remember also a conversation in spring 2000 in Baghdad, at the bar on top of the Palestine Hotel overlooking the Tigris River, where the Iraqi bartender was talking bitterly about the Kuwaitis and the way they spoke disrespectfully about Iraqis. The bartender at the Palestine Hotel in Baghdad had legitimate grievances as a part of his life experiences.

I recall Israelis speaking about suicide bombers who had blown themselves up, and in the process took the lives of young children as well as innocent men and women. I recollect Israelis speaking about the incessant rocket attacks against Sderot and Ashkelon in southwest Israel. The Israelis have legitimate grievances as a part of their life experiences.

I think back on the times when I listened to Palestinians speak, and read e-mails and watched reports on Al Jazeera concerning Israeli bombing reprisal attacks, disproportionate responses to Palestinian terror attacks, that ended up taking the lives of innocent Palestinians, men, women, and children. The Palestinians have legitimate grievances as a part of their life experiences.

Legitimate grievances born of bitter life experiences are carried into my office by good people who are burdened by the nemesis of their angry memories. Good people can recite for me names, dates, places in which some part of their personhood was violated by someone they love or by a stranger. The wounded people who come into my office carry with them legitimate grievances as a part of their life experiences. All of us men and women and children have legitimate grievances.

Human beings repeat our legitimate grievances to those from whom we can find a sympathetic hearing. Many of us are what I call "score-keepers." Scorekeepers are people who self-righteously hold fast to their legitimate grievances and anger. Still, according to our Rabbinic teaching, legitimate anger is a self-destructive emotion. Rabbi Yudin, who taught in ancient Babylonia, likened anger to a boiling kettle, or to someone who spits up in the air, only to end up spitting in his or her own face.[4] If we allow ourselves to become a boiling kettle, the water will eventually evaporate, and fire—the raging anger of the scorekeeper with legitimate grievances—will eventually consume the kettle of the self. When our roiling anger becomes the hostile pursuer of our own well-being, then we are pursued by a hostile aspect of our own being, our own complex nature.

Our human nature, according to our rabbinic tradition, is a struggle between Inclinations—one good and the other evil—which contend with one another inside a healthy human self.[5] We are neither all good nor all evil. The struggle going on inside of us is necessary to make us strong, and at the same time decent, caring, empathetic. However, when we are ruled by the self-destructive and self-righteous anger born of score-keeping, we can become transformed into a hostile pursuer of our own well-being, and thereby spit in our own faces. Judaism teaches that if we

---

[157] *Kohelet Rabbah* 7:9 קוהלת רבה ז''ט

אל תבהל ברוחך לכעוס. א''ר יודן הכמה דמעזיל על פלכתיה כן סליק ליה בפלכתיה הוא נסיב. דקימקומא גליש על גיסיה שפיך. כל דרקק לעיל אפוי.

"Be not hasty in your spirit to be angry" (Ecclesiastes 7:9). Rabbi Yudin said: "According to how the spinner winds [the yarn] on his distaff so he will manage to take it off from his distaff. When the kettle boils over it pours [the boiling water] on its own sides. If a man spits upwards, it will fall on his face."

[158] *Talmud*, Berachot 61b ברכות ס''א

תניא, רבי יוסי הגלילי אומר, צדיקים. יצר טוב שופטן שנאמר, ולבי חלל בקרב. רשעים. יצר רע שופטן, שנאמר, נאם פשע לרשע בקרב לבי אין פחד אלהים לנגד עיניו. זה וזה שופטן, שנאמר, יעמוד לימין אביון להושיע משופטי נפשו'

Rabbi Yossi the Galilean says: "The righteous are swayed by their good inclination, as it says, *My heart is slain within me* (Psalm 109:22). The wicked are swayed by their evil inclination, as it says, *Transgression speaks to the wicked, methinks, there is no fear of God before his eyes* (Psalm 36:2). Common people are swayed by both inclinations, as it says, *Because He stands at the right hand of the needy to save him from them that judge his soul* (Psalm 109:31)." English translation based on *The Soncino Talmud Berakoth,* 385.

are being pursued by a hostile pursuer bent on destroying us, then we have an obligation to save our life and to destroy the hostile pursuer.[6]

People with legitimate grievances, filled with anger, are pursued by a hostile aspect of the nature of the self. God's good children with legitimate grievances wind the yarn after a fashion that creates a twisted and dangerously knotted emotional tangle. Angry scorekeeping leads us astray to the point where we might be tempted—and here I make up a word—to "Hitlerize" our enemies. I have heard angry Israelis, who have legitimate grievances, speak about Palestinians as if Palestinians were Nazis running concentration camps during World War II. Likewise, angry Palestinians with legitimate grievances liken what Israel is doing to them as a "holocaust." We have heard that language in multiple venues of our life experience, especially among the scorekeepers, who become consumed by the concomitants of anger: fear and demonization. Anger is a self-destructive emotion leading to actions that fly in the face of common sense. Israeli bombing of suspected terrorist centers or Palestinian rockets launched into civilian population centers are—and here I borrow a potent phrase—akin to trying to eradicate cancer cells with a blowtorch.[7]

Holding fast to legitimate grievances is like unleashing a blowtorch on an otherwise healthy self. Those who possess legitimate grievances can only defend themselves by forgiving. Judaism, the great gift of our rabbis, teaches us that when an evildoer makes amends, takes responsibility for an evil act and then asks forgiveness, the religious obligation of the injured party, the person with legitimate grievances, is to be forgiving.[8] Our rabbinic tradition is reasonable, and teaches also that if the same person commits the same offense over and over again,

---

[159] See fn. 2.

[7] Sir Michael Howard, *The Captain Professor* (London: Continuum, 2006) 219.

[8] Midrash *Tanhuma*, Buber, Wayyera. par. 30. See also Moses Maimonides *MishnehTorah*, Laws of Repentance, 2:9 where Maimonides explains that וזה "שלא מחל הוא החוטא." "The one who refused to grant forgiveness is the one considered the sinner."

and asks for forgiveness repeatedly, then we should not forgive.[9] But for one with real and painful grievances, forgiving the genuine penitent is obligatory. Why? Because only by forgiving can we defend ourselves from the hostile pursuit of our own burning anger.

Forgiving is complicated. We could debate—and surely some will—the nature of the genuine penitent. Even worse, many have confused forgiveness with acceptance or approval of that which is evil. If I am forgiving of someone against whom I have a legitimate grievance, that does not mean I approve of the manner in which injury was inflicted upon me. Forgiveness is not about approval of the actions of another human being. Rather, forgiveness is a self-defense mechanism to restore our healthy self. Our tradition asks us to forgive, because forgiveness saves us from the angry side of ourselves, so that we will not hurt just because we have been hurt. Forgiveness saves us from ourselves and requires us not to punish because we have been wronged or punished by others. Forgiveness is the healing balm protecting us from the hostile pursuit of our own angry spirit.[10]

Angry spirits call to mind the feud between the Campbell family and the MacDonald family that began with the Massacre of Glen Coe in 1692.[11] Anger fed that self-destructive feud. In Scotland the kettle boiled. Scorekeepers were unrelenting as God's children destroyed each other and themselves in the process. What will others say about all of us

---

[9] Maimonides, Moses, *Mishneh Torah*, The Laws of Repentance, 2:1: אי זו ? היא תשובה גמורה

זה שבא לידו דבר שעבר בו, ואפשר בידו לעשותו, ופרש ולא עשה מפני התשובה. לא מיראה ולא מכשלון כח.

"Who is a complete Repentant? A person who confronts the same situation in which he sinned when he has the potential to commit [the same sin again], and abstains and does not commit it because of his repentance alone and not because of fear or lack of strength."

[10] Rabbi Douglas E. Krantz, Kol Nidre Sermon, Congregation B'nai Yisrael, Armonk, New York, 27 September 2007.

[11] Magnus Linklater, *Massacre: The Story of Glencoe* (New York: Harper Collins, 1982).

today? What shall be said about Israelis and Palestinians, or Iraqis and Kuwaitis? Will not some wonder: Why could they not forgive?

Forgiveness is not easy for any of us. So when I was asked not so long ago if I thought Jews should forgive the Germans for the Holocaust perpetrated against the European Jewish community, those wonderful women in the bakery of my childhood years in West Los Angeles, my response was that those who conceived and perpetrated the Holocaust, and the destruction of the European Jewish community, and the murder of countless righteous Gentiles, and the destruction of those who were maimed or crippled, or homosexual, or mentally retarded, or different because they were deformed—all who were lost in the Holocaust—most of those perpetrators have died. So the question is not, shall we forgive them even if there were a small handful of genuine penitents, but how long shall we hold onto our anger against the dead? If we hold onto our anger born of legitimate grievances, are we not destroying ourselves, like so many benighted scorekeepers? We have to forgive without forgetting.

Not forgetting is why I keep a Yellow Star framed on the wall in my office, in my sight all day long. That Yellow Star was from an outer garment worn by a Jew of Europe under Nazi occupation. On that star is the word "Jude," and some of the threads on that yellow badge were sown onto the garment of a person unknown. The star is a reminder of the atrocities committed during the Holocaust that brought the destruction of some 11 million people, 6 million of whom were Jews, but also what happened to those who poisoned themselves with fires of animus, who could not put out the ragingly destructive fires inside of themselves by learning to forgive.

Forgiveness is not an act of approval, but the means, the path, by which we extinguish raging fires burning fiercely inside of a human heart. Forgiveness is a fundamental obligation to our own well-being, so that we might create the future we want for ourselves and for all of God's children, a world with less enmity, hatred, fewer scars, and fewer dead children to bury from wars and feuds. Self-righteous anger fueled by legitimate grievances has consumed too many Christians, Muslims, Jews, and other religious and irreligious people. Let us then defend ourselves, our own well-being, and advance our hopes for a better world by forgiving.

9

"Correcting Jesus": A Sermon

Bill J. Leonard

> "Lord, if you had been here, our brother would not have died," said Mary the sister of Martha when Jesus finally showed up at the grave of their brother Lazarus. (John 11:32)
>
> "Child, why have you treated us like this? Your father and I have been anxiously searching for you," his mother said. (Luke 2:47)
>
> "They have no wine," Mary said to him at the wedding in Cana when "the wine gave out." (John 2:3)
>
> "True sir, and yet the dogs eat the crumbs that fall from the master's table," said the Syro-Phoenician woman, unashamedly desperate for her daughter's healing even after she had been verbally expelled from the trauma center of Jesus' good presence, by Jesus himself. (Mark 7:28)

Do we ever *really* listen to the women who move across the pages of the New Testament? Think of it. Jesus often seems surrounded by women who argue with him, chasten him, fret over him, and get frustrated with him without the slightest hesitancy to tell him about it.

It started so early. Luke's stories of Jesus' birth are barely over when we encounter controversy between the almost adult Jesus and his weary parents. Remember? They had been to Jerusalem, where the 12-year-old (newly adult) Jesus, Mary, and Joseph experienced the ancient Temple rituals together. When it is over, Mary and Joseph head back to Nazareth and Mary thinks Jesus is hanging out with his friends along the way, but the next day they can't find him anywhere and fear he's lost in the big city. They rush back and spend *three days* looking for him. *Three days!!!* Can you imagine if you couldn't find your 12-year-old in Atlanta, New York, or Orlando for three days? And when they finally find him, does Mary welcome him back with open arms, confessing, "Of course, Son, we should have known you'd be at a prayer meeting"? Hardly! "Child," the New RSV translates (she calls Emmanuel, the Word made flesh, "Child"), "why have you treated us like this?" Can't you almost hear her say, "I don't care if you are the Son of God, you could have told us where you were going"? "You are grounded for at least a week"? And the text says that, even after Jesus gave what Mary surely thought was a totally lame excuse about being about "my Father's business," they "did not understand what he meant."

Now I ask you, at some time in your life, how many of you have ever heard a similar line from the mouths of your own mothers? Raise your hands. (The rest of you are lying.) Apparently, the Holy family had some dynamics that are known to all families. For years, I rushed so quickly to the punch line—"Don't you know I should be about my Father's business?"—that I missed the fascinating exchange between mother and son, virgin and savior, theotokos and logos. Did Jesus learn anything from the moment? I wonder if he learned to tell her the next time that he ran off to be about his "Father's business." Or did she learn to start letting her adolescent son go?

And then there is the wedding, in Cana of Galilee, and Jesus and his mother have the second of only two direct conversations appearing in all the gospels. "They have no wine," Mother Mary says. And Jesus' response shows just a taste of impatience: "O, woman," he says to his mother, "what has this to do with me? My hour has not come." But listen to Mary, who, like many of our mothers, will not take no for an answer. "Do whatever he tells you," she says to the caterer. And you know what happened.

In response to his mother's request, Jesus works what John's gospel says was the first "of the signs" that convinced his disciples that he was the Messiah. And the caterer saves the story with the wonderful two-sentence sermon: "Usually we serve the good stuff first and wait until the guests are a little drunk, but you have saved the best until last." Jesus listened to his mother and the wedding feast turns into a sign of the kingdom of God!

Jesus listened to the grieving Mary of Bethany, who threw accusations out of her broken heart, lifted his voice and Lazarus, three days in the tomb burst forth grave clothes and all. He listened to the nameless woman who covered his head with perfume, when the disciples ridiculed her and made an ethical dilemma out of it.

And then there is this Syro-Phoenician Canaanite woman—what a story, so brief, so momentary, so telling, so troublesome. Jesus and his disciples are in the "Gentile lands" (Tyre, the text says)—and not necessarily because they want to be there—on the road, enemies right and left back. Suddenly this woman throws herself into his path, imploring Jesus to heal her daughter, "overtaken by a devil." Don't you just hate it when hysterical women show up asking for something they do not deserve? And Jesus' response is equally direct, full impatience and ethnic distance—she is a Gentile, after all, and she's a bit demanding, even shrill. So Jesus offers the harsh retort that would surely steal the life out of any human being trembling on the edge of hopelessness: "It is not right to take the children's bread and throw it to the dogs." Case closed. Move along, lady. But she will not be silent or be silenced. Can we listen to the woman one more time? Jesus did. "True, sir," she declares, "and yet even the dogs can eat the scraps that fall from their master's table."

And then Jesus gets it. In fact, Jesus accepts the correction. "For saying that, you may go," he says, "the demon has left your daughter." Stand back, hold on, get ready: Listen to this nameless Syro-Phoenician woman. She corrected Jesus and he accepted the correction.

This story jumps across the centuries, full of issues that will not let us go either.

It's about race and nationality. She is a Gentile, a Syro-Phoenician woman. Some of the early rabbis called "those people" dogs—not all the rabbis, but some; it was a common throwaway word for a castoff people. And Jesus, at least in this story, begins with a sense of his own ministry that precludes a response to folks like her. Is the Father using this woman to stretch the Son's own mission and ministry? The questions abound. In our own struggle with race and nationality, we find ourselves in such situations small and large—indeed, our world is filled with boundaries that mute the cries of those who need and want to be heard. I almost mentioned healthcare, but "itinerant preachers" shouldn't meddle.

It is about gender. To hear the disciples tell it, she is merely another screaming woman, hysterically demanding something she did not deserve. But Jesus listened.

In the mid-nineteenth century, Sojourner Truth, the Black woman abolitionist, was speaking at an anti-slavery convention when a man challenged her ability to speak to a "mixed company" of men and women lest she violate biblical regulations about women speaking in public. Truth replied:

> Some say women can't have as much rights as a man because Christ isn't a woman. I ask you, where did Christ come from? From God and a woman, man had nothing to do with it. If the first woman God ever made was strong enough to turn the world upside down, then all women working together ought to be able to turn it right side up again, and now that they are asking to do it, the men better let them.[1]

From first-century Palestine to nineteenth-century America, women asked to be heard.

It is about theology. Who "qualifies" for the grace of God? Are there groups ahead of the line—chosen people, orthodox people, privileged people? Whose prayers does God hear? Where does the Jesus story begin and end? What the woman teaches Jesus and us is this: Grace is not an entitlement, it is a gift, pure and simple—"even the dogs eat the crumbs from the master's table...." The people who seem farthest off are drawn close. The folks who have no value in this world are valued, since sometimes grace just squeaks by.

In the next segment of this text, Jesus continues healing the broken ones, this time a person with hearing and speech impediments. Crowds flocked to him, bringing with them the lame, blind, speechless, crippled, and many other sufferers; they put them down at his feet, and he healed them. I wonder, did Jesus bother to ask the racial, national, gender, or theological boundaries of any of those people, or did he heal them every one, no questions asked? The text does not say, but we wonder, don't we? Perhaps he never talked of dogs and crumbs again. He listened and learned.

So what might this strange and wonderful story teach us today? I'd suggest three basic points.

---

[1] Carleton Mabee, *Sojourner Truth: Slave, Prophet, Legend* (New York: NYU Press, 1995), 67.

First, sometimes faith and desperation are inseparable. The woman in the story is desperate for her daughter's healing, sure enough. The desperation pushes her faith even as she clings to it. She shouts at Jesus desperately. I've done that on occasion, for the sake of my developmentally disabled daughter, shouted at Jesus and therapists for healing that did not come, but strength to deal with the absence of healing came, still comes, day by day. At those moments, such desperate faith is messy, even impolite, but it is faith nonetheless.

Second, sometimes grace breaks through when least expected, destroying our preconceived notions of God and ourselves. In this story it even seems to have happened to Jesus of Nazareth. Her desperate faith teaches even Jesus a lesson—he has not come only to "the lost sheep of the house of Israel," but to all who are hurting, struggling, and believing. What walls have we constructed today that Jesus and the woman might break down as grace breaks through to us? Who is left out of your "mission" in the world that God might open to you and to grace?

Third, grace is a gift, not an entitlement. Even an ounce of it will help when hope is almost gone. "Lord," she says, "even the dogs eat the scraps from the master's table." Sometimes life and circumstance are so convoluted, so broken, that about all I can do is reach for a crumb, a modicum of grace. That ancient, nameless woman knew that, didn't she? Sometimes even the crumbs of grace can help to make us whole.

So come to this table. Come with the "foreign woman," who for a moment found even Jesus hesitant to bestow the grace she demanded. Grasp the "crumbs" that fall from this table and, in them, find the promise of a whole loaf. In the audacity of deserving nothing, demand an equally audacious gift of grace. In this moment, let us demand of Jesus the hope and help we do not merit, but need so desperately. Then see what happens. Amen.

10

"Unexpected Judgment": A Sermon

Otis A. Maxfield

Our gracious Father, as we continue to worship you in spirit and in truth, we pray for that flexibility which allows us to enter into the unexpected. Even as a fortnight ago we expected spring and this morning we found snowflakes; spring is also a reminder that in the worst of us there's a possibility of something better and that in the best of us there's a possibility of something finer. So this day as we seek to understand the significant truth which became incarnate in Christ Jesus our Lord, may we seek to bring before him all that we are—realizing that in us He sees possibilities and that indeed these possibilities may become our future. So now may the words of our mouths and the meditations of our hearts be acceptable in your sight. Amen.

The text below is found in Saint John, chapter 8, verses 1–11. This account is omitted in ancient manuscripts, but it appears to be an authentic incident during Jesus' life and ministry, though not belonging originally to John's Gospel. It's an interesting story. It reads:

> They went each to his own house. But Jesus went to the Mount of Olives. Early in the morning he came again to the temple. All the people came to him and he sat down and taught them. The Scribes and the Pharisees brought a woman who had been caught in adultery, and placing her in the midst they said to him, "Teacher, this woman has been caught in the act of adultery. Now in the law Moses commanded us to stone such. What do you say about her?" This they said to test him that they might have some charge to bring against him. Jesus bent down and wrote with his finger in the ground, and as they continued to ask him he stood up and said to him, "Let him who is without sin among you be the first to throw a stone at her." And once more he bent down and wrote with his finger on the ground, but when they heard it they went away, one by one, beginning with the eldest. And Jesus was left alone with the woman standing before him. Jesus looked up and said to her, "Woman, where are they? Has no one condemned you?"

> She said, "No one, Lord." And Jesus said, "Neither do I condemn you. Go and do not sin again."

We're lucky to have this story. It seems to be uniquely like Christ and totally unlike anybody else in religious literature. It also seems obvious that the church could not have invented it. Once it heard the story, neither could it forget it. So it's true for most of us who have heard the story all through the years. Our best biblical scholarship tells us that it was not in the original manuscript according to John. In the first place, the language sounds like Luke. In the second place, it appears more appropriate to follow Luke, chapter 21. How it got there is a matter of hypotheses. The Dead Sea Scrolls have some interesting theories. One is at the end of the seventh chapter of John's Gospel, when Jesus, in an argument with the Pharisees, says, "I judge no man by the standards of the flesh." Or as J. B. Phillips translates: "I judge no one by your worldly standards." And the hypothesis is that when the scribes were copying the manuscript sometime in the first century, they came to that potent and vivid sentence (in itself worth a sermon), "I judge no man by worldly standards." Now the scribe had ["heard"] some of the stories about Jesus from the original canon, so in the margin of the text, he penned the following story. Later, as other scribes copied the scriptures by the laborious process of hand, they may have taken what was in the margin and put it in the body of the text. I think the important thing is that the story is so very much like Christ and so very unlike anybody else. And I am persuaded that the church had not invented it, but once they heard it, it could not be forgotten.

A couple of weeks ago we talked about James and John and their desire to be first. Jesus told them that he who would be first must also be least. Last week we talked about Nicodemus's problem of being born again. In this third interview, we find instead of dealing with a woman taken in adultery, Jesus really dealt with the Pharisees. This, to me, says a lot. It says once and for all that, in the New Testament, sex is not made the major sin, nor that the desires of the flesh are put on a plane above those of the spirit. The fact of the matter is that when Jesus was confronted with a self-righteous group of people, on the one hand, and the woman caught in the very act of the other, he chose to make the judgment against those who had committed sins of the spirit! It's almost as if to say that really morality is not a matter of one particular set of acts or another. One may be sexually pure and thoroughly obnoxious on every other level. Or one may never have been lustful, but one may have been so coercive and punitive and so unbelievably judgmental and authoritarian in other things that the sins of the flesh look tame compared to the sins of the spirit.

It's incredible how the church has gone the other route. Let a man commit a sexual sin and all sorts of things break loose. Let him be obnoxious, difficult, manipulative, and judgmental all through his life—yet we put up with him and feed him a lot of nonsense that he's a good man. This story sort of obliterates most of the ways in which, then and now, we make judgments about people. The point is, however, that the Pharisees didn't care about the woman's adultery. They used her as a tool to get at Jesus—not an unfamiliar tactic in our time where we drag up incidents out of a person's biography and smear them on the public record rather than dealing with the issue that happens to be at hand. At any rate, it didn't take him very long to focus on the Pharisees rather than on the woman who was taken in adultery.

There are some other things about the text itself to consider. We read from it that, for a long time, their accusations went on. He bent down and fingered the sand—whether he drew in it or wrote in it, nobody really knows. Finally, when they were all through with their accusations, he said quietly: "Let him who is without sin among you be the first to throw a stone at her." And they went away one by one beginning with the eldest. I don't know why the older ones went away first. There are two possible interpretations. First, if you live long enough, you know more about sin. The other might be that, if you live long enough, you grow more mellow because you begin to realize nobody is perfect, and your own life is scarred enough so that you no longer need to be self-righteous. Often I find this is an affliction of the young, incidentally, and not of the old. I would rather be with older people any time I sin grievously than I would with some of the young adults who want to make it a perfect world or die in the attempt!

They said he fingered the sand. I looked in the commentary and there are a host of theoretical interpretations. I really don't know why he wrote in the sand. I only know my own recollection of other very gracious and thoughtful people who have written in the sand. While I was sitting and trying to brood over this text some days ago, there came back to my mind an incident that I have long since forgotten. In the days of my adolescence, I was all of a sudden very much confronted by the birds and the bees, and a few other things, too! And I was desperately searching for someone who could understand and not berate. Either out of my own adolescence or my own anxiety, I did not find an abundance of such people.

However, while at a summer camp, I met a very wonderful old-time counselor and swimming coach. One afternoon I got up my courage and said, "I want to talk about me." And he suggested we take a walk. We went up the beach and finally sat down in the sand. While the surf pounded in, and the marsh grass waved behind us, and the sandpipers ran in front of us, I sat there trying to tell him about the advent of my adolescence, as if he had never heard such a story before. I noticed that all the time I talked, he sort of had his head down between his legs. He had taken a piece of driftwood and was scratching in the sand. When I finally came to the point of real confession, I looked up, expecting to see him staring at me. But he was not looking up at all—just still scratching in the sand. When it was over and we started back, I asked, "What on earth were you doing with the stick?" He said, "Well, I decided that I better look in the sand and think about myself because you were exposing enough of yourself. There was no sense in having my gaze upon you, too." I have no idea if this was in the mind of our Lord, but I do have a feeling that those who love us often help us conceal all that we need to conceal and only reveal the things that must be revealed.

I would suspect that, in a very human sense, Jesus thought this woman had enough shame and was subject to enough embarrassment without his gaze being upon her, too. You know, a good physician will not expose more of your body than he needs to when he examines you. And so it is in human relationships. Our obsession is not to get all of the facts or to put people in front of an x-ray. Our desire is to help them protect what needs to be protected, and reveal, on the other hand, what needs to be put to the test of the light of the noonday heat. At any rate, it seems to me that the finger in the sand is a wonderful way of saying, "I care enough about you not to strip you naked, but to help you keep concealed what properly ought to be so."

Let's consider another aspect of the interview. Towards the end of it, he took a glimpse of her face and said, "Woman, where are they? Has no one condemned you?" In Aramaic, the word "woman" is a very special term. In our English language we use it all the time. In Aramaic, the best translation of the word "woman" is "beautiful" or "lovely." How incredible that—having been called a "harlot," a "prostitute," and having been caught in the very act of adultery—after the Pharisees had gone, he could look at her and say, "Woman!" It is reminiscent of the time when, on the cross, he looks out to see his mother and says, "Woman (or beautiful lady), behold thy Son." I can't imagine what could have gone on in this woman's mind in such a moment, but I do know what so often happens in me when those who have sought to love me in the midst of my own spiritual anguish have called me "Friend" or have given me an affectionate term. Often we brace ourselves, waiting for some descriptive phrase that will nail us to the tree when we are already broken—and when someone loves us in the way Jesus did when he said, "Woman," this must be an extraordinary kind of experience! Then he says, "Where are they? Has no one condemned you?" When she says, "No one, Lord," he says, "Then neither do I. Go and sin no more." The English poet Robert Browning tried to speculate on how this woman must have felt when he had her say, "Then I knew that I was saved. I never met his face before but on first view I felt quite sure that God had set himself against Satan and toward all the loveliness that I could one day have."

There is one other comment about the story. It may be a difficult one, but I hope one that opens an avenue of thought for you later. It doesn't seem to be accidental that many of the gripping stories of the Old or New Testament all have their roots in a "fallen woman"—whether we take Ruth, or Bathsheba, or Tamar, or Rehab; or whether we take the woman at the well, or the woman in Simon's garden, or this particular woman, or even Mary herself. Around the figure of the fallen woman or the prostitute, in mythology and its symbolic, artistic interpretation (and, I must say, out of our understanding of dreams as a gateway to the soul), we find that the figure of the prostitute on the symbolic level (not on the concrete level) is often the forerunner of that free, untrampled, unfettered love of God that comes and offers itself freely to us.

One tragedy is that we interpret these figures concretely and historically, and therefore we commit that awful sin of judging by worldly standards rather than by spiritual ones. But if you stop to think about it for a moment, you note that in "Never on Sunday," for example; it was not only a great theme song but, in all honesty, if you could put away your moral indignation, it was a story with such sensitivity and pathos and tenderness in it, you couldn't help but come away feeling very perplexed—at least I did. And if you saw our friend "Irma," you not only laughed hysterically at Irma's escapades in Paris, but perhaps you caught a glimpse of what was tied up in this figure. We see an unbelievable distortion of this great symbol in the Key Club, and in the Bunny, and the Kangaroo, and lots of other figures of our times. And it seems to me, beyond the obvious distortion, there's a terrible hunger on the part of sophisticated people to say, "What is there in this feminine symbol that could lead us to God's love?" So you see, what can never be satisfied in the flesh can almost inevitably be satisfied in the spirit. But what I am really trying to say is not that sexuality should be treated lightly or that prostitutes should be exalted, for this figure makes no sense at all unless we turn it around symbolically. If we do this, we begin to see that really to be "born of the virgin" is to know love without the flesh experience, and that this figure is often the carrier, or the vessel, in which some kind of real spiritual transformation can occur.

Well, what about the story for us, apart from these preliminary observations? It seems to me that obviously Jesus had a totally different idea of "sinful people" than most of us have, or at least the culture has. Take an individual—and he is often different alone as compared to when he is in a group. The individual church member is different when he is voting at a congregational meeting, and the same is true of the person. The Pharisees (and I presume we are more in their camp than the ones who are taken in adultery) made the assumption that sinful people were wicked. But our Lord seems to have made the assumption that sinful people were not wicked half so much as they were terribly weak. In our private lives we are weak. Most of us do lead lives of quiet desperation and vainly attempt to cover up or to put things in Fibber McGee's closet. Or we attempt to sweep it under the rug! All these are evidences of the awful weakness of our humanity, for it's tough to be human! It's easier to be a remnant of our animal ancestry. Our Lord seems to have assured that. When a sin occurred, it was a waste of time to berate or condemn. One, rather, had to search for the purpose or the way in which that misplaced longing could be transformed.

At least, it seems to me that Jesus said we need to remember that no phenomenon contains so much destructive feeling as moral indignation. It's destructive because it really permits envy or hate to be acted out under the guise of virtue. I know that whenever I have been morally indignant, and thought that I had a great case, I have always lived to regret the fact that I capitulated to my moral indignation. That may be a way in which one gets some relief, but it is inevitably the way in which one gets caught in an awful, judgmental act. Eric Fromm speaks of this point when he writes, "The indignant person has, for one, the satisfaction of despising and treating the creature as inferior coupled with the feeling of his own superiority and righteousness." And, my! Whenever I have seen people in our community morally indignant, I have really met a Pharisee who ought to be challenged on throwing the first stone. We see this so much around sexual problems, even in our times. I have seen men stay as heads of companies and have status positions in churches whose manipulative and destructive tendencies have tainted lots of people, including their own children.

But over all these years, and in recent months, I have seen good men, sensitive and tender, who have committed sins in the sexual area isolated from our community and fired from their jobs, the intimation being that they ought to leave our community. I have seen it done by people who get such a sense of moral indignation that I worry more about their souls than I do about the sins of the people who have been condemned. It isn't that I treat their sins lightly, nor do they, but they, at least, come with the sense of shame. Maybe just the tangible embarrassment of the sin of the flesh gives us the possibility of forgiveness and reconciliation. The more sophisticated the sin of the spirit, the less aware one becomes of his power needs or of his avarice or his covetousness. The great tragedy is, you see, that when one gets morally indignant, he feels superior himself and acts towards the other as if he were inferior. But our Lord believed that sinful people were more desperately weak than terribly wicked. And secondly, he saw the futility of condemnation. I only worry that I speak too glibly at this point and that I really don't feel as good as it may sound. I am also desperately aware how difficult it is for me not to condemn what I disapprove of in others. But I know that therein lies part of my own shadow.

Dr. Jung, for example, said:

> Condemnation does not liberate, it oppresses. I am the oppressor of the person I condemn, and not his friend and fellow-sufferer. Modern man has heard enough about guilt and sin. He is sorely beset by his own bad conscience and wants rather to learn how he is to reconcile himself with his own nature, and how he is to love the enemy in his own heart, and to call the wolf his brother.

The only kind of condemnation that does any good, says Jesus, is the kind that one makes on himself. And if one has already taken responsibility for his sins, then obviously the only thing to say is, "Go, and sin no more." The only people that he called the "generation of vipers," and the only people he was referring to when he said, "It would be better for them to be cast into the sea with a millstone around their necks," were those who said they thanked God that they were not like other people!

One of my colleagues, Alvin Zunkel, preached a sermon on this particular story, and in it he made some very helpful comments on how we often condemn without even knowing it. One often says, "But I never read the riot act, and I didn't spank my child, and I wasn't vindictive. So why do they feel so guilty in my presence?" As Mr. Zunkel points out, often we become judgmental when we say, "Why?" Over and over again, I listen to people who begin by saying, "Why on earth did he do this to me?" This merely implies, "Why did he act like such a fool and a beast when I have been home being such a good person?" Now, *that's* an act of condemnation! Sometimes I have said to one of our children, "Why on earth did you do that?" The response I get is, "There's no sense in telling you, Dad, if you have to ask the question."

Or we observe people saying, "Well, I don't know why they did that, but at least I have never been tempted in that direction." That immediately removes one from the possibility of helping anything right to come in the situation. And to be asked "Why?" is often to be nailed to the wall. I am so glad that Jesus didn't say, "Why on earth did you commit adultery in broad daylight?" Or, "Why on earth did you let them drag you down here?" Or, "Why on earth weren't you smart enough to peddle your wares after dark?" You see, there was no "Why?" And who knows "Why?" until he has had an opportunity to be loved and to be held?

Another way we condemn in a nice way is by asking for the facts: "Give me the details." Jesus' interview didn't turn like most of the magazines, journals, and novels I have come across recently. No one said, "How many times have you done this before?" No one said, "Was he good-looking?" No one said, "What do you do with the money?" No one said, "How did you feel in the process?" No one said, "What's your technique?" I'm grateful that Jesus didn't need to press for all the historical facts about someone's sin. Is it not as important as knowing what the sin symbolizes? What is the purpose behind it? What did it mean in their lives? Often, helping people to conceal what doesn't need to be revealed is an act of tenderness and fidelity towards them. The only things that need to be brought out are the things that the person feels free enough to bring out as he pursues the course of his own salvation. And to be pressed for facts, as is often the case, particularly when we are morally indignant, is to stain and reduce the possibility that the work of forgiveness and reconciliation can take place. In fact, there is a great deal about many people's lives that I hope never to know, for the only thing I need to know is what is relevant to my continuing relationship between them and me. The more I am involved with them and my soul, the less of the facts I need to know.

The other way in which we condemn subtly, but terribly destructively, is by the threat of punishment. The woman said, "I told him if I ever caught him drinking again, we would be through." So now he keeps a bottle of vodka on the shelf in his office, you'll see, and she'll never know why he is so late coming home and is so hard-working. Or the mother says to the child, "If I ever hear that you have done that again, I'll lock you up in your room and ground you for a month." So the child begins to learn early in life that you don't take it all home. You wall it off and you carefully keep it outside. You only trust certain people with it. The threat of punishment is a form of condemnation and it usually nails a person to further destructive behavior—not a change of behavior.

There are two other things. I think Jesus also had a different idea about forgiveness. What he wanted was for the woman to be restored to a living, real relationship. Alienation and isolation are moods in which no one can recover. This is the danger of our warding off people who've fallen. And to throw the adulterer out is really to reduce the possibility of being restored to love. To take the obnoxious person and put him in a cake of ice and say, "Go somewhere else" is to repudiate the whole responsibility of being an instrument of God's love. It's an "in spite of" quality, not a "because of" quality, that makes us lovers of men.

Really, the incredible thing to me is that our Lord had more concern about the future than about the past. He didn't dwell on all that had gone before he opened a window ever so slightly—that enabled a woman to catch a fleeting glimpse of the dawn of a new day and the possibilities of a new life. I do know that people try suicide when they see no future. And I do know that my own despair has been more than I could bear when I was only looking back to the past. You see, the past is like the rearview mirror. It's there to give us a quick glimpse of the road behind so that we might better navigate the road ahead. But if you keep looking in the rearview mirror, you crash. You can't get from here to there. So when he said, "Go and sin no more," he was saying, "Let's look to the future." Now, the past is always with us because yesterday and tomorrow combine together to make today. But when the past is seen in the light of the future, then it's a great teacher and no longer a millstone.

Someone tells the story of an artist who had a studio downtown. Outside his window, he saw a beggar making his pitch for money. One day the artist took his stool and the canvas and sat in the window and painted a picture of the beggar who was out on the street. When he was finished, he invited the beggar in and said, "Look at the painting." The beggar asked, "Who is it?" "Why," said the artist, "it's you." The beggar said, "Is that the way you see me?" And the artist said, "Indeed, it is." Then said the beggar, "That's the kind of person I must become!"

And to me, the good news about Jesus is that, really, whenever he looks at us, and whenever we let him get close, he sees the possibility of what we might become. So, even to those of us who have sinned far more than the woman taken in adultery, he says, "Go. Neither do I condemn you. Go and sin no more!"

11
Morehouse College and the King Chapel Ministry: A Personal Retrospective

Echol Nix, Jr.

The word "vocation" comes from the Latin word "*vocare,*" which means "to call." *Webster's Collegiate Dictionary* defines "vocation" as "an occupation, either professional or voluntary, that is carried out more for its altruistic benefit than for income."[1] Vocations can be seen as providing a psychological or spiritual need, and the term can also be used to describe any occupation for which a person is specifically gifted or interested. Nancy Duff writes in the *Dictionary of Feminist Theologies*: "The doctrine of vocation affirms that every individual life with its unique combination of gifts and limitations has divinely appointed purpose and that we are called to glorify God in all we do."[2]

Ann Wiginton, in her book, *Awakened to a Calling*, reflects on the "vocation of ministry." She writes: "Each of us holds within our souls the hope for something more—something more than what we experience, accomplish, and consume. Sometimes that hope grows into longing for a life that brings together our dreams, our gifts, our hurts or pain, and our truest loves. That longing is what pulls each of us toward vocation."[3] For Saint Thomas, in his *Summa Theologica* (1273), this pull is a "beatific vision," the striving for a perfect blessedness that consists in a vision of God. Appropriated later by Spinoza, in his concept of "*amor Dei Intellectualis*," "the intellectual love of God" or "the highest happiness of humanity," this concept suggests that the pull is directed towards an intellectual union between God and humanity.

---

[1] *Webster's Collegiate Dictionary* (Springfield, MA: Merriam-Webster Incorporated, 2010) 1323.

[2] Nancy Duff, *Dictionary of Feminist Theologies*, ed. by Letty Russell (Louisville, KY: Westminster John Knox Press, 1996) 35.

[3] Ann Wiginton, *Awakened to a Calling* (Nashville, TN: Abington Press, 2005) 5.

If these suggestions are true, human beings are never fully satisfied. They are restless, and in constant search for ultimate fulfillment. For Augustine, the fifth-century theologian and philosopher, "humans are restless and can never find rest until one finds rest in God."[4] The German Medicval mystical thinker Meister Eckhart best summarizes this "restlessness": "To the one who cleaves to God, God cleaves and adds virtue. Thus, what you have sought before, now seeks you; what once you pursued, now pursues you, what once you fled, now flees you."[5] Everybody at some point asks questions such as: Who am I? Why am I here? Where am I going? What am I to do? These are difficult questions and, for many, will take a lifetime to answer. Like Jacob wrestling at Peniel, my own struggle with these questions grows out of my love for God and my desire to serve humanity.

Ancient Catholic monks thought the pursuit of wisdom includes the desire for God and the love for learning. If true, these two qualities have been at the core of who I am. I was nurtured in a religious household and my family stressed the importance of education. My brother and two sisters had many books—books of poetry, biographies, short stories, mystery novels such as the Hardy Boys and Nancy Drew, dictionaries, encyclopedias, and Bible story books. My Christmas and birthday gifts were often books as well as toys. Neither of my maternal or paternal grandparents completed high school but spent their careers as domestic workers and coal miners. My father, an educator and evangelist, was the first in our family to attend college. My mother later worked as a classroom aide at Dozier Elementary School in Montgomery, Alabama. Around the eighth grade, I developed an interest in Morehouse College, primarily due to the reputation of another "Morehouse man" and former pastor in my hometown, Dr. Martin Luther King, Jr. At that time, Morehouse advertised itself as "a distinguished institution dedicated to producing outstanding men and extraordinary leaders to serve humanity with a spiritual consciousness." That description sounded awesome to me

---

[4] Augustine, *Confessions*, trans. F.J. Sheed (New York: Sheed and Ward, 1942) 3.

[5] Eckhart, "The Talks of Instruction," in *Meister Eckhart*, trans. R. B. Blakney (New York: Harper & Row, 1941) 7.

as an eighth-grader! So, at 13 years old, I told my mother at our kitchen table, "I want to be a Morehouse man."

My interest in Morehouse College continued to grow during high school, and reading Dr. Alton Hornsby's multi-page article in our new set of the *World Book Encyclopedia* entitled "African Americans" further strengthened my decision. My family's income was modest and the reality of attending a private school, opposed to a state institution, was out of our financial reach. So, I decided to raise money by participating in high-school oratorical contests, 4-H cooking contests, essay competitions, and science fairs—all at the local, state, and national levels. I won over 13,000 dollars from these competitions as well as scholarships from civic organizations, fraternities, and sororities. After completing my first year at Morehouse, the Dean of Chapel, Dr. Lawrence E. Carter, awarded me the Martin Luther King, Jr. scholarship, a 15,000-dollar award sponsored by the King Chapel. A requirement of the award was to attend all Sunday-morning chapel services. Instead of joining a local church, I attended the weekly chapel services and had the chance to hear many of the famous ministers and pastors in America.

My first day at Morehouse was exciting. Hundreds of freshmen arrived on a hot, autumn Friday, dressed in long-sleeve White shirts and neckties. Immediately, the freshman orientation leaders began to discuss the Morehouse mystique, a special quality that encourages students to succeed at a level commensurate with their abilities and to give back to their communities. We sat in King Chapel and heard quotations from Dr. Benjamin E. Mays, Dr. Howard Thurman, Dr. Martin Luther King, Jr., and many others. We were told to look to our right and to our left and to remember that one of the two students next to us would not be there at graduation time. We were reminded of the challenges facing African-American men and to remember the ones who were not in college like us.

Although I had an interest in law, the questions I thought about most often were theological and philosophical ones. These questions included: What is a human being? What is the meaning of life? Why are we here? What is salvation and who is it for? What is the church? Are non-Christians going to hell? What is the kingdom of God? During my sophomore year, Dean Carter made me coordinator of the chapel assistants' Bible study, which I named "the Howard Thurman Discussions for Disciples." The sessions met each Saturday through the academic year and discussed the Bible, theology, ethics, sociology of religion, economics, and politics. I also invited Dr. Henry Mitchell, a renowned homiletician, to lead a series on preaching and how to construct sermons.

After class one day, Dean Carter pressed into my hands *A Theology Primer* and *Behind the Masks of God*, two recent books by Dr. Robert C. Neville, professor of Religion, Philosophy, and Theology at Boston University. Dean Carter is an alumnus of Boston University and was impressed with Neville, who had recently assumed the deanship of the BU School of Theology. Dean Carter said: "These books are significant contributions in the fields of metaphysics, theology, and philosophy, and if you are going to be a serious scholar, engage him." I read Neville's books from cover to cover. I was particularly intrigued with his thoughts on Chinese religious philosophy, including Confucian rituals as an alternative to the study of religion and ethics in the modern West. I was a History major at Morehouse but began to feel an "irresistible urge to preach." After informing my parents by phone of my decision to enter the ministry, other conversations were held with Morehouse professors such as Dean Carter, Dr. Roswell Jackson, Dr. Melvin Watson, and a number of prominent clergy such as Dr. Samuel D. Proctor and Dr. Gardner C. Taylor. Both Dr. Proctor and Dr. Taylor strongly suggested seminary because, according to them, "the call to ministry is a call to preparation."

The King Chapel annually sponsored a "seminary swing" to seminaries and divinity schools around the country, and during the year all of this was happening with me, the chapel assistants were planning to visit New England. Several chapel assistants drove northeast from Atlanta and visited Howard University School of Religion, Union Theological Seminary (New York City), Yale Divinity School, Princeton Theological Seminary, Harvard Divinity School, Andover-Newton Theological, and Boston University. Boston University impressed me the most because of Dr. King, who graduated from BU in 1955, and Dr. Neville, whom I was just learning about at Morehouse. Before the trip, I read Edgar Brightman's *An Introduction to Philosophy*, L. Harold DeWolf's *A*

Theology of the Living Church, and Walter Muelder's *The Ethical Edge of Christian Theology*. These texts helped me become more familiar with the social justice teaching of personalism at Boston University and how that school of thought contributed to the intellectual development of Dr. King.

My life took an unexpected turn my junior year at Morehouse. My mother, Mrs. Annie Mae Nix, was diagnosed with multiple myeloma, a rare form of bone cancer. She never asked me to stay close to home, but I wanted to stay nearby so I chose Vanderbilt Divinity School in Nashville, Tennessee. I have often wondered how my life would have been different had I gone to New England then instead of staying in the south. I have no regrets about being close to my mother at a time when she needed me the most. Through her illness, I learned much about God, about myself, and about ministry—perhaps more than I could have ever learned by just attending classes or reading books in the library.

During my senior year at Morehouse, the Business Department invited me to participate in a tour of Hong Kong and Singapore. This was a welcome opportunity to supplement my religion and history courses, and it would strengthen my knowledge of cultures in Asia. In fact, Dean Carter said on the first day of an introductory religion course: "A Ghanian proverb warns, 'Do not claim your mother's stew is the best in the world, if you have never left your village.'" The trip to Asia was centered on international business and changing trends in the free market. As the only non-Business major in the group, I was more interested in the culture and religions of the Far East. We left Hartsfield Airport (now Hartsfield-Jackson) and flew to Tokyo, Japan, and then to Kowloon, Hong Kong, and Singapore. The tour is forever etched in my mind because it opened my eyes to another culture, history, and religious heritage just as important and meaningful as Western civilization.

On a warm spring afternoon, I graduated from Morehouse College with a bachelor's degree in History. Halfway through the commencement ceremony, I looked to my right and to my left and discovered that neither of the two students who sat by me four years earlier during orientation week was present. The ceremony was meaningful and inspiring, especially with family and friends in the audience. Dean Carter gave the benediction by offering two quotations to the graduating class. The first quotation was from Howard Thurman: "Never let God repent for creating you." The second one was from the Apostle Paul, and often quoted by Benjamin Mays: "You shall reap what you sow."

12

The Twilight of Personalism at Boston University: The Testimony of a Participant-Observer

Harold H. Oliver†

After teaching philosophy at Boston University for thirty years, Borden Parker Bowne declared in 1905 that he was a personalist, thus defining the philosophical and theological environment of that institution for many years to come.

Ninety-nine years later, the deaths of Walter Muelder ('30, GRS '33, Hon. '73) and John Lavely ('41, GRS '50) in 2004 brought to a virtual end what many Boston University personalists regarded as "the century of Bowne's theism." My tenure at Boston University—as faculty member and as emeritus—spanned thirty-nine of those years. When I joined the faculty, I knew firsthand only Edgar Sheffield Brightman's ('10, GRS '12) *A Philosophy of Religion*, in which he presented and defended his notion of the finite God, and Harold DeWolf's ('26, GRS '35) *The Case for Theology in Liberal Perspective*. Unlike Erazim Kohak, who reported that, when he became a member of the Philosophy Department, he "fought personalism tooth and nail, with argument and sarcasm," I virtually ignored it, regarding it as "a Methodist philosophy."[1] The effect for the two of us was the same; both of us could say at the time—to use Kohak's further comment—"I would have nothing of it."[2] Twenty-three years would pass before I seriously engaged the personalist legacy, and only then when I was invited, by Thomas Buford ('63), to participate in the program on personalism at Brighton, England, in 1988.

---

[1] Lavely once wrote that it was common for many unsympathetic with the movement to speak of it in these words. John Lavely and Carol Robb, eds., *The Boston Personalist Tradition in Philosophy, Social Ethics, and Theology* (Macon, GA: Mercer University Press, 1986) 259.

[2] Thomas O. Buford and Harold H. Oliver, eds., *Personalism Revisited: Its Proponents and Critics* (Amsterdam-New York: Rodopi, 2002) 72.

While I knew too little about Boston Personalism when I arrived, I knew that it was an important legacy in American theological education. Some of my colleagues were the principal mentors of Martin Luther King, Jr. (GR '55, Hon. '59), whose untimely death at the hands of a White racist occurred in 1968. I quickly realized that the School of Theology had played an important role in the shaping of liberal theology in America and in the articulation of a vision. At the memorial service for Walter Muelder, the distinguished philosopher and theologian Robert C. Neville, who succeeded him as dean, highlighted the virtues of what he called "the great philosophical tradition of Boston Personalism," namely, "an unrelenting rational approach to inquiry, openness to all sources, and a voice that paid attention to the ordinary lives of people in the church."[3] Considering the fact that almost every student who attended the Boston University School of Theology in the twentieth century was taught philosophy of religion and theology by a personalist, it is not surprising that most Methodist ministers and bishops were of the personalist persuasion.

In his masterful multivolume history of liberal theology in the nineteenth and twentieth centuries, Gary Dorrien names the Boston University School of Theology as one of the three most influential liberal seminaries in America, the other two being Union Theological Seminary in New York and the University of Chicago Divinity School. Any movement that spans a century will have a generational sequence and some modifications along the way. While a certain generational awareness was present in the minds of the later personalist, it is easy to trace only the first three generations: Bowne, the Albert Cornelius Knudson (GRS 1900) and Brightman, then Peter Bertocci ('31, GRS '35), Muelder, and Lavely. My former student Father Bogumil Gacka ('95) has rendered us a service by arranging the sequence of the principal subschools:

> Borden Parker Bowne, who championed Personalism; Edgar Sheffield Brightman, whose position was Theistic Personalism; Albert Cornelius Knudson, a theologian, who formulated Theological Personalism; Peter Anthony Bertocci of the philosophy department, whose thought was

[3] Robert Cummings Neville, "Remarks for Walter Muelder's Memorial Service," *Focus* (Fall 2004): 2, 10.

labeled Osychological Theism; and Walter George Muelder, whose philosophy he called Communitarian Personalism.[4]

Boston University faculty used different designations for some of these subschools, usually combining various configurations of terms like "personalistic," "theistic," and "idealistic."[5] Muelder usually referred to the Boston tradition as "personalistic idealism"; the *Festschrift* for Bertocci carried the title *Contemporary Studies in Philosophical Idealism.*

From the time Bowne announced his predilection for the term "personalism," he defined its meaning in association with the term "idealism." Like the absolute idealists, he defined reality as mental; unlike theirs, his idealism contained an element of pluralism bordering on individualism. His appeal to the term "idealism" was a deliberate rejection of all the materialisms of the nineteenth century. He also claimed to be a realist, though we might have some trouble deciding what the terms meant when Bowne wrote a letter to his wife, dated 31 May 1909: "It is hard to classify me accurately. I am a theistic idealist, a *Personalist*, a transcendental empiricist, an idealistic realist, and a realistic idealist: but all these phrases need to be interpreted. They cannot well be made out from the dictionary."[6]

William James, however, who in his lecture "Monistic Idealism"[7] had proven himself an enemy of idealism, appreciated the fact that Bowne's idealism was tempered by a genuine realism, as is apparent from a letter he wrote to Bowne in 1908: "It seems to me that you and I are aiming at exactly the same end. The common foe of both of us is the dogmatist-rationalist-abstractionist."[8]

Theism was a major element in the thinking of all the Boston Personalists, and this at a time when philosophers generally were not given

---

[4] Bogumil Gacka, *American Personalism* (Ofiyna Wydawnicza: "Csaz," 1955) table of contents.

[5] For example, Bertocci described Brightman's philosophy as "theistic personalistic idealism." Buford and Oliver, *Personalism Revisited*, 35.

[6] Gacka, *American Personalism*, 45.

[7] *A Pluralistic Universe* [1909] (Cambridge, MA: Harvard University Press, 1977).

[8] Buford and Oliver, *Personalism Revisited*, 15.

to discussing it. Bowne's somewhat traditional theism (of the Methodist variety) was heavily weighted by what was called "the problem of good and evil." His successor, Brightman, became preoccupied with this same issue so deeply that he altered classical theism to deal with it. Although his new doctrine of Theistic Finitism caught his colleagues by surprise, we should recall that some of his students were shuttling back and forth to Harvard to hear Alfred North Whitehead, who at virtually the same time was articulating a finite theism informed by different assumptions. The doctrine of the infinite-finite God was rejected by Brightman's colleagues Knudson and DeWolf, and was not defended by their successors. The exceptions were Muelder and Bertocci, the latter of whom thought of God as the creator, but—because he accepted Brightman's notion of the non-rational Given "coeternal with the creator God"—left room for the finite hypothesis.[9]

Another development in Boston Personalism portended the shape the movement would take in the legacy of Dean Walter Muelder—the "correction" of Bowne and Brightman's individualism toward a more holistic view of the person. Muelder was fond of telling how he pointed out to Brightman the deficiency of the latter's individualism and was asked by Brightman to draw up a syllabus in social ethics, a concept new to Brightman. Muelder proved to be the chief embodiment of the transformation of personalism in the direction of social ethics. He called his philosophy Communitarian Personalism, and it rested on the redefinition of the person as a "socius with a private center"—Brightman had spoken of God as a socius. Fueled by the social vision of Methodism and the new Social Gospel of Rauschenbush, personalism in the School of Theology moved largely in the direction of theoretical and applied ethics. This was the climate of the School when Martin Luther King, Jr. took his doctorate from Boston University and accounts for its appeal to many of its students in the last half century.

Before turning to what I have called the "twilight of personalism" at Boston University, I feel compelled to give my impression of what Neville calls "openness to all sources." For the first three generations, the Philosophy Department guaranteed the succession of personalism by

[9] Ibid., 35ff.

appointing to the faculty their own graduates. According to Lavely, it was only after Brightman's death that there was a conscious movement by three of his students—Bertocci, Richard Millard (GRS '42, '50), and Lavely—to make the department more "pluralistic," in the belief that "such diversification would be more of a tribute to Brightman than an ingrown, closed personalist department."[10] Another twelve years would pass before Muelder followed suit by appointing four faculty who were trained elsewhere, namely at Harvard, Oxford, Zurich, and Emory. Natalie Jacobson McCracken wrote of this situation in a memorial tribute to Muelder, titled "Spirit Ascendant," for *Bostonia* magazine: "When [Muelder] arrived, the faculty was essentially Methodist; ten of the eleven regular faculty member held BU degrees and doctorates." This state of affairs persisted virtually unchanged until 1965, but by the time Muelder returned in 1972, "twenty-two of the forty-one faculty members had earned their highest degree elsewhere."[11]

For the first twenty-three years of his tenure as dean of the School of Theology, he was content with a personalist faculty. One of the chief failures of the movement at Boston University for the first fifty years was that it kept its gaze fixed on the philosophical and theological problematics of nineteenth-century Europe, principally of Germany, and re flected new developments in philosophy in twentieth-century England and Europe, such as phenomenology (and hence, Husserl and Heidegger), logical atomism and positivism (Russell, Ayer, and Wittgenstein), philosophical and theological hermeneutics (Gadamer), and process philosophy (Whitehead and Hartshorne), and derided the newly emerging dialectical theology (Barth), just to name some of the principals.

[10] Lavely and Robb, eds., *The Boston Personalist Tradition in Philosophy, Social Ethics, and Theology*, 256.

[11] Natalie Jacobson McCracken, "Spirit Ascendant," *Bostonia* (Fall 2004): 62.

I should add that, while Brightman rejected what he called Whitehead's "organic theory of internal relations,"[12] he carried on a friendly correspondence with Charles Hartshorne for many years. Harold DeWolf directed a sustained attack on the European revival of Kierkegaard in *The Religious Revolt against Reason*. Muelder had studied with Tillich at Frankfurt, but expressed no interest in the legacy of Kierkegaard, whose recent "discovery" in Germany was avowedly of such vital importance to Tillich during his student years. Furthermore, Bowne and Brightman claimed to be interested in physics, but, unlike their neighbor at Harvard, Alfred North Whitehead, who wrote a book on theoretical physics and whose philosophy followed closely the rise of the new physics, there seemed to have been no serious response of the personalists to this scientific and philosophical revolution in twentieth-century physics. Einstein, Bohr, and Heisenberg neither interested nor challenged them. In these respects, at least, Boston University personalists in the Department of Philosophy and the School of Theology lived in a closed world largely of their own making. When I, as one of those appointed to the school in 1965, announced to my dean, Walter Muelder, my plans to spend my first BU sabbatical studying cosmology at the Institute of Theoretical Astronomy at Cambridge University, he expressed to me that he had doubts as a theologian about my proposed venture, based upon his belief that the natural sciences have nothing to teach us about God. I went to Cambridge anyway—with his blessing.

I must say in all fairness that, when Brightman created the Personalist Discussion Group in 1938, he raised the question of whether the move was a good thing. Lavely reported in his "History of the Personalist Discussion Group 1938–1988" that "[it] was agreed that if the group were kept open to wide participation and hospitable to different perspective, then the venture would be worthwhile."[13] A glance at the volume of essays drawn from the papers presented to the group in the

---

[12] Gary Dorrien, *The Making of American Liberal Theology, Vol. 2: Idealism, Realism, & Modernity* 1900–1950 (Louisville, KY: Westminster John Knox, 2003) 302.

[13] Written in 1988 and published in Buford and Oliver, *Personalism Revisited*, xxii.

first fifty years should convince the reader that they were widely representative of diverse opinions, many of which were highly critical of personalism. The co-editors of the volume, Thomas Buford and I, ensured that some of the latter were included.

Having expressed my opinions about the strengths and weaknesses of the personalist years at Boston University before I arrived, I turn now to my principal theme, the twilight of personalism at the university in the last forty years. With apologies to Richard Wagner, whose use of the term *Dämmerung* suggested to me this title, I turn now to an account of the school during my years as faculty member and emeritus.

One cannot teach surrounded by those who created this important chapter in American philosophy and theology without an honest appreciation of their talents and wisdom. While I had no interest in personalism for the first decade after my arrival, by then I had begun to read and appreciate the writings of Bertocci, who—in my opinion—was transforming personalistic philosophy in creative ways. In 1975, the year of Bertocci's retirement, I was one of three faculty asked to present papers commemorating the occasion. Also, during the 1970s, I was writing my book *A Relational Metaphysic*, in which I expressed agreement with Bertocci's claim that the self is what it is doing—that the self does not have, but *is* its experiences.[14] I could respond positively to his ideas about time, as when he writes that

> I do not "pass" into a future any more than I "pass" out of the past. My being is always a "now" which is said to be older than a "then," or earlier than a "later," only because of differentiations which we call memories and anticipations.... I *am* my time and the changes which take place "in" me are discriminated as past, present, and future by virtue of my capacity for remembering and organizing my experience, always in a present, as involving a past and anticipating a future.[15]

---

[14] Harold H. Oliver, *A Relational Metaphysic (Studies in Philosophy and Religion, Vol. 4)* (New York: Springer, 1981) 179.

[15] Peter A. Bertocci, *The Person God Is,* (New York: The Humanities Press, Inc., 1970) 58f.

After Bertocci, the Department of Philosophy produced no major successor in the personalist camp. In what may be called—for lack of a better term—"the Lavely era" in the Department of Philosophy, the department became more diverse, as I reported. Lavely wrote major summary articles expressing criticisms of some aspects of personalism and some positive suggestions for moving it in new directions. His contributions included the article on personalism in Paul Edward's *Encyclopedia of Philosophy*; his "History of the Personalist Discussion Group," written for Buford and Oliver's *Personalism Revisited*; and three essays published in *The Boston Personalist Tradition in Philosophy, Social Ethics, and Theology*, edited by Lavely and Carol Sue Robb (GRS '69, '78), in which he writes that he did not teach a course on personalism until 1980 and admits that he produced no major constructive work, although he had completed 90 percent of a book on philosophy of religion by the end of his life.

One of the most distinguished members of the Philosopy Department during my tenure at BU was John Findlay, who became the Borden Parker Bowne Professor. While he had no special interest in personalism, he was invited to present a paper to the Personalism Discussion Group in 1972.[16] Although his paper is on the notion of person, Findlay does not mention the personalists. The same lack of interest in Boston Personalism is evident in the writings of Stanley Rosen, who was Findlay's successor to the Bowne Chair.

The case is different for Erazim Kohak, who in the Philosophy Department turned from an expressed disdain of personalism to a deep appreciation of Bowne's philosophy. In a brief autobiographical statement written for the volume *Personalism Revisited*, Kohak states his debt to Bowne:

> Reading Borden Parker Bowne with total absorption, I began to put things together. I began to see the world as a meaningful whole from which the theories of the natural sciences are an abstraction. Husserl called it *Lebenswelt*, constituted as meaningful not by individual

[16] Buford and Oliver, *Personalism Revisited*, 243–53.

> subjects but by the very presence of purposive activity—of persons, or of transcendental subjectivity.[17]

His debt to personalism is perhaps most evident in his philosophical classic *The Embers and the Stars,* published in 1984. The appearance of this book coincided with the rise of ecological consciousness in the 1960s. This volume seemed to reverse Bowne's devaluation of nature, to whom Kohak's unfolding of the living presence of life in the forest seemed to foster an appeal to immediacy beyond anything Bowne would have imagined, as did his application of Kant's Second Critique to the natural world. Yet, even these notions were informed by the idealism of Bowne—and of Husserl, on my reading.

In the late 1980s, when I gave serious attention to personalism for the first time, I decided that it was not the personalism of the Boston tradition that troubled me, but its idealism. That is not surprising in view of the fact that, in 1981 and 1984, I had published books critical of idealism.[18] At the Brighton meeting, I was expected to speak of the future of personalism. There I argued that I had no serious aversion to the term "person," if I could understand it in terms of Greek patristic theology—that is, as relational, communal, without remainder. The title of that paper, "Relational Personalism," made it seem that my position was nearer to Boston Personalism than was the case. The differences were substantial, as the following comparisons should make evident:

Affirmations of Boston Personalism

Experience is mental and empirical activity.
The agent is fundamental to the act.
Reality consists of the infinite uncreated mind (divine creator) and finite created minds.
The divine mind is the supreme person; finite minds are finite persons.
Nature has only phenomenal reality.

[17] Ibid., 72.

[18] Harold H. Oliver, *Relatedness: Essays in Metaphysics and Theology* (Mercer University Press, 1981); and *A Relational Metaphysic* (Nijhoff, 1981).

Thus, reality is personal.
"God" is a scriptural and metaphysical term calling for rational criticism.

Affirmations of Relational Metaphysics

Pure experience is all there is.
Experience is acting, relating.
The agent is a derivative from the act.
Mind and body are co-aspectual derivatives of relating.
Nature is empirical immediacy.
God-language is mythical, not metaphysical, language.
God-language requires a hermeneutics of myth.
The mythical term "God" arose from conceiving of person as an image totality.
World-language (cosmology) arose from considering nature as a theoretical totality.
The term "self" is less culturally specific than the term "person."
There is no-self (as in pure experience), and it is the relational self (as in I-thou).

This list of my philosophical affirmations is selected from a larger number.[19] These affirmations are at the core of my metaphysics of relation and should serve to show that my differences from Boston Personalism are greater in number than the affinities I have noted along the way.

Who knows whether either of these philosophies has a future? Here I will speculate only about the future of Boston Personalism. Seven years after Paul Deats ('54, GRS '54) and Carol Robb gathered the other remaining Boston Personalists—Bertocci, DeWolf, S. Paul Schilling ('29, GRS '27, '34), and Muelder—to assess this remarkable legacy in its

[19] One will see some development in my thought since my book *A Relational Metaphysic* appeared in 1981. This fact is documented in the later volume, *Relatedness: Essays in Metaphysics and Theology* (1984), and in a forthcoming volume of essays.

halcyon years, I wrote: "Personalism is not moribund nor lacking in progeny, though its potential as a philosophical force will depend on the extent to which it can be made responsive to post-idealistic philosophies."[20]

My former dean, Robert Neville, voiced a similar criticism: "[The] Bownean personalists reassembled the most attractive parts of an expiring German idealism. By implication, they might have done better by at least remaining up to date in their borrowings."[21]

Even so, both Neville and I are fully aware that our predecessors in philosophy and theology carved out a significant role for Boston University in their time. This assessment was shared by many who were—and are—outsiders. One such scholar who recently expressed a guardedly positive assessment is Gary Dorrien, who writes,

> The personalists built a significant school, but not a movement. In the philosophy of religion they achieved a prominent standing through the influence of Bowne and Brightman, though not as dominantly as Knudson supposed. In the field of theology they sustained one of the major streams of American liberal Christianity against an ascending neo-orthodox and neo-liberal reaction, but they never achieved much influence outside the Methodist church.[22]

From the ranks of the true succession, Lavely and Muelder left us in 2004. Only one course on personalism remains at Boston University. Has the sun set on personalism at BU? Not if one counts the many graduates of the school who still carry the torch.

---

[20] Harold H. Oliver, "Relational Personalism," *The Personalist Forum* 5 (1989): 35.

[21] Dorrien, *The Making of American Liberal Theology, Vol. 2*, 343.

[22] Ibid., 352.

13
The Vocation of a Modern-Day Prophet: Dr. Martin Luther King, Jr.

Peter J. Paris

I can think of no one more deserving of a *festschrift* than our distinguished colleague Lawrence E. Carter, who for the past thirty years has served faithfully as the first Dean of the Martin Luther King, Jr. International Chapel at Morehouse University. A significant part of his legacy pertains to his stellar mentorship of students by nurturing their spiritual formation, vocational discernment, academic preparation, and professional excellence for ministry. Inspired by the life and mission of our nation's preeminent preacher, pastor, and prophet (Dr. Carter's primary role model throughout his career), I am happy to contribute a sermon to this volume titled "The Vocation of a Modern-Day Prophet."

Martin Luther King, Jr. was truly one of the world's most esteemed prophetic leaders. Contrary to the views of many, he did not begin the Civil Rights Movement. Rather, it was well underway when he was asked to become its leader. In fact, he initiated few of the major events that ushered him into worldwide acclaim. Most important, his contribution was that of interpreting the meaning of those events not only for the primary actors at the time but for the nation and the world at large. Clearly, no one was more suited for that task than he.

Drawing from the accumulative wisdom of the ages, including the Bible, the Declaration of Independence, and the U.S. Constitution, he persuasively motivated his followers to be steadfast in their resolve and not turn back, because theirs was a mission destined, as he said, "to inject new meaning and dignity into the veins of civilization."

Dr. King's spiritual devotion, political wisdom, moral integrity, and courageous actions were worthy expressions of the Christian faith. Thus, I have chosen a text that captures the essence of his thought and practice. It is Paul's plea to the Christians in Rome: "I appeal to you therefore, brothers and sisters, by the mercies of God, to present your bodies as a living sacrifice, holy and acceptable to God,…" (Romans 12:1 NRSV).

Few other passages of scripture capture more aptly the spirit of his message, which, like that of Saint Paul, was derived from the Sermon on the Mount. In the process of being faithful and loyal to the mission of social justice, many people in the struggle for civil rights were killed and countless others continue to bear the scars of the battle.

Though I never met Dr. King face to face, I was in his presence on several public occasions. I vividly recall the first time I saw and heard him in person. It was at the 1958 Quadrennial Conference of the World Student Christian Federation in Athens, Ohio, where I had brought a group of Canadian students as delegates. His moving reflections on the Montgomery Bus Boycott, coupled with his challenging moral appeal for each of us to join the struggle for racial justice round the world, greatly inspired the entire assembly. Then and now, I could hardly believe that a person not yet thirty years of age could think so profoundly, speak so persuasively, and act so courageously for social justice.

Little did anyone know then that, at the end of the decade, this young man's life would end with an assassin's bullet. Yet, during that tumultuous decade, his leadership made an indelible impact on both this nation and the world at large. His receipt of the 1964 Nobel Peace Prize elevated his influence worldwide, and the 1986 proclamation of a national holiday commemorating his legacy has bestowed immortality on him for all time. From an ancestral lineage of low social esteem, this great-grandson of African slaves became a global exemplar of moral integrity, political wisdom, and religious devotion. Armed only with the weapon of nonviolent resistance, he persuaded his followers to believe that a powerful social system could be dismantled by trusting in the source of their faith and working cooperatively for social justice in the spirit of hope and love.

Contrary to the views of many, the story of Martin Luther King, Jr. is the story of a Black Baptist preacher whose national and international leadership was motivated by the demands of the Christian faith. Whenever that fact is ignored, concealed, or bracketed, his story is inevitably distorted. Like all preachers, Dr. King was not an exemplar of moral or religious perfection. Fortunately, he was all too aware of his own limitations in that regard. Yet, by the grace of God and the loyalty of those who followed him, he was able to achieve a goal that few thought possible in their lifetime. He succeeded in effecting a radical structural change in race relations throughout the south: a victory that sent shockwaves throughout the nation, culminating in the Civil Rights Act of 1964 and the Voters' Rights Act of 1965. Some have considered those legislative actions as the completion of the Civil War and the commencement of first-class citizenship for African Americans.

Undoubtedly, that triumphant accomplishment enlivened the hopes of oppressed peoples both in America and around the world. The inspiration of his personal commitment and the persuasive appeal of his rhetorical excellence inspired many to embrace his method of nonviolent resistance and to do what St. Paul considered a necessary expression of Christian discipleship, namely, "to present their bodies a living sacrifice, holy and acceptable to God…."

Accordingly, African Americans and countless others of every race, creed, and nation eventually joined hands to form an unconquerable spiritual force bent on bringing peace to the nation by nonviolently protesting injustice here and everywhere. As that vast diversity of people swayed together to the familiar tune "We Shall Overcome," Dr. King said that he experienced momentarily the eschatological arrival of what he called "the beloved community."

Now, a prophet is both a social critic and a reformer. He or she abhors social injustice and boldly condemns it without counting the cost to his or her own life. A prophet is single-mindedly committed to the goal of social justice and the rightful practice that will bring it about. The character of the prophet is reflective of the goal that he or she works diligently to realize. A Christian prophet embodies the virtues of courage, discernment, truthfulness, and justice, in addition to the theological blessings of faith, hope, and love.

Our remembrance of Dr. King quickly focuses on the primacy of *love*, which was the guiding principle for all of his public practices. We recall his often stated words, "I still believe that *love* is the most durable power in the world." *Love* characterized his vision of the ideal society. *Love* constituted the goal he sought to realize, which he called "the beloved community." *Love* regulated the means he employed for the realization of that goal, namely, nonviolent resistance, which he advocated not as a strategy alone but as a way of life. *Love* characterized the moral disposition he sought to inculcate in all who joined him in the struggle for justice; a disposition of humility, forgiveness, compassion, and reconciliation with one's enemies. "*Love* is the only force," he said, "capable of turning an enemy into a friend."

Like Jesus of Nazareth, Dr. King persuaded his people to protest with the dynamic power of love as their only weapon. Let us hastily state that, for him, love was no sentimental, warm fuzzy feeling, but a forceful, militant power that looked injustice in the face and condemned it outright. The response to that condemnation exposed the brutality and horror of injustice as witnessed by the televised scenes of water hoses blowing the protestors asunder; mounted policemen beating men, women, and children; teargas pouring into churches; snarling dogs attacking nonviolent demonstrators; and numerous burnings and clandestine killings. Clearly, the public practice of love in the service of justice necessitated much courage, which Dr. King and numerous others, especially students, had in abundance.

For the prophet, religion, politics, and morality imply one another. Dr. King said repeatedly that Christian theological thought is wholly useless if there is no corresponding practice. For example, it makes no sense to call for peace if we do not do the things that lead to peace. Peace is made by peacemakers, who believe that there can be no peace without justice. Herein lies Dr. King's greatness as a prophet. His primary model was Jesus of Nazareth, who embodied love and justice. Secondarily, he was greatly inspired by Mahatma Gandhi, who brought the British Empire to its knees by persuading his followers to embody and practice the soul-force of nonviolent resistance.

Like Jesus, who taught his disciples to turn the other cheek in the face of violence, Dr. King did likewise. *Like Jesus,* who forgave his executors while hanging on the cross, Dr. King forgave the woman who stabbed him in a New York department store; and he forgave those who bombed his home on several occasions; and he forgave those who inflicted countless other abuses on him and his followers, including the death of four little girls in the Sixteenth Street Baptist Church in Birmingham, Alabama. *As Jesus taught* his disciples to seek first the Kingdom of God, Dr. King taught his followers to keep their eyes on the prize, namely the beloved community, and to hold on. Because of his unquestioned belief that their struggle was also God's struggle, he was confident that they would be victorious in the long run. *As Jesus commanded* his followers to serve him by meeting the needs of the least of their brothers and sisters, Dr. King believed unquestionably in the mission of promoting the dignity of all who are oppressed by the forces of racism in America, apartheid in South Africa, colonialism around the world, poverty both at home and abroad, and the ravages of war in Vietnam and elsewhere.

Now, you might ask how the criteria of Martin Luther King, Jr.'s thought and action differ from that of Osama Bin Laden, since both lay claim to religion as the ground for their respective missions and justice as their final goal. I think the difference lies in Dr. King's method of nonviolent resistance, which implies respect for the dignity and humanity of the enemy both in the process of the struggle and its aftermath. Thus, all that Dr. King did and said was commensurate with Jesus' Sermon on the Mount. Neither Jesus nor King would ever justify actions that would diminish the dignity of their enemies by hatred, torture, humiliation, or assassination. That is what distinguishes Dr. King's mission from that of Osama Bin Laden.

Let us not forget, however, that some African Americans opposed Congressman John Conyers's advocacy for a national holiday to celebrate Dr. King's birthday, because they feared that our nation's official image-makers would domesticate Dr. King's memory by enshrining him in the pantheon of national heroes and, consequently, nullify his uncompromising, militant, prophetic leadership. That fear continues in our day. In fact, it is seen most vividly in those many attempts to turn this national holiday into a "day of community service." As important as community services are, Dr. King's advocacy of social justice cannot be adequately translated into a day of social service.

Let no one decry the memory of Dr. King by saying that his teaching was soft and his practices were timid. No one who ever marched with him believed they were doing an easy thing. Rather, to choose to resist hatred, violence, and the threat of violence in a nonviolent way requires more courage than anyone has by nature. That courage can only be developed by the corresponding exercise of courageous practices that require training, discipline, and divine grace. In the process of practicing nonviolent resistance, one eventually becomes a nonviolent person and, most important, one's enemies are amazed and confounded as they witness such a practice. That puzzlement was seen time and again on the faces of policemen and jailors who could not understand why Dr. King and his followers went to prison loudly singing the spirituals: songs of hope that had enabled their ancestors to overcome the many bitter centuries of chattel enslavement.

Clearly, none doubted Dr. King's moral and religious commitments. Yet, they often questioned the nature of his political wisdom, especially his uncompromising devotion to nonviolent resistance. But none questioned the intrinsic goodness of nonviolence as an ideal. Like Jesus, King did not evaluate what was morally good by appealing to the norm of expediency. Rather, he was steadfast in his resolve not to comply with evil and he inspired his followers to resist it by placing their lives on the line.

Certainly, prophets do not fare well in their own homeland and Dr. King was no exception. Yet, ironically, the nation that once abused him has honored him in our day. That poses an extraordinary dilemma since there is much evidence to support the view that the three greatest interrelated problems that Dr. King identified facing America in his day still persist, namely, racism, poverty, and militarism.

Contemporary racism is seen in the disproportionate number of African-American children robbed daily of a quality education in our inner-city schools, as well as the disproportionate number of young African Americans caught in the seemingly inescapable grip of unemployment, drug addiction, incarceration, homicide, the HIV/AIDS epidemic, and much more. Like the unjustifiable Vietnam War, America was led into the War in Iraq by false arguments and an arrogant resolve to force America's will onto the Iraqi people by military conquest. And the conditions of economic disparity continue to increase globally in direct proportion to the affluence, waste, and greed of the American empire.

Like Jesus, who challenged many similar problems in his day, Dr. King and his followers used a similar method of protest by presenting their "bodies as living sacrifices, holy and acceptable to God." So, what does this have to do with all of us? Please do not forget that social injustice is never an abstract idea. Rather, it is always an empirical reality:

specific, concrete, visible, and quantifiable. Social injustice is never very far from where you live, work, and worship. In fact, it may very well be present in each of those places. From the time of Jesus up to the present, social injustice is likely to be encountered in the mundane experiences of our daily lives. Look for the most vulnerable in your midst. They are the ones whom Jesus called "the least of these." Listen to them tell their stories, describe their problems, and state their needs. In our day, such people are legion: the homeless, the hungry, the sick, abused wives and children, illegal immigrants, street gangs, and racial/ethnic/sexual minorities, to mention only a few. Followers of Christ are called to embrace these people with love, which means helping establish structures of social justice that will enable them to flourish and actualize their full potentialities.

Certainly all who accept the vocation to be preachers, pastors, and prophets in our day should embody the model of ministry set by Dr. Martin Luther King, Jr. and, by God's grace, be willing to pursue social justice by presenting their "bodies as living sacrifices, holy and acceptable to God."

14
African-American Liberal Arts Education and the Cultivation of Virtue

Samuel K. Roberts

Ever since Puritan minister John Harvard bequeathed his personal library of 320 books to the college that would eventually bear his name, a discernible moral component has informed the scope, vision, and expectations of American liberal-arts higher education. In the wake of Harvard's founding (1636), and other distinguished schools such as William and Mary (1693) and Yale College (1736), the American colonies fashioned a means of educating leaders for American society complemented by moral values drawn from religious sensibilities. Before the adoption of the United States Constitution in 1789, nine church-related schools had been established in the young nation.[1] While the training of ministers was an important focus, especially with the founding of Harvard and Yale, the training of ministers was not the sole aim of these schools. Early colleges sought to ensure the moral formation of all students, regardless of their vocational interests. As one commentator writes: "The crucial ingredient…was that all learning ultimately was to coalesce into the values and actions of a Christian gentleman."[2]

The men and women who would emerge as the graduates of the first liberal-arts colleges founded for and by Blacks in the nineteenth century were hardly reminiscent of the "Christian gentlemen" who had graduated from Harvard, Yale, and William and Mary. Yet, in reflecting

---

[1] In addition to Harvard, Yale (Congregational), and William and Mary (Church of England), there were Princeton (Presbyterian, 1746), University of Pennsylvania (strong Church of England ties, 1740), King's College or Columbia (Church of England ties, 1754), Brown (Baptist, 1762), Queen's College, the original name for Rutgers (Dutch Reformed Church, 1766), and Dartmouth (Church of England influence, 1769).

[2] John R. Thelin, *A History of American Higher Education* (Baltimore: The Johns Hopkins University Press, 2004) 24.

on the rise of African-American higher education after the Civil War, W. E. B. Du Bois could celebrate the fact that the riches of the liberal-arts tradition should not be reserved only for the sons of privilege. In his characteristically lyrical fashion, Du Bois exulted in the fact that "the riddle of existence [of] the college curriculum that was laid before the Pharaohs, that was taught in the groves by Plato…is today laid before the freedmen's sons."[3] Du Bois was referring to those schools whose heritage harkens back to the work of Black Church denominations and Abolitionist evangelical White missionaries who helped found a significant number of African-American colleges in the nineteenth century, many of whom continue to thrive as member institutions of the United Negro College Fund.[4]

I argue that inherent in the identity, work, and mission of African-American liberal-arts colleges and universities is a moral imperative to cultivate a unique conception of virtue within students. This conception of virtue was essentially, as I maintain elsewhere, "a divinely ordered life that impelled its adherents to struggle against injustice and oppression and to forge communities and structures that could ensure the development of the furthest moral and material possibilities of African Americans."[5] The eventual development of African-American liberal-arts colleges and universities was the result of a combination of various historical forces and cultural imperatives. I contend there are three sources that have shaped the identity of these institutions: (1) the *paideia* notion in Greco-Roman classical thought, which held that an unfettered pursuit of knowledge should be encouraged among students in accordance with the

---

[3] W. E. B. Du Bois, *The Souls of Black Folk* (New York: Dover Publications, 1994) 51.

[4] There are currently 101 HBCUs, or Historically Black Colleges and Universities, existing in the United States, not all understood to be within the liberal arts tradition. On the other hand, the thirty-nine member colleges of the United Negro College Fund, a group subsumed within the HBCUs, typify the liberal arts institutions in that historically they focused curricula on the arts, letters, and sciences rather than technical or vocational training.

[5] Samuel K. Roberts, *In the Path of Virtue: The African-American Moral Tradition* (Cleveland, OH: The Pilgrim Press, 1999) 15.

presumption that humans are rational, self-possessed beings; (2) the conviction within evangelical piety that knowledge should be pursued in accordance with the contours of faith and the presumption that humans are creatures of God; and (3) the presumption that knowledge should serve the interests and aspirations of African Americans, in accordance with a belief that human beings are always historically and socially located. These three sources, while rich and indicative of the essence of Black colleges, and certainly not altogether mutually exclusive of each other, have been fraught with some tension. But the conception of virtue, understood within the cultural framework here, offers possibilities for not only resolving these tensions but also for serving as a foundation for the continued work and mission of these institutions. The essay will conclude with some reflections on how the cultivation of virtue among students might proceed on the campuses of these colleges and universities.

Paideia and African-American Liberal-Arts Education

At the heart of liberal-arts education is the notion of *paideia,* or the "instruction" of human beings in ways consistent with their true form, that is to say, as rational, self-possessed beings. Such a notion envisioned the fullest range of intellectual inquiry on the grounds that the minds of rational, self-possessed beings should know no boundaries. While this was a valued ideal in the Greco-Roman world, two vastly different traditions emerged from this initial impulse and each affirmed a radically different vision as to who could properly be instructed. The earlier tradition, the one of Plato and Aristotle, held that education and intellectual development should be reserved only for men who were privileged citizens. The latter tradition, drawn from the Roman world of Seneca, and ironically inspired by Socrates, was by contrast much more egalitarian. As Martha Nussbaum notes, the earlier tradition presumed the freedom of the few, whereas the latter tradition asserted the quest for freedom of the many. In acknowledging the influence of Seneca in this tradition, Nussbaum asserts that "an education is truly liberal—by which [he] means connected to freedom *(libertas)*—only if it is one that liberates the student's mind, encouraging him or her to take charge of his or her own thinking, leading to a Socratic, examined life."[6] In a Senecan view of education, "only liberal education will develop each person's capacity to be fully human,...self-aware, self-governing, and capable of recognizing and respecting the humanity of our fellow human beings, no matter where they are born, no matter what social class they inhabit, no matter what their gender or ethnic origin." In sum, the essence of this Roman tradition of liberal-arts education focuses on developing the *potential* of human beings rather than merely reaffirming the prior status of inherited privilege, as the earlier tradition had done.

Clearly, the African-American embrace of the liberal-arts tradition is more indebted to the Roman than to the Greek notion of *paideia.* Education, not to mention *higher* education, has always been socially significant for African Americans in that the forced inclusion of Blacks in the American experiment precluded their intellectual development. For instance, only the body of the slave was thought to have any value in slaveholding society and culture. Throughout the antebellum South, teaching a slave to read and write was a punishable offense. In the slaveholding South, even when free Blacks initiated any efforts to provide education for their children, such efforts were often met with violent reactions from local Whites, as evidenced in Bishop Daniel Payne's frustrated efforts to conduct a school for Black children in Charleston, South Carolina, an enterprise that was doomed by the passage of state law in 1835 forbidding the operation of any school for children of color.[7] In the free Northern states, access to education for Black children was not always favored by public opinion. Unless Black communities had the resources to build their own schools, access to public education was limited to racially segregated facilities. By 1850, most Northern communities maintained separate schools for Black children, with exceptions such as Boston, New York, and Philadelphia.[8] Given the meager re-

---

[6] Martha Nussbaum, "Cultivating Humanity," *Liberal Education* 84/2 (Spring 1998): 42.

[7] Daniel A. Payne, *Recollections of Seventy Years* (New York: Arno Press, 1968) 27.

[8] John Hope Franklin, *From Slavery to Freedom*, 6th ed. (New York: McGraw-Hill, 1988) 147.

sources for primary and secondary education, it is no wonder that the number of Blacks who would be able to pursue higher education would be so few. It has been estimated that the total number of African-American graduates of colleges prior to the Civil War was no more than thirty, the first two being John Russworm from Bowdoin and Edward Jones from Amherst in 1826.[9]

With the Civil War and emancipation from slavery, the possibility of access to general and higher education for African Americans seemed to have a promise for fulfillment that slavery had long denied. Yet, by the end of the nineteenth century, a vigorous debate emerged between Booker T. Washington and W. E. B. Du Bois about the purpose of education for a people emerging from slavery. Washington, the founder of Tuskegee Institute (now Tuskegee University), argued for courses of study that would strengthen the economic development of Black people in the southern states, a region where eight out of ten Blacks resided at the time. He envisioned thriving Black communities where relatively self-sufficient farmers, artisans, mechanics, and tradespeople could lead their lives. Believing that economic development would gradually pave the way for political rights, as a concession for the forbearance of powerful Whites, he withheld any challenges to the political order in the Jim Crow South. W. E. B. Du Bois, a graduate of Harvard and Berlin, argued instead that the full exercise of political rights by Blacks should not be deferred and that the surest way to secure these rights would be through the training of an elite vanguard or "the talented tenth." These trained elite would challenge the American social order, thus paving the way for the exercise of political rights for all disfranchised Blacks.

Despite their differences on various aspects of education, it is obvious that Washington and Du Bois shared a common vision that education could transform the lives of African Americans in ways that would liberate them from the shackles of oppression. In a real sense, the torturous debate in which we have always cast them fails to recognize this fact. Washington was no enemy of literature and the arts, nor was he against political activism. Even one of his more critical biographers has

---

[9] Frank H. Bowles and Frank A. Decosta, *Between Two Worlds, a Profile of Negro Higher Education* (New York: McGraw-Hill 1971) 25.

documented how he surreptitiously funded many challenges to racial segregation, even as he appeared to acquiesce to Jim Crow in his daily struggle in Alabama.[10] In practice, over half the instructors at Tuskegee taught literary subjects, and the school quietly developed what one historian described as a "complicated but effective academic program… which provided an almost infinite number of class levels to match up with individual abilities and preparation."[11] While Washington forged his own path toward the upward mobility of African-American life as he labored in the segregated South, he certainly would not have disagreed with Du Bois, who was of the opinion that a valued expectation of liberal-arts education would be a "loftier respect for the sovereign human soul that seeks to know itself and the world about it; that seeks a freedom for expansion and self-development."[12]

The Tutored Heart: The Notion of the Christian College and African-American Liberal-Arts Tradition

A second source that has informed the genesis of the African-American liberal-arts tradition is the notion of a Christian college, an institution that owes its existence to evangelical Christian faith and to an even longer tradition within Christian faith that sought to reconcile faith and human knowledge. The Judeo-Christian tradition has long recognized the valued role of the human mind in glorifying God and in discerning the will of God so that proper moral discernment and behavior might ensue. As early Christianity gained a footing in the Greco-Roman world, it could not help but absorb prevalent notions about education, many of which presumed the philosophical heritage of Greek and Roman traditions. Augustine believed that the human intellect was critically

---

[10] See Louis R. Harlan, *Booker T. Washington: The Making of a Black Leader, 1856–1901* (New York: Oxford University Press, 1972).

[11] Virginia L. Denton, *Booker T. Washington and the Adult Education Movement* (Gainesville: University of Florida, 1993) 139–42. See also Adam Fairclough, *Teaching Equality: Black Schools in the Age of Jim Crow* (Athens: University of Georgia Press, 2001) 18.

[12] W. E. B. Du Bois, "Of the Training of Black Men," *The Souls of Black Folk* (New York: Dover Publications, 1994) 66.

important in understanding God's intent for humanity. In the medieval period, Aquinas insisted that reason is not averse to faith; to the contrary, reason could be a justifiable aid to faith. Monasteries continued the Greco-Roman courses of study that had nourished the minds of so many earlier scholars: the Greek emphasis on grammar, rhetoric, and logic (the trivium); and the Roman emphasis on arithmetic, geometry, music, and astronomy (the quadrivium). The Reformation, emphasizing the notion of the priesthood of all believers, encouraged all believers to become literate in order to engage the Bible personally. Moreover, Reformers, notably Calvin and Luther, emphasized the importance of a learned and trained clergy.

In an effort to train African-American clergy and provide some access to higher education for Blacks, northern religious bodies aided the genesis of African-American colleges greatly by establishing Wilberforce University in Ohio in 1856 (Methodist Episcopal Church) and Lincoln University in Pennsylvania in 1857 (Presbyterian). After the Civil War, a more vigorous role for African-American religious bodies in establishing schools could proceed. In fact, the African Methodist Episcopal church assumed control of Wilberforce, thus making it the first Black-controlled campus in the country.[13] As such, Black denominations were intent on educating clergy for service in their churches. Against many difficulties and with meager resources, Black churches exemplified ingenuity in helping to establish schools. In *The History of the Negro Church*, Carter G. Woodson writes: "With these striking examples of sacrifice in behalf of the education of their race, the Negro churches themselves began to participate in the extension of education as a means to spread the gospel through an intelligent ministry and to enable the laity to appreciate it as the great leverage in the uplift of the man far down."[14] By 1868, a dozen of these colleges had been formed. Forty of the fifty-four private Black colleges in existence in the 1870s were formed in the quarter century

---

[13] William C. Ringenberg, *The Christian College: A History of Protestant Higher Education in America* (Grand Rapids, MI: Baker Academic Books, 2006) 86.

[14] Carter G. Woodson, *The History of the Negro Church* (Washington, D.C.: Association for the Study of Negro Life and History, 192) 184.

after the Civil War. African-American Baptists established Shaw in 1865, Morehouse in 1867, Leland in New Orleans, and Benedict in 1871. Northern Methodists founded Rust at Holly Springs in 1866, Morgan at Baltimore in 1867, Claflin at Orangeburg in 1869, and Clark College in Atlanta in 1870. The American Missionary Association, an agency of the Congregational Church, was instrumental in the founding of Fisk University in 1866, Talladega in 1867, Hampton in 1868, and Tougaloo and LeMoyne in 1870; the Congregationalists also founded Howard University in 1867. Colored Methodists founded Paine College in Augusta, Georgia in 1884. W. H. Crogman, president of Clark College and also professor of classics, proclaimed that "these schools are Christian schools."[15] Rev. Henry L. Morehouse, after whom Morehouse College was named, stated that the "ruling idea in this educational work has been the formation of strong, intelligent Christian character; education dominated by a positive Christian spirit."[16] A rather inspired alumnus and historian at Hampton University wrote in 1918 that Hampton was "essentially a spiritual enterprise conceived as a form of missionary service."[17] While the initial aim of virtually all of these schools was the preparation of ministers and missionaries for Africa, the curricula gradually broadened and they began to prepare students for a variety of

---

[15] W. H. Crogman, *Talks for the Times* (Cincinnati: Jennings and Pye, 1896), quoted in Roberts, *In the Path of Virtue*, 126.

[16] Henry L. Morehouse, "The Work of the American Baptist Home Mission Society for the American Negro," quoted in Roberts, *In the Path of Virtue*, 126.

[17] Francis G. Peabody, *Education for Life: The Story of Hampton Institute* (New York: 1919) xii. See also Richard I. McKinney, *Religion in Higher Education among Negroes* (New York: Arno Press, 1972) ix, 3. See also H. M. Bond, "Origin and Development of the Negro Church-Related College," *Journal of Negro Education* (Summer 1960): 219; Dwight O.W. Holmes, *The Evolution of the Negro College* (New York: Arno Press, 1969); Rayford W. Logan, "Evolution of Private Colleges for Negroes," *Journal of Negro Education* (Summer 1958): 213–16; August Meier and Elliott M. Rudwick, *From Plantation to Ghetto* (New York: 1966); and Elizabeth Geen, "Morehouse College," in Keeton and Hilberry, *Struggle and Promise.* (New York: McGraw-Hill, 1969).

other vocations. By 1900, the percentage of Black college graduates who entered the ministry—11.3 percent—was not significantly different from the percentage of ministerial graduates in other colleges. By comparison, of the 1,900 graduates from thirty Black colleges in the South by the end of the century, 37.2 percent had become teachers in Black schools, 4 percent had entered the medical profession, and 3.3 percent had entered the legal profession.[18]

The Imperative of African-American Higher Education

The third source in the genesis of African-American colleges has been the desire to respond to the historical and cultural exigencies of the Black experience in light of the realities of post-Civil War American society. Any assessment of the role of Black education after the Civil War must assume that an implicit goal of any educational philosophy was helping Blacks escape a subordinate status or of meeting the needs of the "man far down," as Carter Woodson put it. For the most part, the first generation of graduates of African-American colleges were the sons and daughters of former slaves. Like her cohorts, one of the founding members of the Fisk Jubilee Singers, Samuella Sheppard, had been born a slave in 1851.[19] "In many ways, African Americans viewed education as the ultimate emancipator, enabling them to distance themselves from slavery, move past their subordinate status in society, and achieve social mobility."[20] These colleges presumed that they were producing graduates who would be crucial to building an American society after the Civil War, in which the sacrifices made during that war and the pain of enduring slavery would be made good. However, in order to achieve the goal, the leaders of these institutions believed that the moral formation of

---

[18] Henry A. Bullock, *A History of Negro Education in the South* (Cambridge: Harvard University Press, 1967) 175.

[19] Andrew Ward, *Dark Midnight When I Rise: The Story of the Jubilee Singers* (New York: Farrar, Straus and Giroux, 2000) 3.

[20] Walter R. Allen, Joseph O. Jewell, Kimberly A. Griffin, and De'Sha S. Wolf, "Historically Black Colleges and University: Honoring the Past, Engaging the Present, Touching the Future," *Journal of Negro Education* 76/3 (2007): 267.

students would be required. It was hoped that the confluence of the three sources that inspired the genesis of these colleges—the full development of human potential within a religiously grounded context in which service to one's people was expected—would produce worthy graduates. It was further hoped that these graduates would be exemplars of virtue in their personal lives and vocations.

Tensions Within the Sources

So far, I have argued that three sources have contributed to the identity and mission of African-American colleges and universities in the liberal-arts tradition. These sources have not only enriched these schools but have accounted for the continuing vitality of these historically important institutions. Yet, the reality of tensions within these sources must be acknowledged. At some level, the *padeia* idea may resist the constraints and dictates of faith. James Tunstead Burtchaell has offered a fascinating study of colleges that eventually severed formal relations with church bodies in the twentieth century in order to secure a public image more in line with that of major research universities.[21] Moreover, as Black students became even more politically radicalized at a certain point in the Civil Rights revolution, many came to charge that appeals to faith traditions and classical notions of knowledge (not perhaps fully understood to have been consistent with the Roman version) inhibited a more forthright appropriation of student demands for "Black power" on not a few college campuses during the decade of the 1960s.[22] And to be sure, there is now afoot vigorous movement among many church-related colleges to reconcile the fullest expectations of academic freedom and research with the vitality

---

[21] James Tunstead Burtchaell, *The Dying of the Light: the Disengagement of Colleges and Universities from their Christian Churches* (Grand Rapids, MI: Eerdmans Publishing Co., 1998). See also George Marsden, *The Soul of the American University: From Protestant Establishment to Established Nonbelief* (New York: Oxford University Press, 1994).

[22] See Daniel C. Thompson, *Private Black Colleges at the Crossroads* (Westport, CT: Greenwood Press, 1973) for a discussion of the tensions on Black college campuses during this era, esp. ch. 2.

of faith traditions.[23]

African-American Appropriation of Virtue

The unique conception of virtue that became so evident in the thought of African-American thinkers and social activists from the eighteenth century onwards is amazingly reminiscent of the three sources that informed the development of Black liberal-arts colleges and offer a means of resolving the tensions inherent in these institutions. The general thrust for the affirmation of this African-American notion of virtue comes from a basic affirmation that resisted the assumptions of slaveholders that Blacks were naturally inferior and, thereby, fit for slavery.

Rather, there was the general affirmation that God had created them as equal to all other human beings. Moreover, all means should be pursued to cultivate the mind, including education. Finally, the pursuit of virtue was seen as being consistent with—indeed obligatory—as Black activists conducted the struggle against slavery and the full integrity of the Black community.

In 1779, a group of Connecticut slaves had the temerity to issue the following petition to the state General Assembly:

> Reason and Revelation join to declare, that we are the creatures of that God, who made of one blood, and Kindred, all the Nations of the Earth; we perceive by our own Reflection, that we are endowed with the same Faculties with our Masters, and there is nothing that leads us to a Belief, or Suspicion, that we are any more obliged to serve them, than they us, and the more we Consider of this matter, the more we are Convinced of our Right (by the laws of Nature and by the whole tenor of the Christian Religion, so far as we have been taught) to be free.[24]

Another prominent African-American minister was Lemuel Haynes. He was the pastor of a predominantly White Congregationalist church in Rutland, Vermont who pushed this logic even further in an 1801 "Fourth of July" sermon when he declared that there exists a

---

[23] Douglas V. Henry and Michael D. Beaty, eds., *Christianity and the Soul of the University: Faith as a Foundation for Intellectual Community* (Grand Rapids, MI: Baker Academic, 2006).

[24] Roberts, *In the Path of Virtue*, 23.

mutually inimical relationship between slavery and true virtue. For him, slavery attempted to destroy a sense of self-worth. During slavery, Blacks were taught to view themselves as a "rank of beings far below others, which suppressed, in a degree, every principle of manhood, and so they become despised, ignorant and licentious." [25] Virtue is a natural ingredient of the free life; it is the necessary characteristic of free persons. Therefore, as Haynes and the Connecticut slave petitioners reasoned, the continued enslavement of those who would aspire to freedom and the virtue that is inherent in such freedom is an unnatural act in God's universe. This presumed natural incompatibility between slavery and virtue, between slave existence and the virtuous free life, was echoed years after Haynes's sermon by an anonymous "free Negro" who reminisced about his former life as a slave. "The condition of the slave is," he recalled, "nothing more deplorable than in its being so unfavorable to the practice of every virtue."[26]

We have, therefore, within the thought of slave petitions for freedom in the late eighteenth century and the affirmations of preachers such as Lemuel Haynes, the genesis for what can rightly be called the African-American pursuit of virtue. The antislavery agitation of later abolitionists such as Maria Stewart and Frederick Douglass embodied the pursuit of this understanding of virtue as well. After an intense religious experience, Stewart was inspired to mount the podium and call for the end of slavery. In what might have been one of her earliest speeches, given at the African Masonic Hall in Boston in 1833, she expressed her belief in the acquisition of knowledge as a critical component in the life of virtue. Stewart held that the attempt of racist society to deny humanity to Blacks, and the fact that Blacks were "looked upon as objects of pity and commiseration [has filled my] soul with a holy indignation, and compelled me thus to come forward, and endeavor to turn their attention to knowledge and improvement," adding defiantly, "for knowledge is

---

[25] Lemuel Haynes, *The Nature and Importance of True Republicanism* (Rutland, VT: N.p., 1801) 11–12.

[26] A Free Negro, "Slavery," in *Negro Orators and Their Orations*, ed. Carter G. Woodson (New York: Russell and Russell, 1925) 25.

power."[27] Other African-American proponents of virtue insisted that the virtue of perseverance and, overall, moral character would be critical in their fight against oppression. In encouraging fellow Blacks to maintain a sense of urgency in the struggle against slavery, James Forten, Jr. urged fellow members of the American Moral Reform Society, "It is perseverance we want; let us get hold of it."[28] Virtue and character were very important for Frederick Douglass as well. Douglass wrote: "A change in our political condition would do very little for us without this."[29] Without a sense of character, the correlate of self-possessed moral agency, the fruit of political activism would be to no avail. Douglass further wrote:

> Character is the important thing, and without it we must continue to be marked for degradation and stamped with the brand of inferiority. With character, we shall be powerful. Nothing can harm us long when we get character. There are certain great elements of character in us which may be hated, but never despised. Industry, sobriety, honesty, combined with intelligence and due self-respect, find them where you will, among Black or White, must be *looked up to*—can never be *looked down upon*.[30]

There is a confluence between the liberal arts as it developed in African-American colleges and universities and the notion of virtue in Black social thought. In a very real sense, the confluence of these three sources that have informed the liberal-arts tradition in African-American colleges may now be considered a context where virtue can be intentionally cultivated on contemporary college and university campuses. Among the common features of Black liberal-arts education and

---

[27] Maria Stewart, "Address Delivered at the Masonic Hall," in *The Productions of Mrs. Maria W. Stewart* (Boston: Friends of Freedom and Virtue, 1835) 64.

[28] James Forten, Jr., "An Address Delivered Before the American Moral Reform Society," 17 August 1837, in Howard Brotz, ed., *Negro Social and Political Thought 1850–1920* (New York: Basic Books, 1966) 226.

[29] Frederick Douglass, "What Are the Colored People Doing for Themselves?" in Brotz, ed., *Negro Social and Political Thought,* 207.

[30] Ibid.

virtue is the affirmation that the purpose of education and intellectual inquiry is to allow students to develop their potential as human beings. The real question becomes: How can contemporary liberal arts institutions be more intentional with developing this notion of virtue among students?

Closing Reflections on Virtue Formation in African-American Liberal-Arts Colleges and Universities

One obvious implication is that African-American liberal-arts colleges and universities must intentionally become places where virtue can be cultivated. The *ethos* of an institution denotes the network of prevailing norms and values that undergird the daily life of people. *Ethos* denotes a set of expectations and norms that govern the behavior and actions of all members of a community—in this case, students, faculty, and administrators. Another significant aspect of *ethos* is found in the narratives, stories, even legends, that inspire people to strive for a more moral and virtuous life. This is precisely why Alasdair McIntyre argued that "I can only answer the question 'What am I to do?' if I can answer the prior question 'Of what story or stories do I find myself a part?' Deprive children of stories and you leave them unscripted, anxious stutterers in their actions and in their words."[31] The young men and women who enter Black liberal-arts colleges and universities are obviously not children who miraculously show up on first-year dormitory steps. They bring with them powerful stories and backgrounds as well, some of which have provided confusing or misleading scripts about what ought to be valued in life, about what path to success ought to be pursued, and what even is to be considered "success." It is the role of the liberal-arts college to provide an environment to engage questions and encourage students to challenge assumptions. Moreover, extracurricular activities should be conceived as contexts that contribute to this general *ethos* for moral formation. Within the full range of college activities—in and out of the classroom—there should be ample opportunities to develop the following: critical self-examination; the formation of an imaginative

[31] Alasdair MacIntyre, *After Virtue* (Notre Dame, IN: University of Notre Dame Press) 216.

moral vision, with accompanying aspects of religion and spirituality; and finally, opportunities to enact the norms of virtue through specific practices, such as service or volunteer work.

Martha Nussbaum offers a compelling vision of the role of liberal arts in her overall vision of "cultivating humanity." For her, essential to the cultivation of humanity in today's world is the capacity for critical examination of one's self and one's own tradition.[32] This means, of course, the capacity to challenge tradition and convenient orthodoxies. It is the capacity to reason logically and keep an open mind, even in the face of opposing ideas and perspectives. After all, it is the very earmark of the liberal-arts tradition to provide a place for the free exchange of ideas and points of view. In Nussbaum's view, this means "the ability to think what it might be like to be in the shoes of someone different from oneself; to be an intelligent reader of that person's story; and to understand the emotions and wishes and desires that someone so faced might have, including the many ways in which social circumstances shape emotions and wishes and desires." Moreover, the formation of virtue requires some measure of change in the imagination and openness to the spiritual and religious experience. Diana D. Akiyama, speaking before the 2008 meeting of the Association of American Colleges and Universities, affirmed that as colleges and universities continue to move toward more diversity, they rethink "the common assumption that religious belief and persons of faith are anathema to liberal learning." She continues:

> There are profound nonrational or spiritual qualities that can be recruited to sustain communities. These spiritual resources are not creeds or statements of belief; rather, they are resources like trust and courage. Framed by a spiritual perspective, trust and courage are generated by an awareness that we are not, ultimately, in control, that there is an element of transcendent wisdom that can sustain us as we struggle to do the right thing.[33]

---

[32] Martha Nussbaum, "Cultivating Humanity," *Liberal Education* 84/2 (Spring 1998): 42.

[33] Diana D. Akiyama, "Diversity: A Corporate Campaign," *Liberal Education* 94 (Summer 2008): 18.

For Akiyama, it was

> no coincidence that the civil rights movement was grounded in the spiritual values of courage, trust, love, forgiveness, compassion, and peace. Martin Luther King, Jr.'s professional training as a minister and his unwavering faith provided a foundation for his work as a civil rights leader. While he and his staff developed rational strategies to push for equality, spiritual values grounded and centered their work.[34]

King's alma mater, Morehouse College, has a long and distinguished history of providing an exceptional educational experience that meets the intellectual and spiritual needs of students and is known for producing outstanding men.

Finally, the full inculcation of virtue always demands the embodiment of certain practices in the lives of students that are consistent with virtuous living. There must be opportunities to embody the values and ideals inherent in the conception of virtue. Awareness of an imperative to be available to others, to engage in acts of service, is in part an outgrowth of the prior regimen of self-examination that the liberal-arts regimen demands. Given the historical context out of which the notion of virtue has emerged within African-American social thought, it would seem that opportunities for service to persons in distressed environments or crises would seem obvious. The volunteer efforts of Black student groups in tutoring young people and providing services to the elderly, and the volunteer efforts of fraternities and sororities in the aftermath of the Katrina crisis, along the Gulf coast, among other crises, are good examples of virtue.

African-American liberal-arts colleges and universities have a rich history that is informed by the confluence of the three sources discussed here. As these institutions face the challenges and opportunities in the third millennium, it should be the prayer of all of us—graduates and those whose lives will be touched by them—that their lights will continue to shine.

---

[34] Ibid.

15

Cultivating a Culture of Peace

Prince El Hassan bin Talal

April is a special month for our faith: the joy of Palm Sunday for Christians, the birthday of Buddha, the Jewish Passover, and for Muslims throughout the world, the commemoration of the Hijri New Year and of the martyrdom of the Holy Prophet Muhammad's (peace be upon him) grandson, Hussein ibn Ali. Here was a man who, fifteen centuries ago, spoke of humankind's need to cast off the yoke of oppression when he declared that it was far nobler to accept annihilation than to submit to tyranny. "If you are indifferent to oppression," he said, "you are part of the machinery of oppression."

More recently, Gandhi was the pioneer of *satyagrapha*, a method of direct social action based on the principles of courage, nonviolence, and truth. He believed that the way people behave is more important than what they achieve. He promoted nonviolence and civil disobedience as the most appropriate methods for obtaining political and social goals and inspired movements for civil rights and freedom across the world. In some ways, the two men were not dissimilar, in that both were motivated deeply by a sense of purpose, expressed in the following quote from Gandhi:

> There are times when you have to obey a call which is the highest of all, that is the voice of conscience, even though such obedience may cost many a bitter tear, and even more, separation from friends, from family, from the state to which you may belong, from all that you have held as dear as life itself. From this obedience is the law of our being.

It has often been said that possibly the longest distance in the world is between the mind and heart, and I quote Dr. Martin Luther King, Jr. from his *Strength to Love* (1963):

> Like an unchecked cancer, that corrodes the personality and eats away at its vital unity, hate destroys a man's sense of values and his objectivity. It causes him to describe the beautiful as ugly and the ugly as beautiful, and to confuse the true with the false and the false with

> the true. Darkness cannot drive out darkness; only light can do that. Hate cannot drive out hate; only love can do that. Hate multiplies hate, violence multiplies violence, and toughness multiplies toughness in a descending spiral of destruction. The chain reaction of evil—hate begetting hate, wars producing more wars—must be broken, or we shall be plunged into the dark abyss of annihilation.

I have had the privilege of working for peace in many parts of the world. You may find it strange that a series of conferences we held a few years ago was given the title, "The Fear of Peace." It might have seemed more natural, particularly to those of us who have had the misfortune of seeing and smelling death firsthand, had it been called "The Fear of War," but it was titled "The Fear of Peace." We started by discussing fear of the other: would it be possible or conceivable to shake hands with an enemy? We moved on to fear of the folks back home: would we be censured, or accused of consorting with the enemy, if we shook hands and exchanged views? Finally, we moved towards considering what might be called a sort of agoraphobia, a fear of unfamiliar places or situations—in this instance, peace—and how we could make known to the world that we were committed to peace whatever the personal risks involved. It is this ethic of human solidarity that first attracted me to the work and principles of Dr. Martin Luther King, Jr.

A global world needs a global ethic, and in the words of the World Council of Churches and communiqués from many hundreds of other meetings on the subject of improving and deepening conversation between the adherents of the faiths, we share in the following: the empowerment of the poor, the development of civil society, and governance with a human face. A Byzantine Sophist who lived at the height of the Byzantine Empire had the following epitaph inscribed on his gravestone: "He was touched by the love of the public good, of the common good." That common good is what we have to find once again. Can we move from a culture of existing to a culture of involvement, of participation? The cornerstones of such a culture are surely: respect for life; responsibility towards future generations; the protection of the human habitat; and above all, echoing the altruism of Dr. Martin Luther King, Jr., marked by mutual respect and a recognition of each person's dignity and worth.

It was with this in mind that, in the early 1980s, working in conjunction with the international NGO movement, we set up the Independent Commission on International Humanitarian Issues, which included, among others, Desmond Tutu, who became a colleague on the commission's study on the ethic of human solidarity. We looked at pressing global issues—population, environment, poverty, and development. We discussed the forces of change—new nations, peoples' movements, women, and youth. We focused on vulnerable groups such as Street Children and Child Soldiers. We listened to the mothers in Plaza de Mayo in Argentina. We studied the cases and listened to victims of torture, displacement, and neglect. We examined studies on diseases, famine, deforestation, and natural disasters. Further, we focused on emerging issues with commercial nuclear power, genetic engineering, and industrial disasters.

We presented our recommendations to the Secretary General of the United Nations, and every year there is a renewed call for a New World Humanitarian Order at the General Assembly. Sadly, however, when the NGOs said, "We came to you as the lobby for the powerless," I could only reply, "I am sad to say that I am the powerless lobby for the powerless." I think nonetheless that we have to preserve. Despite the importance of political power in reference to a New World Humanitarian Order, I think it is important to remember something Walter Sisulu said to me in Soweto in January last year. He said we have to stop working against xenophobia, against apartheid, and against occupation, and rather start working for a sharing of cultures and a sharing of perceptions.

The late Yehudi Menuhin's proposal for the establishment of a Parliament of Cultures inspired me, in an address to the International Parliamentary Union, by emphasizing that culture should not be an afterthought, relegated to the bottom of the list, after security and economy. Culture is identity, culture is security, culture is the meaning of life to so many of us. In Arabic, we say comprehension precedes understanding, and I would like to suggest that no worldwide proposal—such as "globalization"—can be understood if it is not first comprehended. If you use the term "globalization" in our part of the world, people will ask whether you mean "universalization of values," which is something they can understand and feel they could participate in. Any new worldwide proposal, in order to have legitimacy for all concerned, must be described in terms that are relevant to the various religious, cultural, and legal traditions. Only then can they resonate. If globalization can be presented in such a comprehensible way, it will no longer be perceived as a western imposition on the rest of humankind, but accepted as a means of modernizing and enlarging through participation, allowing each tradition to remain faithful to its roots. By the same token, each tradition will discover that the challenges human beings have faced for centuries were met in more or less similar ways. In doing so, different civil societies might be inclined to accept the other as brothers, sharing the same human destiny, rather than viewing them as potential enemies or barbarians.

President Daisaku Ikeda, in his daily guidances, says:

> True happiness exists in faith alone.... No matter what awaits us in the future, we have no alternative but to pursue the road toward enlightenment, peace, and the salvation of mankind. Faith means courage. Faith means vitality. Faith means continuation. Faith also means good common sense. Faith enables us to live with a peaceful mind in the scope of the eternal flow of life; to objectively observe transient phenomena, based upon the eternal and absolute Mystic Law.

I was saddened as a Muslim to see the wanton destruction of places of worship sacred to the Buddhist faith in Afghanistan. I was more saddened still that the *terra media*, the middle ground that has existed for centuries between faiths, is now addressed in political terms. I would have liked to see Muslims being asked to travel to Afghanistan to represent the United Nations. As people with cultural affinity, they would have been able to say to the Taliban: "What you are contemplating is unconscionable for Muslims." However, we cannot allow this deterioration to continue; otherwise, the middle ground, *terra media*, will not survive. We cannot continue to claim to be moderate and centrist if we are not dynamic in promoting that centrism, in promoting that middle ground. If we are not dynamic, if we do not stand up, and if we are not counted, then the middle ground will continue to erode and extremists on all sides will fill the vacuum with slogans of hatred and of confrontation.

Only two days ago, the World Conference on Religion and Peace (WCRP), of which I have the privilege of being the moderator, convened a meeting of religious leaders, Muslims and Christians, in Uganda—where there are 1.8 million orphans, orphans of families infected with HIV—to address the common challenges that confront them and that cut across their communal boundaries. Our project in conjunction with PLAN International, CARE, Save the Children, and the Society for Women Against AIDS in Africa will be addressing up to 10,000,000 such children in Africa. The religious leaders of Uganda have committed themselves to work shoulder to shoulder to face this challenge, and I believe that this is one practical way by which the faith communities can disseminate altruism. I think the time has come to emphasize the importance of positive peaceful initiatives.

How can we build a culture of peace? It is certainly long overdue. Although agreements and treaties have long been recognized as essential instruments for regulating the conduct of states, far less attention has been given to a more comprehensive approach engaging individuals—the citizens of those same states. In Tehran, Iran, only three weeks ago I addressed 48 governments. The theme was "xenophobia, discrimination, and different forms of intolerance." I spoke of the importance of developing a code of conduct, the importance of involving civil society, and the importance of involving non-governmental organizations. To my surprise, over the course of the three long days of the conference, the NGOs were given a mere ten minutes to speak. I find it tragic and shortsighted that the involvement of the common man is not encouraged. Governmental treaties on refugees, for example, go back to 1951. You may not believe it, but 70 percent of the world's refugees are Muslims. Yet, Muslims are accused of extremism. I am convinced that addressing the causes of despair—the economic, social, and political causes of despair—by inviting people to participate, and by taking steps to encourage the will to stay rather than to flee the homeland, is an important point of departure if we are to underline the importance of the right to a dignified life free from terror and free from despair.

A few months ago, I was invited to visit Auschwitz (Ozviecim). Many were surprised that I accepted the invitation. Yet had I, as Moderator of the WCRP, refused, people would have accused me of hypocrisy, of calling Western Judeao-Christian values "exclusive" and then rejecting an opportunity to participate, to triangulate the conversation into one between Christians, Muslims, and Jews. They would have had a point, so I went. My wife's late mother (God bless her soul) worked, under the guidance of Eleanor Roosevelt, on the Committee on the Charter of Human Rights. One of her colleagues was the late Professor Lemkin, who invented the term "genocide" and who lost twenty-four of his kin. At the "Chemra Lomdei Mishnayot," the place where the last synagogue was dedicated, I was thanked by the Catholics for triangulating the conversation. I also took the opportunity to remind my Christian friends that Christianity was born in our part of the world. My Jewish friends recognize the fact that the killing has not stopped: in Gorazde, in Kosovo, in Sarajevo, in Rwanda, and in so many parts of the world.

I am convinced that, in pursuing the concept of what I call "developing that noble art of conversation"—of involving people—one day we will achieve a new code of conduct. One of the practical steps that might be taken would be to consider the creation of a multidenominational peace corps. We hear a lot about blue helmets in the United Nations. As a friend once said: "What about blue overalls?" I don't care what color overalls they wear, as long as we select our best surgeons, our best doctors, our best social workers to go and give of themselves, and I have had the privilege of seeing the effectiveness of such action when working with the lepers of Sudan. This is a practical manifestation—putting words into deeds. We know societies are vulnerable. We are all vulnerable, but can we take the risk of doing good things in bad times—can we make a difference?

Someone once said there are three priorities in peacemaking: peace at home, peace with our neighbors, and peace with the modern age. I wonder whether a moment cannot come where we see, drawn up and adhered to, a charter for civic and human rights for different regions of the world, fundamental rights in which we all share, and responsibilities that we give of ourselves to meet. Can we not speak of alms? For twenty years, I have worked to try and create a Muslim *Zakat*, alms, foundation, echoing the pension funds in Europe, where people have agreed to work together to alleviate poverty through a clearly defined program with a clearly defined objective. I think this is one aspect of real people-to-people involvement, worthy of serious consideration. Much has been said on the subject of a universal code of conduct, but it took twenty-five years of conversation to come up with one sheet of paper outlining such a code. It started by emphasizing the association between theology and practicality, beginning with commonality and taking into account the Enlightenment tradition. In his "Answer to the Question: What Is Enlightenment?" (1784), the great philosopher Immanuel Kant said that, "if it is now asked whether we live at present in an enlightened age, the answer is 'No.'" However, Kant added that "we live in an age of enlightenment." For him, Europe, including Germany, was in the throes of becoming enlightened. How? To secure "a man's release from his self-incurred immaturity," Kant thought people must think for themselves under the watchword "*Sapere Aude*!" which means "Dare to know," from the Roman poet Horace.[1]

Can we not speak of embracing the principle of "No coercion?" Can we not uphold the right to proclaim one's own religion? To reconsider the content of education? Can we not ensure a free flow of information? Yesterday, Dr. [Walter] Massey spoke to me regarding the digital divide, which to me implies the divide between data and information on the one hand, and knowledge on the other. First, in looking afresh at our own and, second, each other's texts, heritage, and history, can we develop a framework for disagreement as well as accept responsibility for words and actions at all levels and recognize the political and economic dimensions of our interfaith dialogue? I believe that it is incumbent on all of us in whichever field we are in to seize the moment, like Gandhi and Hussein ibn Ali, and together work towards a better and more caring world, where mutual respect and human dignity coexist.

All my adult life, I have treasured the words of the Muslim scholar Ibn Al Arabi, who lived in Spain and the Middle East between 1165 and 1240:

> My heart is open to all the winds:

---

[1] Roy Porter and Allen Lane, *Enlightenment: Britain and the Creation of the Modern World* (New York: Penguin Press, 2000).

It is a pasture for gazelles
And a home for Christian monks,
A temple for idols,
The Black Stone of the Mecca pilgrim
The table of the Torah,
And the book of the Koran.
Mine is the religion of love.
Wherever God's caravans turn,
The religion of love
Shall be my religion

And my faith.

Chapter 16

It's Not Easy Being Dean: From Kelsey to Carter and the Case for the Importance of Religion in the Historically Black College and University Context

Harold Dean Trulear

In 1938, George Kelsey returned to Morehouse College, his *alma mater*, as a professor of Religion. In 1945, he became Director of the Morehouse School of Religion. Such a position carried significant influence on the campus, as evidenced by the testimony of Martin Luther King concerning Kelsey's role in his life.[1] While teaching Morehouse, Kelsey concurrently pursued and completed his Ph.D. in Christian Ethics at Yale University. His career reflected a clear commitment to teaching and scholarship. For Kelsey, research and scholarship were not separate from personal devotion. He was both a scholar and a preacher.

Kelsey was determined to teach religious studies in a manner that reflected both piety and intellectual rigor. His work as a scholar and preacher was consistent with the vision of President Benjamin E. Mays. As president, Mays, like Kelsey, was a Baptist minister with a Ph.D. in religion from the University of Chicago. Mays spoke weekly in chapel during his twenty-seven years as president, influencing countless Morehouse students and graduates, including Dr. Martin Luther King, Jr., Class of 1948.

However, during the Mays-Kelsey era, there were debates on campus about the role of religion in a liberal-arts college setting as well as the role of religion in the larger society. Kelsey discussed these

---

[1] The King papers at Stanford and the Kelsey papers at Drew contain significant correspondence between the two of them. Kelsey was the only person to give King an "A" at Morehouse, and, according to King, Kelsey convinced him that behind the legends and myths of the Bible are many profound truths that one cannot escape. See *Papers*, 1:42–43, Stanford University. The Kelsey papers contain George Kelsey's letter of recommendation for King to attend Crozer Seminary.

tensions in a paper presented to the Joint Committee on Negro Ministerial Education of the Northern Baptist Convention, Southern Baptist Convention, and National Baptist Convention, Incorporated in 1948. In this paper, Kelsey noted that "religion is peculiar among all fields in that it is both an experience and a body of knowledge in a manner that other fields are not." This often resulted in a tendency to "substitute piety for scholarship," disregarding the fact that, "as preachers and teachers of religion, [students] need piety and knowledge." [2] He noted that religious studies in general, and theological education in particular, suffered because of an environment where people "believe that learning dries up the living waters of the 'spirit.'" "The 'spirit' to which many students referred was manifested in an overt emotionalism in religious services."[3]

Kelsey, along with others in Black colleges, had the dual responsibility of providing leadership in both undergraduate and professional programs in Religion. For Kelsey, many African Americans were unable to distinguish between "essential religion" and the "crude manifestations of religion." He noted:

> The standards of the churches are low while those of other professions are high.... In other professions education and skill count. And the richest prizes are available only to those who have scaled the highest heights in education and technical efficiency. These professions are therefore marked by a dignity and status among all people.... Since the Negro ecclesiastical establishment environment demands very little preparation on the part of its ministers, and since the capable and alert boys are neither encouraged to enter the ministry nor attracted by it, theological education among Negroes is statistically at a low ebb.[4]

---

[2] Kelsey, "The Present Crisis in Negro Ministerial Education," *The Papers of Martin Luther King, Jr.*, Volume VI (Berkeley: University of California Press, 2007) 104. I give additional attention to Kelsey's legacy in "George Kelsey, Christianity and Race: A View from the Academy," in *Princeton Theological Review* (Spring 2004): 35–40.

[3] Kelsey, "The Present Crisis," 1.

[4] Ibid., 2.

In his paper, Kelsey also discussed the tension with balancing the study of religion with the practice of religion. He was not the chaplain, but he made a powerful impact in the Religion Department and influenced many of the religious activities on campus. Unfortunately, a lack of resources is one reason for his eventual departure from Morehouse.

The issues that Kelsey wrestled with continued to exist throughout the Mays era, and when Hugh Morris Gloster became president in 1967, he strengthened the place of religion at Morehouse. During the Gloster administration, the chapel program moved from George Sale Hall, where religious services were previously held, to the Martin Luther King, Jr. International Chapel, which was dedicated in February 1978. The Dean of Chapel position would be a position of visibility and influence at an institution that valued strong religious leadership and produced great leaders, including Dr. King, for whom the new chapel would be named.

President Gloster already had in mind some idea of what he wanted and expected of the new dean. Prior to assuming the presidency of Morehouse, Gloster held teaching and administrative positions at several institutions, including Hampton Institute (now Hampton University). As Dean of Faculty at Hampton, he supervised the United States Agency for International Development's USAID program in Sierra Leone as well as several foreign studies programs in Europe and the Middle East. He brought this international experience with him to Morehouse as well as a knowledge of Hampton's respected chapel program. Faculty, staff, and students participated in the service, and the chapel opened its doors to local residents and visitors in the city of Hampton and surrounding areas. Those in attendance often heard prominent speakers, especially renowned pastors and scholars. In addition, Gloster knew of the annual Hampton Ministers' Conference, which has served as a week of continuing education for clergy since 1914.

Gloster wanted the King chapel program at Morehouse to rival the chapel program at Hampton and to develop a national forum that would be comparable to the Hampton Ministers' Conference, not necessarily in terms of numbers, but in terms of intellectual exchange and stimulating engaging enrichment programs. Further, the new dean at the King Chapel would have to build a Sunday-morning congregation, virtually *ex nihilo,* to function like a church, similar to Howard University's Rankin

Chapel and Harvard University's Memorial Church. These expectations were a part of the job description and a related one was fundraising. The Dean of Chapel would have to develop the King Chapel ministry programs and develop an annual budget. Although Gloster secured most of the funds for the construction of the chapel and the adjacent administration building bearing his name, the ongoing work of the chapel, such as day-to-day operations, staffing, weekly services, community outreach, and all other developmental aspects, would be the responsibility of the dean.

President Gloster conducted a nationwide search for the position of Dean of Chapel and interviewed many candidates, including alumni. Lawrence Edward Carter's name surfaced to the top and news of his selection was circulated at the funeral of Dr. Sandy F. Ray, pastor of the Cornerstone Baptist Church in Brooklyn, New York. Carter is not a graduate of Morehouse College, although he was recruited by Dr. King in a church office in Columbus, Ohio. Carter attended and graduated instead from Virginia University of Lynchburg with a bachelor's degree in Social Science and Psychology, and received the Master of Divinity, Master of Sacred Theology, and Doctor of Philosophy degrees, all from Boston University. Carter was chosen for the position that many alumni thought would be reserved for one of the college's "established" or "up-and-coming" graduates. After all, Morehouse is known for its outstanding graduates, including Martin Luther King, Jr., Howard Thurman, Mordecai Johnson, Miles Mark Fisher, George Kelsey, and other prominent alumni in the fields of Religion and Theology. However, thirty-five years of extraordinary service is proof that Dean Carter was the right choice.

Another challenge that further proves Carter was the right choice is the way he has negotiated the tensions discussed earlier that characterized the Kelsey-Mays era. These tensions carried over, and there were new challenges to the academic study of religion in colleges and universities, as well as the shifting political and religious landscape in America. Carter began his administrative duties in Georgia at the end of President Jimmy Carter's administration. Carter, also a Georgian, was a self-proclaimed "born-again Christian." The 1970s and 1980s were marked by a rise in evangelicalism, televangelism, and church growth, and sociologists have long debated reasons for these phenomena in light of what was happening socially and politically in America and abroad. In the early 1990s, Stephen Carter's *The Culture of Disbelief: The Trivialization of Religion in the Public Square* elevated the discourse regarding religion by insisting that religion in the United States is often trivialized by American law and politics, and that those with a strong religious faith are forced to bend to meet the viewpoint of a "public faith," which is largely faithless. In the book, Carter argues that there is a place for faith in public life, yet adheres to the separation of church and state.

The debate about the place of religion in a liberal-arts curriculum is an ongoing one that is also a part of the "culture of disbelief." One of the casualties at many liberal-arts colleges and universities is a religion requirement, a traditional part of liberal-arts education but one that is being more and more designated as an elective instead of a requirement. For Carter and other professors of Religion at Morehouse, there was no threat of eliminating Religion from the curriculum, but there was a need for Carter and Aaron Parker, among others, to resist the current of popular culture and its influence in terms of religious theories and methodologies. At the time of his appointment, Dean Carter's approach was social-scientific, like the approach of Kelsey and Mays. Carter's course load includes introductory Religion courses for which he uses a number of texts by classical and contemporary thinkers. His psychology of religion courses integrate clinical, theoretical, and empirical literature, as well as biographical information of the lives of significant psychologists and their works. He incorporates new research on meditation, the correlational study of religion, religion and mental health, object relations theory, pluralism, and social constructionism.

Also, the Dean of the Chapel had a significant fundraising responsibility as part of his job description. President Gloster raised the money for the construction of the chapel, but the ongoing life and work of the chapel required additional resources. Dean Carter stepped into a position that had a development component, along with an additional "to-do list." This vision elevated the chaplain's role and responsibilities beyond what they had been during previous administrations. These would be major challenges for the founding dean. While Carter's challenges applied directly to the development of the chapel, Carter also assumed the religious leadership of an institution of higher education at a time when religion found itself marginalized in the public square. He began his deanship at the end of the administration of President Jimmy Carter, who was a self-proclaimed "born-again" Christian during a time when White, evangelical Christianity, televangelism, and megachurches grew to unprecedented levels.

The rise of evangelicalism was a reaction, in part, to the secularization in society. Stephen Carter's *The Culture of Disbelief*, previously mentioned, appeared after Dean Carter's installation. At Morehouse and at other religiously affiliated institutions, "pre-professional" majors and concentrations such as Youth Ministry and Ministry Studies were debated as a part of the liberal-arts curriculum. Dean Carter and Religion professor Aaron Parker, among other faculty members, resisted the emphasis on "pre-professional" areas of concentration within the Religion major. They pressed for a more broad-based, liberal approach ("liberal' in the sense of accepting the sciences in the academic study of religion). These sciences, which grow out of the modern period (following the death of Descartes), include: modern history, modern philosophy, sociology, anthropology, psychology, and other human sciences studying religious phenomena. As a psychologist of religion, Carter appreciates the sciences as a methodological tool to study religion. He also appreciates and practices spiritual disciplines, like prayer and meditation, as a part of ministry to college students. In a real sense, Carter's work and ministry dovetail with the Mays era in establishing religion as a useful discipline in the church and academy.

Many historically Black colleges and universities, including nonsectarian or public institutions such as Howard University, Morgan State University, and the University of Maryland Eastern Shore, have religious roots and were started, specifically, to address the need for Black professionals, especially preachers and teachers. Some other historically Black colleges and universities like Fisk, Morehouse, and Spelman, among others, are still "religiously affiliated," and religion is taught in a liberal-arts context. The fundamental mission for many of these colleges has not changed from the schools' historic origins. Many of these schools serve first-generation college students and administrators, and faculty encourage them to give back to their communities. A consumer-driven, market economy presents an ongoing temptation for graduates to forget those who still struggle and who have not accomplished at their same level. The motto of the National Association of Colored Women's Clubs, "Lifting as We Climb," captures an important mission of HBCUs in the late nineteenth and early twentieth century.[5] Morehouse is no different than other HBCUs in terms of producing graduates who want to make a desperately needed contribution to their communities.

At Morehouse, as with other institutions, religion is discussed in terms of African-American history and sheds light on Middle Eastern, African, and Asian cultures, among others. Dean Carter's interest in ecumenism puts the chapel program in line with the idea of Morehouse as a "world house" (from an ancient term, "oikoumene," which is engraved in stone near a side entrance of the King Chapel) and supports former president Robert Michael Franklin's vision of the "Morehouse Renaissance" based on Morehouse students' being "well read," "well spoken," "well traveled," "well dressed," and "well balanced."

Let me close with an experience from a panel on which I participated as part of the Tercentennial Celebration at Yale University in 2001. As panelists, we responded to a presentation from Yale Law Professor Stephen Carter about the role of religion in politics and the public square, primarily from his book *God's Name in Vain*. The panel consisted of a diverse group of religious leaders: clergy and lay; Black and White; Protestant, Catholic, and Jewish. A Muslim community activist was the last to speak, and he talked about "cooperation" and "working across faiths for the common good." He said:

> This has been an interesting discussion, but the reality is that each of us represents a religious tradition that is both universalistic and monotheistic. That means we all believe in one God, and that that God is the right God for all people. Which means that while we politely seek a crass common ground that enables us to work together, deep within, each of us thinks our religion is right and the others are wrong, we just don't say it.

---

[5] See Cheryl Sanders, *Empowerment Ethics for a Liberated People* (Minneapolis: Fortress, 1995), which includes a chapter titled "Lifting as We Climb" detailing how this ethic framed Black professionalism in this era.

Many do not understand the need for “interreligious dialogue.” Dean Carter not only says it—he understands it, encourages it, and does it.

17
The Civil Rights Movement and the Role of Nonviolence in Promoting Healthy Communities

Edward P. Wimberly

Introduction

The presentation takes seriously a public health orientation to the prevention of violence. It grows out of the Institute of Faith Health Leadership (IFHL) at Interdenominational Theological Center (ITC).[1] In this presentation, the public health model presented seeks to foster optimal health of the community by securing, maintaining, preserving, and promoting the relational ties of the village, social networks, neighborhood, cross-generational bonds, strong mediating structures (marriage, family, extended family, churches, fraternities/sororities), communally based healing practices, and oral traditions that promote images and expectations of healthy marriage and family life among African Americans, particularly youth and young adults. The approach takes seriously the practices that promote public health, including public policy efforts to promote relational ties that value the role of care and nurture, which support African-American males' responsible roles in family life.

The model of public health promoted here also focuses on primary prevention, secondary prevention, and tertiary prevention. The model takes seriously both the public health and community mental health movements grounded in the Harvard School of Public Health Community Mental Health Program in the 1950s and 1960s, and whose

---

[1] The IFHL sought to respond to the Administration for Children and Families, Office of Family Assistance, and the Responsible Father and African-American Healthy Marriage Initiative sponsored by federal legislation. This model was originally developed through the work of Edward P. Wimberly, Rueben Warren, and Anne Streaty Wimberly.

influence is present today in public health and community mental health emphases.[2]

Both the public health and community mental health approaches assume that prevention involves the widest possible level of intervention including the public dimension and especially public policy. Moreover, it assumes that promoting social policies, consultation and education within governmental organizations, social agencies, urban planning entities, and community groups would impact the lives of people throughout the total community. Attacking public health and community mental health at this broad community level is called "primary prevention." Closely related to primary prevention is the level of secondary prevention, which is focused on early case-finding and intervening into the lives of people who show the early signs of disease or relational problems. Finally, the model focuses on tertiary prevention, which focuses on the rehabilitation of people who have been sick physically or emotionally and need to return to the community following rehabilitation. Tertiary prevention prepares the community for the return of the rehabilitated to the community.

The approach presented in our discussion today focuses on all three levels of prevention, and the purpose of such a focus is to point to the need to permeate thoroughly the entire African-American community with values that grow out of the nonviolent Civil Rights movement. More precisely, this presentation focuses on developing a mentoring model of prevention of violence of African-American men toward African-American women, children, and the more vulnerable in our society. Toward this end, the presentation explores the potential use of an antisexist and generic understanding of nonviolence growing out of the Civil Rights era applied to domestic relationships.

---

[2] This model shaped the thinking of Rueben Warren, who got his master's and doctoral degree in public health from Harvard in the mid-1970s, and Edward P. Wimberly, who studied community mental health at the Solomon Carter Fuller Mental Health Center at Boston University in the 1970s. The community mental health orientation influenced the Consultation and Education program where Edward P. Wimberly did his student internship from 1972–1974.

Such an approach is preventive in that it seeks to promote intimate justice values at the widest possible public level that will impact how people live their daily lives in marriage and family life. This approach promotes optimal health by setting forth positive images of male and female relationships and parenting rooted and grounded in the concept of intimate justice.

Key Assumptions

Before exploring the specifics of a mentoring model for the prevention of domestic violence growing out of the Civil Rights Movement, it is important to set forth the assumptions that undergird this presentation.

This first assumption concerns the meaning of intimate justice. Intimate justice is all about promoting health in domestic relationships, especially between males and females, through commitment to ethical values that support mutuality, reciprocity, and collaborative styles. This understanding grows out of the sharing of power in intimate male and female relationships, and it reflects one model that has emerged from the research into African-American male and female relationships.[3]

Defining the nature of domestic violence is also important at the outset.

> Severe violence between African-American spouses relates to kicking, biting, hitting with fists, hitting with objects, physical beating, threatening with guns or knives, and the use of guns or knives. A study of severe violence between African-American husbands and wives concludes that between 1975 and 1985 severe violence perpetrated toward African-American women decreased from 169 per 1,000 persons in 1975 to 64 per 1,000 in 1985. The reasons given for the decline are (1) rise in median income of Black males during this period,

---

[3] Alongside more traditional approaches to power in male and female relationships, there is also a tradition where African-American men and women collaborate in decision-making. See Elaine B. Pinderhughes, "African-American Marriage in the 20th Century," *Family Process* 41, no. 2 (2002): 276.

(2) rise in the age of first marriage, and (3) declining rates of unemployment.[4]

The cause of African-American male violence toward African-American females was jealousy, but research reveals that collaborating in decision-making and egalitarian values in the spousal relationship fostered less violence than that used in relationships dominated by the traditional or patriarchal model. Moreover, research reveals that the significant use of violence depends on the homes in which the males were raised, particularly the socialization process of both males and females.[5]

Violence and nonviolence are learned behaviors that are the result of socialization.

The nonsexist dimension of the Civil Rights Movement, especially the imaginative model of the Ten Commandments of Intimate Justice, serves as a good model for mentoring.[6]

Contemporary models of masculinity fueling domestic violence have grown out of stereotypical images of manhood grounded in the arena outside the home. The values of self-interest and competition, seeking one's own self-interest; denying the importance of relationships, and the need to care for and nurture those relationships; valuing the marketplace over the home; talking rather than listening; self-confidence without humility—all are characteristics that shape manhood in the U.S.A.[7] The key conflict is that African-American men historically have been cut off from avenues of achieving this image of masculinity economically, but nonetheless, they have sought the disconnection and detachment from relationships. One result of a history of distorted images of masculinity and increased detachment is the abuse and exploitation of women.[8]

---

[4] Edward P. Wimberly, *Counseling African-American Marriages and Families* (Louisville: Westminster John Knox, 1997) 117.

[5] Ibid., 117–18.

[6] Ibid., 44–45.

[7] Edward P. Wimberly, "Men, Pastoral Care of," in *Dictionary of Pastoral Care* (Nashville: Abingdon Press, 1990) 704–705.

[8] Erik Eckholm, "Plight Deepens for Black Men, Studies Warn," *nytimes.com* (20 March 2006).

The Civil Rights Movement

It is documented that the Civil Rights Movement was a sexist movement, and it did not transcend the traditional and stereotypical roles that women, and especially Black women, were expected to play. Despite the sexist beginning, there are certain lessons that can be gleaned from the Civil Rights Movement that can be drawn on in the contemporary effort to implement intimate justice. The key issue being raised is that violence and nonviolence are both learned behaviors passed on from generation to generation.

The first lesson is that somebody defines reality, and it is not unusual for the dominant race in the United States, namely Whites, to define reality. One of the imaginative and important contributions of the Civil Rights Movement was that it taught African Americans that they had the power to redefine reality for themselves.[9] Learning to define reality for Dr. King was grounded theologically in the belief that our worth and value were conferred on us by God and not by society. This fundamental conviction led to transcending the negative attitudes toward Black people held by wider society, and it helped us not only to redefine reality, but also to redefine the meaning of manhood. Manhood was redefined as the ability to refocus our lives on the God-given strength within us, which remained dormant as long as we were preoccupied with the violence of Whites against us. Thus, nonviolence became a new strategy of expressing our determination to be free.

Second, the training in nonviolence has a great deal of similarity to the training in intimate justice. For example:

> Socio-drama was used to prepare people for nonviolent demonstrations. Through socio-drama, demonstrators were prepared to respond nonviolently and to resist striking back when verbally and physically attacked. In fact, every volunteer had to sign a commitment card which contained the Ten Commandments of nonviolence. As part of the training in nonviolence, each demonstrator had to pledge to meditate on the teaching of Jesus, to remember that nonviolence sought justice

[9] Wimberly, "The Civil Rights Movement," 39. *Journal of Religion and Abuse*, vol. 2(1) (New York: The Haworth Press, 2000) 39.

> and reconciliation, to walk in God's love, to pray for freedom, to sacrifice personal wishes for a higher goal, to treat friend and foe with courtesy, to be service oriented, to refrain from the violent use of the fist or tongue in fighting back, to pursue good spiritual and bodily health, and to follow the leadership of those who led the movement.[10]

Towards a Model of Intimate Justice

Promoting health at the widest possible public policy levels involves assuring the existence of relational connecting values and ties of the village; of social networks; of neighborhood; of cross-generational bonds (at least three generations); of strong mediating structures, institutions that stand between the individual and wider culture, such as the family, extended family, churches, schools, neighborhood organizations, Boy Scouts, recreation centers, churches, and others.

For example, since domestic violence seems to decline because there is a rise in median income of Black males, the rise in the age of first marriage, and declining rates of unemployment, it seems important for public policy to address issues related to access to better-paying jobs, job training, marital preparation, and discrimination in jobs.

Support through public policy for regular and consistent involvement of husbands and wives across at least three generations, since such connections do enhance marital success except where there are generations of domestic abuse. In the cases where domestic abuse exists across generations, secondary and tertiary models of early case-finding and intervention might be helpful.

Assure the establishment and continuing of voluntary associations and community agencies that support marital preparation and proper relational values that support intimate justice and egalitarian models of marital and family life.

Make sure that government, school systems, and social agencies address education and employment opportunities existing in specific areas.

---

[10] Ibid., 40.

Identify and support community revitalization projects that support marriage and family life through involvement in base community groups, community development organizations, charter schools, and others.

Develop character education in schools focusing on intimate justice and power issues in close and interpersonal relationships.

Primary Prevention

Primary prevention is very much related to the health promotion model outlined above. One key issue not addressed above is how images of what it means to be men are defined.

Since one of the key factors in addressing racism in the Civil Rights Movement was redefining reality, primary prevention needs to address the way masculinity is defined. For example, manhood is increasingly being defined by the competitive models existing in the marketplace that do not support the relational values of caring and nurturing. Therefore, manhood should be defined not only to include values related to earning, but also in terms of the relationships that exist within families, such as son, husband, father, uncle, and grandfather. The point is to recapture what it means to be a relational person.

Key also is to make public transportation available to places of employment.

Secondary Prevention

Secondary prevention is the level at which the Civil Rights Movement comes into full force.

Here, consultation and education are used to educate marriages, families, extended families, neighborhoods, churches, boys' and girls' clubs, schools, and wherever adults and parents gather to promote intimate justice.

One key approach is to use men who have not used violence against women to educate youth and young adults about nonviolence. The education should use accountability and socio-education in the approach. Accountability means fostering links between males and females that enable youth and young adults to redefine what it means to be men and women beyond the control and power over others. It also means talking about responsible behavior as men, lovers, husbands, fathers, and mentors. For women, it means breaking with the traditional norms of subservient femininity and affirming important roles inside and outside the family for women. Social education helps both males and females critique the negative roles that males and females play and how race and culture foster these negative roles.

Through consultation and education, teach men such values as mutuality, reciprocity, empathy, accommodation, nurture, respect, and accountability.

Help males and females understand traditional patriarchy and how it undermines male and female relationships, promoting violence among those who are not well grounded in relational values.

Through consultation and education, teach the Ten Commandments of Intimate Justice. The Ten Commandments of Intimate Justice can be used at both secondary and tertiary prevention levels. The preamble of intimate justice reads as follows: "I hereby pledge myself to participate in a process of learning to relate with care, equity, and fairness in my relationships with my spouse and mate. Therefore, I will keep the following commandments of intimate justice:"[11]

- To meditate daily on the life and teachings of Jesus related to the treatment of others with respect, care, fairness, and love.
- To remember that nonviolence and intimate justice seek not only the welfare of my mate and others, but they also assure that my basic needs for love and connections are met as well.
- To pray daily for those whom I have abused verbally and physically that the harm I caused them is healed.
- To ask God to show me daily those dimensions of my beliefs/convictions that cause me to behave in ways that limit the freedom and growth of others.
- To cooperate daily with insights from God through others who help me become aware of and change the attitudes, convictions, and beliefs that lead me to abuse others.

[11] Ibid., 44–45.

- To participate fully in group processes with my peers and mentors, no matter how uncomfortable it becomes.
- To refrain from the use of violence of any kind—whether physical, verbal, or nonverbal—within or outside the group, and particularly with my mate.
- To strive for physical health through recreation and exercise.
- To perform community service so that I learn the importance of serving others.
- To take seriously the opinions and ideas of others, though they might not be similar to my own.

Tertiary Prevention

This level of prevention involves work with men who seek to achieve certain ends through the use of domestic violence through the use of the following: "physical abuse, emotional abuse, economic abuse, threats and intimidation, isolation and entrapment, sexual abuse and exploitation, control and abuse of children, and isolation through job relocation and language barriers."[12]

Key here is the fact that rehabilitation of actual perpetrators of abuse is very difficult and often unsuccessful. Methods that have some validity, however, include confrontation, challenging, exploring, and awareness-building. Here, men who have overcome their own battering of women, or men who have not battered their wives, help men who batter confront the destructiveness of their behavior as well as the impact that this behavior has on their mates and children. As indicated, these efforts often fail, and those who work with batterers need to make sure of the safety of the ones battered.

It is crucial to realize that prevention of domestic violence is very important when compared to the lack of success in trying to rehabilitate those who use violence in intimate relationships. Consequently, we need to redouble our efforts to promote intimate justice at the widest public

[12] Rhea V. Almeida and Tracy Durkin, "The Cultural Context Model: Therapy for Couples with Domestic Violence," *Journal of Marriage and Family Therapy* 25 (July 1999): 313.

level as well as through primary and secondary levels. Drawing on the nonsexist version of the Civil Rights Movement is a legacy that should not be ignored in our effort to promote nonviolence in intimate relationships.

18

Ripping the Veil, Weaving Meanings: The *Text*ures and Therapeutics of African Diaspora Formation

Vincent L. Wimbush

I aim in this essay to build upon my work on the history of African Americans' engagement of the Bible as part of a project in cultural-criticism. Here I address some of the larger ongoing implications and ramifications of this fraught history as part of an attempt to understand these peoples and their orientations and expressivities and sensibilities. This I do by engaging some of the challenges of humanistic scholarship on African-American history and culture, and by using "scriptures" as analytical wedge "to think with," that is, as complex social-cultural comparative phenomenon through which African-American expressive traditions in particular and the politics and forms of expressivity of societies and cultures in general are refracted and can be problematized. The two problematics I focus on in this essay have to do with (1) the concept of the "veil" that names and positions the Black self as "other"; (2) the imperative of naming, analyzing, and "ripping" (resisting) the "symbolic order" or structure that establishes and protects "the veil"; and (3) the need to discover and recover the use of tools and strategies and practices by which the "weaving" (construction) of meaning for the sake of psycho-social empowerment and healing "beyond the veil" can be sustained.

Du Bois and the Veil

Because of his prescience and sharp sensitivity to issues having to do with interpretation and consciousness, I find still challenging and useful as expansive, critical and sensitive perspective on the existence and challenges of persons of African descent in the United States the language and argumentation found in W. E. B. Du Bois's classic collection of essays, *Souls of Black Folk*, originally published in 1903.[1] In this collection as part of his attempt to name the major challenges faced by the "folk"—or perhaps, more accurately, the challenges faced by the type of Black person he knew himself to be, thereby speaking in complicated ways for so many others—Du Bois refers again and again to the "veil."[2]

Notwithstanding their internal differentiations and infrapolitics, about which he as historian and social scientist was very much aware, all Black folks, Du Bois argued, had been placed—no, forced—behind the "veil." Referred to (by my count) more than thirty times, the metaphor of the veil in *Souls of Black Folk* is Du Bois's attempt to define the existence of Black folks in the United States as those forced into divided consciousness—thus, the poignant meaning of the plural term "souls": not as reference to the many souls as in many persons, but as reference to the two "souls," two orientations, sentiments, in the one representative body, or in each body, divided, warring against each other. This division was for Du Bois the deep, internal, psychologically felt reflection of the external sociopolitical existence of Black folks as the chronic persistent other, as the subaltern, as the enslaved/colonized living next to, and reduced to looking at themselves through the gaze of, the enslaver/colonizer.

Recall some of the famous references carried by the sometimes riveting, haunting, but also elegiac florid language: "…Then it dawned upon me with a certain suddenness that I was different from the others…shut out from their world by a vast veil…" (2); or "…After the Egyptian and Indian, the Greek and Roman, the Teuton and Mongolian, the Negro is a sort of seventh son, born with a veil…" (2–3).

---

[1] W. E. B. Du Bois, *Souls of Black Folk* (New York: Bantam, 1989 [1903]). All quotations are from this edition.

[2] The term "veil" has interesting etymology: Middle English *veile*, taken from old North French, taken from Latin *vela*, plural of *velum*=sail, awning: used allusively in various prepositional phrases, such as behind, beyond, or within the veil: Tyndale 1528; Wollaston 1722; Tennyson 1850; E. Fitzgerald 1859; A.J. Ross 1877; to conceal from apprehension, knowledge, or perception; to disguise: D'Israel 1841. At the time of Du Bois's writing, these uses were very much in the air of popular discourse and in letters.

Modified variously in terms of the "veil of Race" (55, 56), "Veil of Color" (127, 142), as that which imprisons (64), as that within which Black folks are born and in which they grow up (147, 148, 150, 156, 159, 165), as that which casts a shadow (149), as that against-over and beyond—which the Black self strives to live (76, 153), as that world beyond which White folks live (56), as that phenomenon or haunting which the Black self overcomes only in death (151), and that which, based on hope, is to be rent (187).

Literary critics Shamoon Zamir[3] and Arnold Rampersad[4] have argued that in the metaphorization of the veil Du Bois drew most directly from (Plato via) Hegel, then from Emerson, and some other late nineteenth- and early twentieth-century persons of letters; from nascent psychology; and from the Bible. These scholars suggest that Du Bois took from Hegel the idea of the veil and its effects on consciousness and wedded them to the Bible's stories regarding transformation. Du Bois needed language and concepts through which he could articulate what he understood to be the profundity of the crisis of divided consciousness as well as the ascetics and performativity of transformed consciousness. Hegel's concern had been about the "unhappy consciousness" as part of the dialectics of the master-slave relationship and that moment in which such consciousness is transformed, when self-consciousness discovers itself beyond the realm of appearances, that moment in which the "curtain" is drawn aside.[5]

The pertinent references from the Bible in relationship to the "veil" have to do with the experience of enlightenment and transformation—in the book of Exodus (26:33) the "veil" (LXX: *to katapetasma*) separates the Holy of Holies, the sanctuary for the Ark of the Covenant, from everything else; in 1 Corinthians (13:12) Paul makes reference to

[3] Shamoon Zamir, *Dark Voices: W. E. B. Du Bois and American Thought, 1888–1903* (Chicago: University of Chicago Press, 1995) pt. 2.

[4] Arnold Rampersaud, *Art and Imagination of W. E. B. Du Bois* (Cambridge: Harvard University Press, 1976) ch. 4.

[5] G. W. F. Hegel, *Phenomenology of Mind*, trans. J. B. Baillie (New York: Harper Textbooks, 1976 [1807, trans. 1910]) 211, 212–13. Quoted in Zamir, *Dark Voices*, 135.

humans, even repentant ones, being able to see only partial truths—"darkly as through a veil" (*en ainigmati*); in the letter to the Hebrews (6:19) the unknown writer refers to entering into the domain of the "veil" (*eis to esoteron tou katapetasmatos*) to mark the change in those who although having been enlightened, have in the face of persecution "fallen away"; and, perhaps, most poignantly, the Gospel of Matthew (27:50–54), having depicted Jesus crying out loud and dying on the cross, indicates that "the veil" of the temple was "rent in two" from top to bottom (*to katapetasma tou vaou eschisthe eis duo_apo anothen hoes kato*).

A great part of the purpose of *Souls of Black Folk* was to celebrate the social power and social gifts and contributions of the people forced behind the veil. The way of doing this was through emphasis on the forms of Black expressivity—music, literature, religion. To be sure, Du Bois understood the veil itself and Black folks' forced positioning behind it as problematic, to be gotten rid of, ripped. He and others during his times constantly challenged Black folks to strive to rend the veil. Although after many decades of intense engagement and strivings Du Bois removed himself from the situation here in the United States, there is no doubt that the legal changes that were wrought here in connection with the civil rights struggles of the 1950s and 1960s and 1970s represented a degree of rending of the veil for which Du Bois had fought and hoped.

Yet even as the matter of the degree of amelioration of socio-economic position among Black folks continues to be debated, it is clear that "the veil" as a metaphor for Black existence has proved to be rather elastic and expansive, communicating more than one message. At the end of *Souls*, after having consistently and dramatically used the term "veil" to describe and provoke strong emotions about the separation and hegemony of Black folks from "the kingdom of culture," Du Bois used it in a rather different, more positive sense, as the language of the slave songs that encodes or conceals the most profound and sensitive sentiments:

> In these songs…the slave spoke to the world. Such a message is naturally veiled and half articulate. Words and music have lost each other and new cant phrases of a dimly understood theology have

> displaced the older sentiment...the music is distinctly sorrowful. [They] tell in word and music of trouble and exile, of strife and hiding; they grope toward some unseen power and sigh for rest in the End.

The words...cleared of evident dross...conceal much of real poetry and meaning beneath conventional theology and unmeaning rhapsody.

> ...Over the inner thoughts of the slaves and their relations one with another the shadow of fear ever hung, so that we get but glimpses here and there, and also with them, eloquent omissions and silences....The things evidently borrowed from the surrounding world undergo characteristic change when they enter the mouth of the slave. Especially is this true of Bible phrases. (182–85)

These songs seemed to have been for Du Bois evidence of a serious grappling with the "veil" of the other valence—the "veil" that was not so much to be overcome but to be understood as complex communication. Here Du Bois was pointing to a certain type of veiling as a critical layered interpretive strategy and form of expression. Yes, to an extent veiling was needed by those forced behind the veil (of White dominance and violence). But Du Bois also seemed to understand that beyond the basic and perhaps original issue of safety, Black folk had come to express their deepest sentiments in veiled terms, indirectly, "in other words" for other reasons. They had begun to "hide" the meaning of their hard, deepest sentiments—hide from the (White) public gaze and ears, not so much in terms of being always out of view and out of earshot, but hide in terms of clear and straightforward apprehension. Their expressions were deemed "naturally veiled and half articulate." This was an-other knowing, an-other epistemological system an-other form of expressivity. To be sure, this other knowing was framed by "conventional theology," but it went underneath it with the strategy of "eloquent omissions and silences." The meanings of the "conventional" changes radically in the mouths of those singing about "trouble and exile, of strife and hiding."

And then Du Bois indicates, almost as a throwaway assertion—at least as the lack of explicit elaboration seems to suggest—that all that he had argued about the Black slaves' power of expressivity was "especially" true with respect to "Bible phrases." Now it seems clearer that "conventional theology" Du Bois understood to be interpretive frameworks associated with Christendom, determined by and reflective of the Bible. So it is all the more significant that he understood that Black folk understood that the "Bible phrases" were "especially" strategic for their articulations, allowing them to "hide" (their true selves) as they felt they must.

Zora Neale Hurston and "Hidden Meanin'"

Some of the powerful implications of this thinking about veiling and hiding were not lost on critics and scholars of African-American culture who followed Du Bois. As a provocative folklorist who documented and narrativized the veiling aspect of African-American expressivities, Zora Neale Hurston comes immediately to mind. And most interesting for me, although she also failed to elaborate on and problematize it, she also noted the uses of the Bible (and other sacred texts) in the folkways and language forms of Black folk. That veiling, indirection, encoding, signifying were prominent in the forms of expressions of the folk is powerfully indicated in that favorite saying that Hurston picked up on in her field work and offered as handle for "reading" the world and the self—"hitting a lick with a crooked stick." In the manner in which she picked up on the full array of the lore and rhythms, the textures and gestures of Black folk, and in the connection she made between the use even of the Bible and free liquid self-authorized interpretations among them—"...even the Bible was made over to suit our vivid imagination..."[6]—Hurston named some of the critical issues involved in critical interpretation about and among Black folks. Her reading of Black "readings" of the world highlights the mysterious, the fantastic, the elusive, the uncanny that constituted the (re)constructed worlds of the Black Atlantic:

> ...Now all y'all heard what Ah said...
>
> Dat's just an old time by-word...
>
> I done heard my gran'paw say dem very words many and many a time...There's a whole heap of them kinda by-words...They all got a

[6] Zora Neale Hurston, *Mules and Men* (New York: Perennial Library, 1990 [1935]) 3.

> hidden meanin', jus' like de Bible. Everybody can't understand what they mean. Most people is thin-brained. They's born wid they feet under the moon. Some folks is born wid they feet on de sun and they kin seek out de inside meanin' of words...[7]

That the Bible and certain Black traditions of communication were associated with "hidden meanin'" is important; the conjuncture is rather powerful: not only can one read the Bible to find in it veiled meanings, one could also use it as key to unlocking the meaning of veiled communication, and one can use it to veil meanings. But most important, in the assertion of the folk claim about veiled meaning as it is compared to the Bible is the arrogation of nothing less than the authority and power of scriptures. In others words, Black folk were claiming not only to understand the Bible as container of esoteric knowledge, but also that they were themselves inventors of esoteric knowledge—that is, inventors of scriptures. That such claims have been downplayed or denied or rejected within the culture of Black folk or explained away by critical interpreters is very much evident and also very astounding. Critical historians and historical critics (theologians and biblical scholars) have preferred to focus simply on Black peoples' different interpretations of the content of the Bible.

Morrison and the (Un)Veiling of the Veil

Very much related to both Du Bois's insight about the sorrow songs and the Bible and Hurston's representation of the Bible as a depository of the uncanny, the mysterious, the "hidden meanin'" is Toni Morrison's focus on memory and on self-revelation within the African diaspora. Her focus brings us back to Equiano and the meaning of his story. Morrison picks up on the connection between the Du Boisian metaphorical use of the veil and the folk/vernacular uses of the Bible illuminated by Hurston in order to problematize Black existence and interpretation. Regarding the veil, she deepens and widens and problematizes Du Bois's metaphorical rendering. The veil has to do, she argued, not (merely) with racial segregation and other-ing. She expands the Du Boisian notion of divided

---

[7] Ibid., 125.

consciousness into an argument about a type of shutting off, occlusion and silencing—of the interior life/self. In an essay entitled "The Site of Memory," published in 1987 in a collection edited by William Zinsser that is hauntingly and poignantly entitled *Inventing the Truth*, Morrison addresses the matter of the veiling of the interior life of the Black self—the muting of deeply felt sentiments, pain, stresses, trauma. With special attention to what were among the first of African-American literary works written in English—the autobiographical slave narratives of the 18th and 19th centuries—she identifies what is for Black folk the perduring problem of uniting the divided consciousness and accessing and probing and articulating the movements of the interior life:

> ...no slave society in the history of the world wrote more...about its own enslavement. The milieu, however, dictated the purpose and the style...popular taste discouraged the writers from dwelling too long or too carefully on the more sordid details of their experience. Whenever there was an unusually violent incident, or a scatalogical one, or something "excessive," one finds the writer taking refuge in the literary conventions of the day. "I was left in a state of distraction not to be described" (Equiano). "But let us now leave the rough usage of the field...and turn our attention to the less repulsive slave life as it existed in the house of my childhood" (Douglass). "I am not about to harrow the feelings of my readers by a terrific representation of the untold horrors of that fearful system of oppression...It is not my purpose to descend deeply into the dark and noisome caverns of the hell of slavery" (Henry Box Brown).
>
> Over and over, the writers pull the narrative up short with a phrase such as, "But let us drop a veil over these proceedings too terrible to relate." In shaping the experience to make it palatable to those who were in a position to alleviate it, they were silent about many things, and they "forgot" many other things.[8]

Morrison's perspective is or seems diametrically opposed to those I have associated with Du Bois and Hurston. It is clear that for Morrison

[8] Toni Morrison, "Site of Memory," in *Inventing the Truth: The Art and Craft of Memoir*, ed. William Zinsser (Boston: Houghton Mifflin, 1995) 109–10.

the slave narratives represent more than anything else the phenomenon of the silencing and forgetting of, the hiding and receding from, the self. Morrison's quotations of selected slave narratives quoted above do not actually include the term itself. She did not make the argument turn around the use of the term "veil" as euphemistic registration of or shorthand allusion to every instance of the narration of the experiences of the phenomenon about which she argues. Yet there is no doubting the examples' support of what seems to be her general argument. She used the pointed metaphor of the veil as a way to think and make the point about what she seems to consider the great occlusion.

The one selection from which she quotes which includes actual reference to the term comes from Lydia Maria Child's introduction to Linda Brent's "tale" of sexual abuse. It seems to be the reference that for Morrison makes clear the problem faced and suggests the language with which a solution can be found:

> I am well aware that many will accuse me of indecorum for presenting these pages to the public; for the experiences of this intelligent and much-injured woman belong to a class which some call delicate subjects, and others indelicate. This peculiar phase of Slavery has generally been kept veiled; but the public ought to be made acquainted with its monstrous features, and I am willing to take the responsibility of presenting them with the veil drawn [aside].[9]

Morrison goes on to make her most important point—that it was striking it was to her that in the narratives there was "no mention of their [the slaves'] interior life." As a writer thriving "not much more than a hundred years after Emancipation, a writer who is Black and a woman," she saw her responsibility to be to instruct persons "how to *rip that veil* [my italics] drawn over 'proceedings too terrible to relate.'" She argued that this project was "critical" for all who belong to the "marginalized category" in society, because "we were seldom invited to participate in the discourse even when we were its topic."[10]

---

[9] Ibid., 110.

[10] Ibid., 110-11.

Morrison's research into the slave narratives led her both to problematize and to provoke more thinking about the occlusion that is effected by divided Black consciousness. But it seems to me that notwithstanding her lack of acknowledgment of it—at least in "Site of Memory"—Morrison was surely aware of Du Bois's uses of the "veil." She was if not dependent upon him, at least in conversation with, Du Bois. Here I have in mind in particular her conversation with him about his intimation of what the "sorrow songs" signify, what they beckon, what they hold out as possibilities in helping contemporaries to "rend the veil," to unite a divided consciousness, to articulate powerful and difficult sentiments and yearnings. As I have already pointed out, it is ironic that the term Du Bois used to point to this work is (a form of) "veil." That is, he thought that one powerful response on the part of Black folks to the dividedness of the Black soul was the music—especially, but not exclusively, the "sorrow songs." The music was understood to be evocative, powerful; Du Bois found himself undone by it; he first experienced and then understood it as powerful carrier of veiled sentiment. The music, then, should be compared to the slave narratives as expressive form—with respect for the obvious differences and shared possibilities and limitations of each form.

From her different social historical positioning Morrison saw more sharply the limitations of both the music (especially but going beyond the sorrow songs) and the literature (especially but going beyond the slave narrative). Regarding music, she argued in an interview that it "kept us alive, but it's not enough anymore."[11] No surprise that she favors literature: she has made it clear that she thinks that fiction—in particular, the novel—can now speak most directly and powerfully to and for the people having migrated to the cities.[12] She seems to see music, including the music that profoundly moved Du Bois, as a continuing part of the veiling, understood as a problem, needing to be ripped. The veiling here

[11] See Thomas Leclair, "'The Language Must Not Sweat': A Conversation with Toni," in *Toni Morrison: Critical Perspectives Past and Present*, ed. Henry Louis Gates, Jr. and K. A. Appiah, Amistad Literary Series (New York: Amistad, 1993) 371.

[12] Ibid., 370–71.

is that which keeps Black folks from probing their interiority—on their own terms. Such a problematic and the way outward seem to be precisely what Morrison addresses in most of her novels, most profoundly in the novel *Beloved*.[13]

Beloved has been and continues to be interpreted in myriad ways, with many different types of interpreters representing many different angles, agenda, perspectives, responding to what appears to be the author's invitation to read and probe and discuss the book. There is raging debate still about many issues around the character Beloved—whence she comes, who or what she represents; the meaning or import of this or that statement or action attributed to her/it, whither it/she goes. But all interpreters generally agree that Beloved is a story about a haunting. The haunting of those who are survivor-heirs of the "sixty million and more" made to undergo the Middle Passage (and to whom the book is dedicated). It is a story about the failure on the part of all of us to remember those who died in such an experience. It is about the refusal of those who died to go away and remain forgotten; it is about the haunting of the memory of those who died. It is about why and how the memory of those who died is prevented, held back, made difficult to impossible to embrace. Why the memory persists. Why it hurts, traumatizes. It is about consciousness, the impact the haunting has upon the Black soul, upon the Black consciousness. It is about the impact of the loss of memory, the prevention and refusal of memory upon the Black soul. It is also ultimately about how the Black soul may be reconstituted, healed, united. So it is, then, also about consciousness, interpretation and articulation—about the terms on which, the framework within which, the Black self, the one who is survivor-heir of the middle passage may now look back, remember, see/interpret, negotiate and speak to the world about what it thinks, how it feels, what it knows, how it travels and experiences. More specifically, the book is made to be about "ripping the veil" that prevents the Black self from remembering and healing itself. It is a pointing in the direction in which the psycho-social-cultural stitching and weaving work can be carried out.

---

[13] Toni Morrison, *Beloved* (New York: Penguin, 1987).

Although it is clear what character in the book does the haunting, not entirely clear in every part of the book is the matter how the haunting is to be understood, that is, how the haunting works, why it persists, what the haunting is really all about. It should occasion little surprise that I would notice and want to exploit—as very few other interpreters have—Morrison's epigraph, which is taken from Paul's letter to the Romans (9:25), and which also supplies the name of the character for whom the book is entitled: "I will call them my people, Which were not my people; and her beloved, which was not beloved."

No argument need be made here about the importance of epigraphs in summing up a writer's agenda; this should be a no-brainer. What I want to stress here is the importance of the epigraph in naming the issue behind the (narrative plot-line) issue. In order for this interest is to be made clear it is important that the larger discursive context of Paul's statement (actually a quotation of Hosea 2:25, with actual word agreement with the LXX version of 1:9) be established. The larger discursive-argumentative context is Paul's effort to address the believers at Rome, who are of mixed religious background, viz., Jews and Gentiles (of different cultural backgrounds), regarding what appears to be, in light of the success of the Pauline mission, an ironic even paradoxical twist of fate and circumstance—the phenomenon of the turning to God in great numbers on the part of Gentiles. Since the promise of God's favor was given first to the Jews, how has it come about that the non-Jews, the Gentiles, are turning in what seems to be great numbers and so many Jews in comparison seem not to be accepting God's "call"?

Paul tries his best to clarify matters; but his arguments are halting, contradictory, elliptical, confusing. It is very much worth reciting a part of the larger rhetorical context—at least from 9:22 to 9:26:

> Yet what if God, wishing to display his wrath and make known [God's] power has endured with much long-suffering those vases of wrath, fashioned for destruction? This was done to make known the riches of [God's] glory for the vases of mercy, which [God] had fashioned beforehand for such glory. Even for us [believers], whom [God] called, not only from among the Jews, but also from among the Gentiles, as indeed [God] says in Hosea,

> Those who were not my people
> I shall call "my people";
> And her who was not loved
> I shall call "my beloved"
> And
> In the very place where it was said to them,
> "You are not my people,"
> there they shall be called "children of the living God."

I think it important to note that the end of the larger rhetorical section—chapters 9–11—in which the prophetic statement that Morrison used for her epigraph is found, Paul sums up how he thinks the matter having to do with the turning and selection should be understood: "…I do not want you to be ignorant of this *mystery*…" (11:25). Paul engages in wonderful play—specifically on the words "call" (*kaleo*) and "mystery" (*musterion*). These words and Paul's play with them—that is, signifying on them as markers of paradox—draw Morrison's attention and inspires her to play with the passage.

Morrison seems to have applied the Pauline "mystery" that equated "the call" (as election) and being called "beloved" to her book and Black existence: she renders the historical and perduring exclusion and marginalization, the historical enslavement, other-ness, and subjugation and the hoped-for elevation and self-possession among Black peoples mysterious. Paul's (use of the text in which Hosea is called) "beloved" is translated by Morrison as Black folks' coming to be loved and loving themselves. So it seems that what for her is most mysterious is the matter of *why* Black peoples were first enslaved and *how* they can or may come to be healed, elevated. In Morrison's thinking—drawing on Paul's language—Black peoples are the "Gentiles," the ones thought at first to be outside, at first considered marginals, strangers, slaves. And just as a mysterious thing happened with the Gentiles of Paul's day, as *even* they were brought into the fold, so Black folks, according to Morrison, are destined to be "called," to be loved.

Morrison argues for addressing Black existence—how it evolved, the survival strategies, and the terms of self-acceptance and healing and empowerment—as a mystery. But what is first required, her essays and novels, especially the book *Beloved*, seem to suggest, is the work of identifying and "ripping the veil." With *Beloved* Morrison makes narratological, thus, more complex and layered, the identification of both the problem and the direction of the healing for the characters. No matter how one interprets *Beloved* the book, it is very clear that it is not a straight stick that hits a clean lick. Whatever *Beloved* means, it does not mean in a straightforward manner. So Morrison's criticism of some of the all too veiled, all too indirect expressions of folk culture notwithstanding, her story that is called *Beloved* is also a "crooked stick"; it is also a type of veiling—even as it may be considered an effort to address the problem of veiling in the African diaspora.

The characters of the story force readers into a scrambling of any kind of simple narrative line. Instead of a line circles come to mind—the characters tell versions or aspects of the same story; or they tell multiple stories, stories that are varied and overlapping. For all of the characters, but most especially for the main character Sethe, the "symbolic order" that the language of the master represents cannot translate her experience. For example, the horrific incident involving the killing of her baby girl cannot be told simply or directly, through the words of the master. It was to prevent her from having to undergo the humiliation of slavery that Sethe killed her baby girl. This experience was deemed by Sethe and by all observers to be horrible. But it was as a horrible representative act, resonant with classic apotropaic (Gk. *apotrepein*: that which averts or wards off evil) tradition, that it was traumatic, "unspeakable": there were really no words that could translate the meaning of the act, the depth of the impulses and feelings involved.

It is the "symbolic order" that Morrison stresses must be ripped in order for Black folks to come to be called beloved. Not just the slave narrative and its formal and rhetorical elements, but dominant western discourse itself, with its need and tendency, as Pierre Bourdieu puts it, to "occult the aphasia,"[14] to veil the veiling, as Morrison might put it. This phenomenon must be ripped. This ripping is signaled in the book by the multiple repetitive and varied tellings throughout the story by the

[14] Pierre Bourdieu, *Outline of a Theory of Practice*, trans. Richard Nice (Cambridge: Cambridge University Press, 1977) 170.

characters about their horrible experiences and hauntings. But the matter was brought to a head by Sethe's effort finally to come to speech about what happened to her. It is Morrison's description of Sethe's movements as she comes into speech that is important to notice here: she was found "...spinning. Round and round the room...turning like a slow steady wheel...Circling [Paul D] the way she was circling the subject" (151, 153). This spinning seems to reveal Morrison's understanding of knowledge, self awareness, self-consciousness, critical interpretation in terms of indirection and fragmentation, perhaps, functioning in terms of therapy or psychoanalysis. Her actions seem to represent for Morrison some sort of critique—of the master narrative and its fixed views about her existence and self. It also seemed to point toward reconstitution and healing. The circling/spinning suggests critique of and resistance to linear discursivity and politics. It also reflects an effort to reconstitute the self. This difference in movement and orientation suggests that the ripping of the veil is accomplished not so much by a refusal to engage language and texts and textuality as a refusal to accord them the power to carry meaning in the same way, on the same terms, that is, in uncritical naturalized terms, as though they were part of what Bourdieu termed the realm of doxa, the domain of the taken for granted, the un-discussable.[15]

Sethe's circling/spinning critiques and explodes this arrangement and structuring. It is really functionally much like the "silence" that Houston Baker discussed in his essay "Lowground and Inaudible Valleys: Reflections on Afro-American Spirit Work." He argues that the interpretive orientation he associates with Black folk culture is to be understood as silence—that is, as holding back from normal/traditional uses of language, a turning away from the regular forms in order to express critique and healing. Drawing upon Susan Sontag's essay on silence, he calls for a "criticism of silence" in order to "match the depths of a magnificently enhancing Black sounding of experience." This seems to me to resonate with Morrison's language about "breakin' back of words." Here is the radicalism and power of the interpretive stance taken and shared by Morrison and Du Bois and Hurston and so many others here registered by Baker: that for Black and subaltern critical

[15] Ibid., 168.

consciousness there is no meaning in any narrative, and script, any text, and tradition unless such is first ripped, broken and then "entranced," blackened, made usable for weaving meaning. "Merely arranged in a traditional...problematic...words are ineffectual. Only when they enter into entranced performance...do they give birth to sounds of a new order." [16] The entranced performance about which Baker speaks is realized only when there is an addressing of the low-ground and inaudible valleys of experiences of Black folks. Then the canonical arrangements and structures are exploded, the veil is ripped.

Morrison's related argument is that for African Americans, for whom there is so much loss, what is particularly important is the recovery of images for the flow of memory. For her, this meant beginning with images—images especially of ancestors or something in association with them:

> [Memories] are my access to me; they are my entrance into my own interior life. Which is why the images that float around them—the remains, so to speak, at the archaeological site—surface first...
>
> ...the act of imagination is bound up with memory...
>
> You know, they straightened out the Mississippi River in places, to make room for houses and livable acreage. Occasionally the river floods these places. "Flooding" is the word they use, but in fact it is not flooding; it is remembering. Remembering where it used to be. All water has a perfect memory and is forever trying to get back to where it was. Writers [=readers/interpreters] are like that: remembering where we were, what valley we ran through, what the banks were like, the light that was there and the route back to our original place. It is emotional memory—what the nerves and the skin remember as well as how it appeared. And a rush of imagination is our "flooding"...like water, I remember where I was before I was "straightened out."[17]

---

[16] Houston A. Baker, Jr., *Afro-American Poetics: Revisions of Harlem and the Black Aesthetic* (Madison: University of Wisconsin Press, 1988) ch. 3, esp. 106, 109. Susan Sontag, "The Aesthetics of Silence," in *A Susan Sontag Reader* (New York: Vantage, 1983) 181–204.

[17] Morrison, "Site of Memory," 119–20.

"Ripping the veil" for Morrison means not allowing the self to be "straightened out," which means refusing to veil the self, refusing to think according to and live within the realm of doxa, the realm of the canonical. It means accessing the sites of memory and then from such sites allowing the waters of memories to flow, in complex relationship to the received (master, canonical) scripts, but outside the artificially established banks of dominant discursivity, the most important instantiation of which we have historically called and may for sake of argument and analysis continue to call "scriptures." Only when these memories carry their own significance, not behind the veil of script/ure/s as canonical structures and modes of existence—only when these are woven together and are retextualized and recontextualized in critical/signifying relationship to "scriptures" (broadly understood) can some sort of social therapy and healing of the sort that Morrison and others have hoped for truly begin.

19

A Biography of God's Dream

Virgil Wood

> Then they said to one another, "Look, this dreamer is coming! Come therefore, let us now kill him and cast him into some pit; and we shall say, 'Some wild beast has devoured him.' We shall see what will become of his dreams!" (Genesis 37:19–20)

> But as for you, you meant evil against me; but God meant it for good, in order to bring it about as it is this day, to save many people alive. (Genesis 50:20)

There is an important difference between biography and autobiography. Biography is the story that is written about someone's life, and autobiography is the story one writes of his or her own life. Some people write both or they write multiple biographies or multiple autobiographies. In fact, W. E. B. Du Bois wrote his autobiography at three different times during his long life, and the final one was published a year after his death. I will examine a biography of God's dream with special reference to the life of Joseph.

As I look back over my life as a Christian of more than seventy years, it becomes clear to me that God has been up to some things in my life that I am just now discovering. God has blessed my journey with so many unexpected twists and turns, which at first felt like misfortune but turned out to be God's special blessing. Many times we think we are in charge, planning and plotting our lives, but then God brings the unexpected into our lives and showers us with uncommon and significant things.

Further, God plants people in our lives and after we bless each other, we pass on. The Preacher rightly observes: "To everything there is a season" (Ecclesiastes 3:1). As I think about the ten years I had the privilege of working with Dr. Martin Luther King, Jr. and the twenty-six years I worked with Dr. Martin "Daddy" King, Sr., I now see things that I had not seen before. For example, the unique impact of Jesus' life and ministry on Martin's life and leadership, and the same impact on Daddy

King's, are awesome stories in and of themselves. We were contemporaries and their witness continues to impact my own life in so many ways.

When I think of the Martin Luther King, Jr. International Chapel at Morehouse College, I am reminded of its founding dean, Dr. Lawrence E. Carter, Chaplain and Professor of Religion at Dr. King's prestigious *alma mater*. I first knew Lawrence Carter as his New Testament Professor at Virginia Seminary and College in Lynchburg, Virginia (now Virginia University of Lynchburg) at the beginning of his student career. I was privileged later during the time of his doctoral studies at Boston University to preach his ordination sermon at First Baptist Church in Brookline, where he interned under Dr. Victor Scalise. It is my delight to salute him as a faithful servant of God's dream, in which, I, too, have sought to be faithful. The major spotlight in this text is on Joseph as a preeminent and faithful servant of God's dream. We will discover through the twists and turns in his life a pathway for believers, whose desire is to become faithful servants of God's dream.

Bishop Desmond Tutu states in his book *God Has a Dream: A Vision of Hope for Our Time:*

> Before we can become God's partners, we must know what God wants for us. "I have a dream," God says. "Please help Me to realize it. It is a dream of a world whose ugliness and squalor and poverty, its war and hostility, its greed and harsh competitiveness, its alienation and disharmony are changed into their glorious counterparts, when there will be more laughter, joy, and peace, where there will be justice and goodness and compassion and love and caring and sharing. I have a dream that swords will be beaten into plowshares and spears into pruning hooks, that my children will know they are members of one family, the human family, God's family, my family."[1]

Likewise, Dr. Martin Luther King, Jr. had a dream as the "Shepherd of America," declaring on 28 August 1963, "I Have a Dream." After five more tumultuous years of struggle and challenge, he made it

---

[1] Desmond Tutu, *God Has a Dream: A Vision of Hope for Our Time* (Colorado Springs, CO: Image Books, 2010) 19–20.

clear on 3 April 1968, the night before his death, that he still had a dream and had been to the mountaintop. Look now at God's dream, as it unfolds again and again through the ups and downs in the life of Joseph. The text today gives us a brief sketch of God's dream and how it was focused throughout the life of Joseph, desecrated by his brothers but culminated in a story of nonviolence over violence, forgiveness over resentment, and abundance over famine. Look at the text for clues about how we can become faithful servants of God's dream by feeding the hungry and uplifting the brokenhearted. Joseph's story is a simple but powerful one. We see him evolving and being faithful to God through his "developmental phases of life." Joseph is in a predicament but he is also a prospect for potential greatness.

First, Joseph is on his high horse. He is gifted but arrogant in his demeanor and temperament. He is gifted and seems to know it. He is slated for greatness, but he is arrogant. His behavior probably stems from that as well as from the partisan treatment he received from his father, elevating him to a position of favoritism over his other eleven brothers. He has a dream. Obviously, it is from God but he thinks it is his dream. His brothers are outraged after he tells them that he will rule over them. Their budding resentment reaches a fever pitch when his brothers decide to throw him into a pit. They are satisfied by throwing him into the pit, hoping this would rid them of his dream.

Second, Joseph is in the pit. He was a co-conspirator in his own enslavement. His pit didn't just start when he was thrown into the dungeon; it started somewhere in the dynamics of his father's dysfunctional family. We see some of his brothers conspiring to get rid of him and others doing all they can to save him. There seem to be few saving elements operating on behalf of this boy's future or the future of his whole family. There appears to be little hope for bringing healing to this extended family. He is in the pit, enslaved to Potiphar, survives the charge of rape by the charge of rape by his master's wife, and, finally, thrown into prison.

Third, Joseph is in prison. It is here that he once again shows his faithfulness to God's dream, even when he did not seem to be conscious of the impact God's dream had on his journey. In prison he interpreted two prisoners' dreams. Specifically, he interpreted the dream of a butler and a baker. The butler promises to remember Joseph for interpreting the dream that freed him from prison. After two years, Pharaoh had a dream and discovered that none of his advisors or magicians could interpret the dream. Upon the recommendation of the butler, Pharaoh sends for Joseph, who does, in fact, interpret his dream and advises Pharaoh on the necessity of implementing a strategy to prepare for an upcoming famine. The dream involved seven fat cows and seven skinny cows, seven healthy stalks of wheat and seven sickly stalks, and how the sickly ones devoured the healthy ones. At this point, Pharaoh appointed Joseph as governor, or second in charge. Interestingly, prison gave him the experience needed to govern Egypt.

Fourth, Joseph is made governor. Like Nelson Mandela, he moves from the prison to an executive office. It was his own faithfulness to God's dream even while he was unaware of what God was up to that prepared him for service. Joseph suggested a strategic plan for preparing the nation through the good times and the bad, and he was given full authority to implement the plan. Just as his dream showed, Joseph was in a position to save lives, including those of his own family.

Fifth, Joseph is a provider. He is now in a position to provide abundance for Egypt. He not only feeds them, he binds up their broken hearts. Egypt was broken and, while they had the resources, national leaders didn't know how to fix the dilemma. Joseph's faith and trust in God's dream evolved and now had clarity and focus. He provided an example of strong leadership by overseeing a "homeland security" plan and, through the process, overcame the long-held resentment of his brothers and forgave them.

What does this story mean? First, Joseph himself comes to understand that God's dream was God's, not his, although he was the human representative. When he realized this, he forgave his brothers and reconciled with his family. All this happened before his father passed. The brothers came to realize that the dream they had meant to kill was not yet Joseph's, but God's alone, and would one day be their economic and spiritual deliverance. They came to understand that they would one day indeed come to bow down before him, but not in submission to his arrogance, but in deep humility to God alone, and in thanks to the God whose dream and presence brought them to a place of deliverance and abundance. Perhaps God has brought the Black Church movement, its friends and allies, to a similar situation. What significance do African Americans have in America? Perhaps God is leading us likewise to acknowledge Genesis 50:20. Joseph for the first time could say to his brothers: "But as for you, you meant evil against me; but God meant it for good, in order to bring it about as it is this day, to save many people alive."

Many of us ask: "What is God up to?" We are reminded that the genius of King was his spiritual legacy growing out of his personal relationship to Jesus as the resurrected Christ. It might be a good idea to take a 100-day, "Jesus-intensive" course starting on the first of January of any year, exploring Dr. King, Jr.'s intellectual and spiritual journey. This would begin with Emancipation Day in January, proceed through King's birthdate, through Easter and the anniversary of King's death, on to Pentecost Sunday, and beyond. It will be a clarion call to join as servants of God's dream, what King saw from the mountaintop when he declared that "we as a people will get to the promised land." Hence, the Church should put more emphasis on Pentecost. Easter celebrates the resurrection of Jesus, but Pentecost represents the beginning of the church and its historic mission. Joseph is an early exemplar.

There is this wonderful tale that is told about a group of people who were interested in a short trip to see for themselves what heaven and hell were like, so they could make up their minds about their plans for a final resting place after this life is over. The first stopover was in hell. Much to their surprise, they were led into this large banquet hall, where they witnessed a lot of people sitting around long tables, with all types of delicious food. Then, there were these long spoons in their hands. The visitors thought, "Hell must not be so bad"—that is, until they noticed that all of the people looked sickly, emaciated, unhealthy, and weak. The next stop was heaven, and to their surprise, heaven looked just like hell—that is, until they noticed that all the people looked well fed, happy, strong, and healthy. The visitors said to themselves, "What's going on here?" Both hell and heaven have the same environment, the same resources, every material advantage, plenty of good food, and other things, but the people seem so different. Then they discover why. The people in hell, with their long spoons, spent all of their time trying to feed only themselves—and they were poorly nourished!

However, the people in heaven, with their long spoons, learned that, to get well fed, everyone has to feed each other. They functioned as a beloved community, in heaven, and when humanity wakes up to God's dream, we will also care and share and participate in each other's blessings and burdens. The visitors returned to earth, thinking, feeling, and doing, just like Jesus. They remembered that he said: "On earth, as it is in heaven" (Matthew 6:10). The predicament of every nation on the globe today is still what Martin Luther King, Jr. said it was: that too few have too much and too many have too little, so that the nation becomes an island of prosperity in a sea of poverty. Our prospect as a nation founded on biblical Jubilee principles is to gather all that we have and transform it into all that we need so that there will be bread on every table. Then, a hungry world is fed, a hurting world is healed, and a broken world is fixed.

When any nation's dream, including the American dream, is aligned with God's Dream, famine gives way to abundance. If America becomes "a beloved community," surely the nations of the world will find inspiration from the American dream, and we can paraphrase Dr. King: "Free at last, Free at last, we thank God Almighty, we are all, free at last! *Shalom…Asalam Alakum… Hallelujah!*"